D1130516

195?—837

263—314

Under the General Editorship of

Taylor W. Meloan *University of Southern California*

HOUGHTON MIFFLIN ADVISER IN MARKETING

Consumer Behavior and Marketing Management

James H. Myers · William H. Reynolds

PROFESSORS OF MARKETING, GRADUATE SCHOOL OF BUSINESS ADMINISTRATION
UNIVERSITY OF SOUTHERN CALIFORNIA

Houghton Mifflin Company · Boston
NEW YORK   ATLANTA   GENEVA, ILL.   DALLAS   PALO ALTO

To Gary Steiner

Editor's Introduction

KNOWLEDGE OF CONSUMER MOTIVATIONS and buying behavior is at the heart of the marketing concept. Without adequate quantitative data and qualitative insights about the market targets that a firm now serves or hopes to penetrate in the future, it is difficult, if not impossible, to marshal corporate resources optimally to achieve planned objectives and enhance the profit position of the enterprise. There is vast quantitative data which a firm may draw upon in formulating its marketing plan of action. Or if the necessary information is not available from secondary sources, it can often be developed rather easily using established survey, observational, or experimental techniques.

By contrast, there is a paucity of useful literature, and pertinent research pertaining to buyer behavior and motivation. Most behavioral scientists have little interest in marketing or in business generally. The major professional journals in psychology and sociology contain little which can be used per se in helping to develop marketing strategies. But there is a wide range of scholarly literature about human behavior. In this book selected constructs and concepts from this literature pertaining to sensory and perceptual processes; learning, memory, and cognition; motivation and emotion; cultural and social group interaction; and family characteristics are reviewed and interpreted in a marketing context. This objective cannot be fully achieved by a readings book which only contains selections from the literature of psychology, sociology, anthropology, and other behaviorally based sources. Typically the business implications of such citations must be interpreted by the reader. By contrast, this book bridges the gap between selected aspects of the behavioral sciences and decision making in marketing.

The authors are well qualified to undertake this task. Professor James H. Myers holds a Ph.D. in psychology from the University of Southern California. Prior to returning to his alma mater in 1959 as a Professor of Marketing, he was Manager, Research Division of the Western Home Office of Prudential Insurance Company. Professor William H. Reynolds has his Ph.D. in political science from the University of Chicago. Before joining U.S.C. in 1963 as a Professor of Marketing, he was in corporate and divisional marketing research with the Ford Motor Company where he did much of the pioneering research work which led to the introduction of the Mustang.

Until recently the principal exposure which students of business had to the behavioral sciences was in courses in liberal arts. The relevance of such work to their upper division or graduate courses in business often eluded them. This book is part of an incipient body of literature which directly infuses knowledge from the behavioral sciences into marketing. It should be a valuable source book at both the undergraduate and graduate levels.

TAYLOR W. MELOAN

University of Southern California

Preface

THE AIM OF THIS BOOK IS:

— To select from the vast body of knowledge about human behavior those concepts and principles which seem to have particular relevance to the understanding of consumer buying behavior,

— To review some of the research which has provided evidence for these principles,

— To illustrate the relevance and application of these basic behavioral principles to the buying situation by examples from current marketing practice.

Our intention is at once modest and ambitious. It is modest to the extent that we have selected only a few behavioral principles from the many which might be examined and have reviewed only a portion of the available research evidence for each principle (which amounts to several hundred studies for some behavioral topics). Yet it is ambitious in that we have tried to sample from the *total spectrum* of the behavioral science disciplines: psychology, social psychology, sociology and cultural anthropology.

Obviously no two authors are fully equal to this task. The more any behavioral scientist knows about his parent disciplines, the less he tends to know about the marketing implications of this knowledge, and vice versa. We make no claim to having done a complete and thorough job. We did not try to be exhaustive either in *selecting* the behavioral principles which are relevant to consumer behavior, in *reviewing* the basic knowledge in each area selected, or in *presenting* all marketing implications of each principle. Rather, our goal was to provide a fresh perspective by looking at consumers through the eyes of behavioral scientists. Only in very recent years has proper attention been given to the potential which lies in doing this.

Several benefits derive from an approach of this type. The college student can view the consumer in a more meaningful, perhaps more rational way. He can better realize the enormous complexity of the task facing firms which offer products and services to the consumer public today. The businessman can develop a better understanding of the basic forces which direct and govern human behavior, so as to plan product and market strategy more effectively. And, finally, the consumer will benefit from the greater selection of products and services which become available to him and from the more efficient marketing practices which keep prices in line so that he can enjoy more of the fruits of our free enterprise economy.

We wish to thank Professors Allen R. Solem and James D. Thompson, who reviewed the psychological and sociological portions respectively of this manuscript. Thanks are also due Professor Taylor W. Meloan, who not only reviewed the entire manuscript but who also made every effort to provide additional time and facilities toward its completion. Without the book *Human Behavior: An Inventory of Scientific Findings* by Berelson and Steiner, the preparation of this book would have been much more difficult and the content less scholarly. This book also benefited from a thorough reading by Melvin Newhoff. And finally, special thanks are due to our wives for the "usual" amount of "extraordinary" patience required for husbands so deeply immersed and preoccupied.

JAMES H. MYERS
WILLIAM H. REYNOLDS

University of Southern California

Contents

Consumer Behavior and Marketing Management

I

Sensory and Perceptual Processes

THE FOCUS OF THIS BOOK is upon the consumer. This includes men, women, teen-agers, children, senior citizens — anyone who buys anything for his own use or for family use. Consumers ultimately provide the basis for nearly all economic activity. The increasing attention on the part of marketing management to consumer behavior attests to its importance.

Consumers are vulnerable creatures. Nature did not provide them with the physical and mental attributes necessary to become sensitive and discriminating buyers in this modern society of ours. In a complex purchasing situation, the consumer's senses often betray him, his powers of rationality fail him, and he often becomes confused. And the seller knows it!

The rush is on among marketers of consumer products and services to discover those basic principles which explain how the buyer behaves in a purchasing situation, why he behaves this way, and the implications of this knowledge in terms of total marketing strategies. This book is devoted to precisely these questions. The aim of this book is not exploitative in the sense of providing the seller with additional tools with which to manipulate or influence consumer buying decisions. Rather, the objective is to review what we know about human behavior *as it relates to the buying situation,* in the hope of better understanding the forces which are operating.

Interest in human behavior is as old as man himself. However, the *systematic study* of behavior begins as recently as the 1800's when the modern sciences of psychology, sociology and cultural anthropology were born. These constitute the primary reservoir of organized knowledge we have about human behavior. It is to these "behavioral sciences" that we must first turn for a more basic understanding of *how* people behave and *why* they behave as they do. Once the groundwork of principles and knowledge has been established for a particular aspect of human behavior, we are in a position to relate this to the more specific problem of consumer buying behavior.

This book first examines the discipline of psychology, to determine the various physiological and psychological processes which govern individual behavior. Then to social psychology, to see how the individual interacts with others and how others influence him. Sociology is reviewed next, to see how social groups, institutions, and whole societies interact and regulate themselves. Finally, cultural anthropology presents insights into how cultures around the world behave and differ from one another.

The total task is impossible in a book of this size, of course. It is possible only to make a start, to cover selected behavioral topics which have been found to have particular relevance in understanding consumer buying decisions. In this way at least the general approach will be demonstrated, so that consumers are likely to be regarded less as buyers than as what they are — human beings in a buying situation.

SENSATION AND PERCEPTION

An understanding of the consumer should properly begin by considering the manner in which he maintains contact with the world around him. Most of what he knows of this world comes initially through his major senses — sight, hearing, taste, smell, and touch. These might be termed "sensory input" mechanisms which establish contact between an individual and his environment. (Extrasensory perception is moot and will not be discussed here.)

"In its purest, perhaps hypothetical form, sensing does not involve the use of learning based upon past experience." (Ruch, 1958, p. 265.) The sensory processes, in other words, tend to be largely physiological in nature. They are not of as great interest to the marketer as *perception*, which, in effect, involves the sum total of sensory impressions from the environment *plus* the individual's own "filling in" to complete the picture.

"The process of perception stands midway along a continuum from sensing to thinking. . . Perception uses *both* the sensations aroused by stimuli and the learning gained from past experience." (Ruch, 1958, p. 265.) This is the primary area of interest to the marketer, who needs to know the *total impression* his products and promotional efforts create in the buyer's mind — what the buyer senses (e.g., the size and color of a package, the texture of a fabric, the fragrance of a cologne) *and* the way in which he adds to or changes his sensory impression by mental (cognitive) processes in accordance with his accumulated experience.

For most of human history, it was assumed that what was perceived was the same as what was there to be perceived; that is, that the sensory and perceptual processes reflected fairly accurately the realities of the external world. Only in recent years, after behavioral scientists began examining human behavior in a more scientific manner, has the fallacy of this assumption been fully appreciated. The evidence today suggests that what we perceive is very often as much a product of what we *want* to perceive as of what is actually there. This does not mean, of course, that we would see a house as a tree or as an automobile. It refers more to the subtle expressions and meanings that we attribute to objects, that is, what the objects *mean to us*.

For example, any child can distinguish a car from a house. Cars clearly belong to a different class or set of objects than houses. Older children can distinguish between objects within a class on the basis of small differences in sensory impressions; e.g., a Cadillac is larger than a Ford, it may have tail fins, a different grille design, or other distinguishing features. It is only as we mature that a Cadillac takes on additional meaning. Such a car is likely to be owned by a person who lives in a large home, who is a business leader or successful professional man, and who belongs to a country club. Knowledge of this sort, when added to the sensory impression, results in our *total perception* of a Cadillac.

Many factors contribute to the total perception of an object or product and these will be discussed throughout this book. These factors are extensive and complex; all are not yet known. Before proceeding to the total perception, however, it is well to examine the basic sensory processes, since these structure an individual's response to stimulation from the outside world.

Perception of an object or event is based, then, upon two types of factors:

Stimulus factors. These are characteristics of the physical object such as its size, color, texture, and surroundings.

Individual factors. These are characteristics of the person himself, his basic sensory processes in operation plus his past experience with similar items or situations plus his expectations, basic motivations, and affective states of the moment (e.g., whether he is happy or depressed).

Neither stimulus nor individual factors taken alone can explain a consumer's reaction to a marketing situation or even to some small part of it, such as the package or advertisement. Both enter into the total perception, and often it is virtually impossible to separate them.

Attention

Before perception can occur, attention must be aroused. Without attention to an item or situation, there is no awareness and, hence, no perception. Attention in this sense functions as a selective device, sorting out from all available stimuli only those which will be noticed and therefore perceived.

Both stimulus (external) and individual (internal) factors determine whether or not attention is produced. In general, the two operate in complementary fashion: the greater the intensity of one, the less the required intensity of the other in order to produce attention. Thus, loud sounds, bright colors, or large sizes are noticed even when there is little or no interest on the part of the individual, while soft noises and other weak stimuli produce attention only when the individual has great interest, motivation, or expectation. For this reason, when the consumer has little basic interest in a product or service (e.g., financial services such as banks and insurance companies, or certain types of household furnishings such as light bulbs) the marketer must often rely upon relatively strong stimulus factors to draw attention to his advertisements.

STIMULUS FACTORS

Many characteristics of stimulus objects determine how much attention will be produced. We can understand these characteristics better by looking briefly at a phenomenon closely related to attention — human *adaptation*. One of our most remarkable and distinguishing human features is our ability to adapt to a wide range of physical, psychological, and social conditions. Often, our senses show *negative adaptation*, that is, after a period of continuous, unchanging application, a stimulus may cease to produce its characteristic sensation. For example, a beam of light projected on the retina becomes unnoticeable after a few minutes. A sharp needle applied with steady pressure to the forearm produces little or no pain after half a minute or so (try it.)

Extension of these and similar findings leads to the conclusion that individuals develop a familiarity with everyday objects and events, particularly those seen or experienced with some degree of continuity or regularity. This familiarity leads to an *adaptation level* for each object or event. We scarcely notice anything which occurs in a state near its adaptation level, but if an object moves away in either direction from this level, sensitization occurs, producing attention in the individual. Thus, it might be said that we "perceive by exception," noticing mainly those objects or events which appear different to our senses. The problem for the marketer, then, is to present stimuli which depart sufficiently from prior adaptation levels to be noticed. Some of the more common *stimulus* factors for accomplishing this are discussed here.

Size. Large sizes normally produce more attention than small sizes. This is common knowledge. However, by doubling the size of, say, an advertisement, will we double its attention value? For advertisements in printed media, the answer is usually no. Doubling the size increases attention value by approximately 50%, not 100 per cent, although this varies with an individual's interest in the topic. (Rudolph, 1947.) Extensive research in this area led to the formulation of the so-called "square root" law, which states that attention increases as the square root of the size: to *double* attention, you must increase the size of an advertisement by *four times*, other factors being equal.[1] As we will see later, this is merely a special case of the more general Weber's Law in psychophysics.

Intensity. Loud sounds and bright colors produce attention. But, again, by doubling the loudness or brightness, we do not get double the attention value but only a exponential increase in attention, as in the case of size. Since both intensity and size can be measured easily (ruler, decibel scale, etc.), it is possible to establish *how much* increase in sensation would be produced by a given increase in size or intensity. Means of measuring sensations are of great help to the marketer and are discussed later in this chapter under Sensory Thresholds.

Color. Generally, color produces more attention than black and white. But do color ads in magazines produce enough more attention to justify their greater cost? No, according to one researcher who found that color ads in the trade publication *Industrial Marketing* produced more attention, but did not attract as many readers *per dollar* as did black and white ads. (Rosberg, 1956.) Findings of this kind must be interpreted carefully in view of the total situation — the type of publication, the proportion of color and noncolor ads, etc.

[1] Note, however, ". . . An increase of 100 per cent in the size of the *illustration* portion of the ad produces an increase [only] of 20 per cent in attention value." (Rudolph, 1947, p. 54.)

Position. The upper half of a printed page produces more attention than the lower half, and the left-hand side more than the right-hand side. Thus, the upper left-hand corner may be several times as favorable as the lower right-hand corner, other factors being equal. [There are cultural variations in this of course. For example, since Orientals and Arabs read from right to left on the printed page, they would be expected to notice the right side of a page more than the left side. (Yamanaka, 1962.)] On the other hand, whether an advertisement appears on a right-hand or left-hand *page* ordinarily seems to make no difference whatever. (Media/Scope, 1964).

Proprietary research suggests that people "read" the design of an automobile from the rear to the front. A sculptured line or a chrome strip which starts from a low point at the rear of a car and ends at a high point at the front is seen as an *ascending* diagonal and seems to connote speed (Arnheim, 1960). A line high in the rear and low in the front appears to droop. When a car is pictured facing left, the tendency to "read" it from the rear to the front conflicts with the normal tendency of people to read the printed page from left to right. Consequently, some manufacturers always show their cars facing to the right.

Movement. Motion produces attention. Point-of-purchase and other sales promotion displays often incorporate a moving device to attract notice. Many outdoor billboards now contain three-way displays which rotate to produce a different picture every few seconds. More attention is produced with no increase in the size of the space. (This approach has been so successful that some authorities consider such billboards to be traffic hazards!) Quasi-motion can also be produced by skillful artwork which carries the eye forcibly along a predetermined path. Even if completely nonrepresentational, some designs are exciting and others quiet. Jagged lines and a vertical design in an advertising layout produce more "movement" than smooth horizontal designs. (Actually, our eyes are in constant movement, "scanning" the visual environment, even when we are not aware of it.)

Contrast. The greater the contrast, the more attention that is aroused. Alternating loud and soft noises, bright and pastel colors, or large and small sizes will produce greater attention than will either of them alone. An automobile in a summer setting in one half of an ad and in a winter setting in the other half will produce attention by contrast. Some of the effectiveness of other attention-producing factors (e.g., size, intensity, movement, color) can ultimately be reduced to their contrast value. As noted earlier, color ads normally produce more attention than noncolor ads, but a black and white ad appearing among color ads might well produce the greatest attention because of its high contrast value in this setting. (In a nation of blondes, would Clairol ads suggest that *brunettes* have more fun?)

Isolation. A small object pictured in the middle of a large space draws attention. A picture of a cold-pill, electronic relay switch, or other small object in the center of a nearly blank page catches the reader's eye.

The concept of adaptation level must be kept in mind when we consider the stimulus factors which produce attention. Since attention is generated primarily by objects or events which are *different* from the usual, a small illustration among many large ones may produce more attention than any of the large ones. This partly explains why advertising seems to run in cycles. The attention value of a new approach may be high at first, but extensive plagiarism of the basic idea by other advertisers leads to adaptation. A fresh approach must then be tried in order to overcome the previous adaptation level.

INDIVIDUAL FACTORS

The stimulus characteristics mentioned above are generally the most favorable for producing attention, other things being equal. But seldom are other things equal. Such factors as the consumer's *interest* in the product or service and his momentary expectation or "set" often have far more to do with attention value than the stimulus factors. Women tend, for example, to be especially receptive to pictures of babies and children regardless of size, color, or other stimulus factors, whereas men tend to notice cars, athletics and power tools. For this reason, commercial advertising effectiveness-rating services usually present ratings for a given ad in relation to other ads of the *same product class or type* so as to eliminate the effects of basic product interest when evaluating ad layout or copy. In general, the less the basic interest of the product, the greater the efforts necessary to produce attention by stimulus factors.

The matter of interest applies even to *brands* within product groups. A Chevrolet owner is more likely to notice Chevrolet than Rambler ads, and vice versa. Popular-brand ads score higher in the conventional ratings than those of less popular brands. This sometimes leads marketing executives in companies with relatively small market shares to blame their advertising for their lack of popularity. The converse is more often true.

Another "individual" factor which affects the attention process is the limited human *span of attention*. "When the requirement is simply that the *number* of objects shall be correctly reported . . . the average span for keen adults is about 8 objects. Individual averages range from 6 to 11, and every individual varies about his own average. . . ." (Woodworth & Schlosberg, 1960, p. 93.) Our span of attention under everyday conditions is, of course, even lower, setting a limit upon our visual input. This fact emphasizes the necessarily "selective" nature of our perceptual processes. On the other hand, *fluctuations in attention* occur frequently, with a minimum of one shift every five seconds or so. We are simply unable to concentrate on any object or thought for a longer time, although we can sustain attention to a large object or event by shifting to different portions of it.

The above suggests that a message or object (e.g., a package) should be kept relatively simple for maximum impact. The current Volkswagen advertising campaign demonstrates, among other things, the effectiveness of keeping the ad layout simple, thereby not exceeding an individual's span of attention as he looks at the picture. These advertisements have encouraged a trend toward simpler printed layouts using familiar words or phrases which have meaning (internal factors) for the consumer. Rosser Reeves, a national advertising authority, has even insisted that a successful ad should not try to make more than *one* selling proposition.

The rapid fluctuation rate of our attention is reflected in radio ads which use two announcers alternately for a single message so that normal shifts in attention are directed to the *same message* from another announcer, rather than away from the commercial entirely. For the same reason, television advertisements must frequently change picture and/or sound to hold attention. It is important, however, for sight and sound to be delivering the same message. Advertisers sometimes try to use an interesting visual sequence (e.g., bikini-clad models) to hold attention while "audio over" delivers the sell. This is almost always ineffective because the attention of the viewer does not stray from the interesting picture to absorb the relatively less attention-getting spoken commercial. One advertisement for an office photocopy machine which showed a bikini-clad model got high "attention" ratings, but produced only 52 coupon returns. When the ad was changed into a cartoon format with two men discussing the benefits and features of the copier, coupon returns jumped to 109 (Baker, 1961.)

It is often a good idea in television commercials for words to appear on the screen as they are spoken, thus holding the viewer as his attention shifts from audio to video and back again.

Attempts to produce attention sometimes backfire because of "individual" factors. One large distiller devised a liquor store display rack which ejected a bottle as a shopper walked by. As the bottle started to fall, the shopper would invariably lunge, only to find that the bottle was held in place by a concealed wire. Attention was produced, but sales actually declined. Apparently the gimmick made shoppers feel foolish and, consequently, hostile feelings were aroused towards the manufacturer and his product.

A considerable amount of money is spent by manufacturers, advertisers, and the entertainment industry in measuring the attention value of various package designs, point-of-purchase displays, printed advertisements, television shows, and movies. For this, a wide variety of instruments (many of which are described in textbooks such as Woodworth & Schlosberg, 1960) has been borrowed from the experimental psychology laboratories.

Sensory Thresholds

Every human sensory process (sight, hearing, etc.) has an upper and a lower limit of responsiveness to stimulation. The upper limit is far below, and the lower limit far above, the actual extremes of physical stimuli. We know, for example, that dogs respond to whistles whose pitch is beyond the audible range for human beings. Whistles of still higher pitch are not audible even to dogs.

The study of the relationship between the *actual physical stimulation* (e.g., the brightness of light, loudness of sound) and the corresponding *sensation produced in a person* is called *psychophysics*. It is the study of the relationship between the psychological and physical worlds. This relationship is not at all what we might expect it to be.

There are three thresholds for each sense:

Lower threshold — the point below which lower physical intensities of the stimulus (light, sound, etc.) can no longer be noticed by an individual.

Terminal threshold — the point beyond which further increases in stimulus intensity or frequency produce no greater sensation.

Difference threshold — the smallest *increment* in stimulus intensity which will be noticed by an individual. This is also known as the "just noticeable difference." (j.n.d.).

The Latin word for threshold, *limen*, is sometimes used, as in difference limen, lower limen, and subliminal advertising (advertising presented below the lower threshold of the sense mode).

WEBER'S LAW

A pioneer in the study of psychophysics was Weber, who in 1834 proposed a mathematical expression to describe the relationship between change in a *physical stimulus* and the corresponding change in the *sensation* which would be produced in the individual. The following is known as Weber's Law:

$$\frac{\triangle I}{I} = K$$

where

$\triangle I$ = the smallest increase in the intensity of a physical stimulus that will be just noticeably different from the previous intensity.

I = the intensity of the stimulus at the point where the increase takes place.

K = a constant (which varies from one sense mode to another).

This means that the smallest *increment* in the intensity of the stimulus that will be *just noticed* is a function of the intensity of the stimulus at the point where the increase takes place; that is, the higher the intensity is, the greater the amount of increase in intensity that is necessary in order to be just noticed. For example:

> We might find that 1 gram was a sufficient addition to a 50-gram weight on the palm [of the hand] to be just noticeable. But starting with a 100-gram weight, we should have to add 2 grams before the difference was noticed, and starting with a 200-gram weight, we should have to add 4 grams. The j.n.d. (just noticeable difference) would seem to be always 2 per cent of the starting weight. (Woodworth & Schlosberg, 1960, p. 194.)

This type of relationship has been found to hold throughout the middle ranges of stimuli for all of the senses, although the constant factor, K, (e.g., 2 per cent in the example just given) varies from one sense to another. In general, our pitch discrimination seems to be the most sensitive (K = 0.3 per cent), while taste and light skin pressure seem to be least sensitive (K = 20 per cent).

We thus find that physical and psychological worlds do not have a one-to-one relationship. However, a relationship does exist as indicated by Weber's Law, and this gives us a basis for understanding many aspects of consumers' perceptual behavior.

The ideal conditions for accurate comparison of various stimuli have been studied intensively. Asked which of two packages is the larger, people judge most accurately when: (1) the packages are close together, (2) both packages are seen together at the same time, and (3) if color and other factors are held constant so that size is the only difference. A marketer with a product inferior in some respect sometimes arranges comparison tests so that the competitive product is used on one occasion and his on another. This minimizes the likelihood that the consumer will notice the difference even if the time lapse is brief. A few minutes of conversation after a prospective buyer has listened to a stereo set will make it extremely difficult for him to compare it with a competitive stereo he is then asked to listen to. Differences in wood finish, control knobs, and other features further confuse the consumer.

(Simple psychophysical measurements, of course, do not vary nearly as much from individual to individual as other psychological and sociological measurements. Most people can compare weights, sizes, levels of brightness, and so forth with reasonable accuracy. This is a major reason that samples in market research studies concerned with psychophysical problems can thus be much smaller than in those concerned with attitudes and preferences.)

Weber's Law is illustrated rather well by consumer response to pricing. An increase of $200 in the price of an American compact car would certainly be perceived as being much greater than *the same $200 increase* in the price of a Cadillac or a Continental. Weber's Law is also the psychological underpinning of the retail practice of marking down items (i.e., lowering the original price, as during a sale) on a *percentage* rather than an absolute basis. The higher the original price, the greater is the dollar amount of markdown required to produce an adequate customer response. Also related to Weber's Law is the fact, "Many retail outlets have found, by experience, that too many price lines (often too close together) cause confusion for some customers and that sales tend to concentrate on only a few of the price lines." (Miller, 1962, p. 59.)

In the area of product design, to make a pastry or confectionery product (e.g., cake, candy, soda pop) *just noticeably sweeter*, the manufacturer would have to add disproportionately more sugar if the product were already rather sweet than if it were only slightly sweet. The same law applies to other flavors such as lemon, garlic, or salt. Similarly, if a manufacturer of hi-fi equipment wished to make his product noticeably louder than his competitor's, he would have to seek an intensity higher than his competitor's highest level in accordance with Weber's Law.

The consumer's perception of the size of a package also follows Weber's Law. A large package would probably require a greater *absolute* increase in its height or in frontal area than would a small package in order to look noticeably larger.

The square root law which states that ad size must be increased by four times in order to double attention is merely a special case of the more general Weber's Law, as was pointed out earlier.

SUBLIMINAL ADVERTISING

Subliminal perception involves the lower threshold or limen rather than the difference threshold. It has long been known that subliminal stimuli can produce certain behavioral effects under laboratory conditions, even though the individual is not aware of these stimuli because they are below his lower sensory threshold. (Lazarus & McCleary, 1951; Klein, Spence, & Holt, 1958.) But could subliminal stimuli be useful in a commercial setting? Could consumers be motivated to purchase a product by subliminal advertising?

James Vicary, head of a marketing research consulting firm, felt that they could. In the middle 1950's, over a period of six weeks, he flashed the messages, "Eat popcorn" and "Drink Coca Cola," for 1/3000 of a second each time on the screen in a motion picture theater in New Jersey. According to sales figures, popcorn sales increased 57 per cent, and Coca Cola sales 18 per cent. (Brooks, 1958). Imagine the excitement among advertising agencies. However, extensive subsequent investigation by Vicary and many others has failed to verify the initial study, and its success was probably due more to changes in certain physical arrangements within the theater than to the subliminal advertising. At present, "There is no scientific evidence that subliminal stimulation can initiate subsequent action, to say nothing of commercially or politically significant action. And there is nothing to suggest that such action can be produced 'against the subject's will,' or more effectively than through normal, recognized messages." (Berelson & Steiner, 1964, p. 95.)

There are probably several reasons for this: (1) because a subliminal message must be brief and simple, not much information can be conveyed; (2) as explained in our discussion of attention, stimulus factors must be strong unless there is great consumer interest and motivation to begin with; (3) subliminal impressions are, at best, too weak to trigger large responses; and (4) individuals vary widely in their lower thresholds for visual, auditory, and other stimuli, just as they vary along the "normal curve" in I.Q. and in grades in most college classes. This means that what is just below the sensory threshold for the "average" individuals is rather easily noticeable to people with unusually low thresholds. An intensity set low enough to be subliminal to these individuals would be too far below the threshold of those with "average" and "high" thresholds to make any sensory impression on them at all, as shown in Figure 1.1.

It is better, perhaps, that subliminal advertising is not effective in motivating consumers to action. If it were, we would be faced with penetrating questions of ethics and regulation which would undoubtedly place further restrictions upon the process of mass communications in the United States.

Sensory Discrimination

Sensory discrimination is of interest to marketers of many types of consumer products although the matter is not usually discussed in these terms. Sensory discrimination refers to our ability to distinguish between similar stimuli presented to one sense mode. Thus, sensory discrimination occurs when stimuli are different enough to be beyond the difference threshold, or just noticeably different. A marketer is interested in knowing if his product is *at least* noticeably different from his competitor's product so that consumers can distinguish between these products in the absence of label identification.

One of the earliest studies in this area involved discrimination among four popular brands of cigarettes. Subjects were told only

Figure 1.1

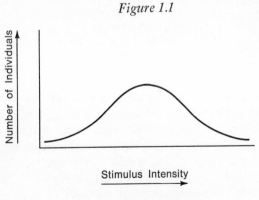

Lower Sensory Threshold

that their regular brand was one of the four, and all identifying marks were removed from the cigarettes used. Under these conditions, the investigators found that correct identification of the cigarettes was little better than could be expected by chance, that is, by sheer guessing. And they noted, "Camels are identified as Chesterfields more often than as themselves." (Husband & Godfrey, 1934, p. 222.)

A later study of cigarette identification involved 200 men and 200 women who normally consumed at least one pack of cigarettes per day. Three brands of cigarettes were used: Camel, Chesterfield, and Lucky Strike. Subjects were divided into two practice groups. The first was asked to smoke each of the three brands interchangeably — with all brands lit at the same time. The other group smoked one brand at a time, putting each one out before going on to the next. Subjects were allowed to practice until they felt they would be able to distinguish among brands when identification was removed in later tests. Results showed that brands were identified correctly 44 per cent of the time, only a slight improvement from the 33⅓ per cent accuracy which would be expected from sheer guessing. There was no difference in correct identifications between the two "practice" groups. However, the people who smoked the brands tested were able to identify their own brand more times than the people who usually smoked other brands. The authors concluded:

> It would appear that claims of cigarette advertisers and habitual smokers to the effect that there are discriminable differences among various brands are technically true, but actually of small magnitude. No data of this study indicated greater discriminability of any particular brand, or greater discriminatory capacity by smokers of any particular brand. (Ramond, Rachal, Marks, 1950, p. 284.)

Although we might expect it to be somewhat difficult to distinguish among cigarettes of the same general type (i.e., filtered, mentholated, etc.), one early study even found that blindfolded subjects were frequently unable to distinguish between real tobacco smoke and warm, moist air inhaled through a pipe mouthpiece! (Hull, 1924.)

Similar results have emerged in the case of cola beverage identification. Studies in the late 1940's showed that subjects could not reliably distinguish among unidentified samples of three well-known, nationally distributed brands of cola beverages: Coca Cola, Pepsi Cola, and RC Cola. (Bowles & Pronko, 1948; Pronko & Bowles, 1948, 1949; Pronko & Herman, 1950.) This made the investigators wonder what would happen if three relatively *unknown* cola beverages, Hyde Park Cola, Kroger Cola, and Spur Cola, were presented for identification. A study showed that these beverages were identified almost invariably as one of the three well-known brands and that there were no correct identifications of any of the three lesser-known brands. Not one of the subjects said he did not know or could not recognize the samples he tasted. On the basis of their studies, the authors concluded, "The seven brands of cola beverages employed in our series of studies (the six we named plus Vess Cola) appear to have the same stimulus function for our subjects and may be said to be 'equivalent stimuli.' " (Pronko & Bowles, 1949, p. 608.)

Later, Thumin questioned these findings on the basis of poor methodology and undertook a study which differed from earlier approaches in three ways: (1) an indication of subjects' previous cola consumption habits was obtained, (2) subjects were told in advance what beverages they would be asked to identify, and (3) the different samples were presented in pairs, rather than three or four at a time, so as to provide a better basis for making comparisons. Under these conditions, Thumin found the number of correct identifications shown in Table 1.1. The last line of this table shows the number of correct identifications that would be expected by chance alone, that is, if subjects were unable to discriminate at all and were simply guessing or drawing names out of a hat.

Table 1.1

IDENTIFICATION OF COLA BRANDS

NUMBER OF CORRECT IDENTIFICATIONS

	0	*1*	*2*	*3 or 4*
Coca Cola	13	23	24	19
Pepsi Cola	12	20	26	21
Royal Crown	18	28	29	14
Chance	15.6	31.2	23.4	8.8

The number of times subjects were able to make correct judgments was greater than the number of times that would be expected by chance alone. For example, Coca Cola was identified correctly three or four times out of four possible choices by 19 subjects, more than double the "statistically expected" number of 8.8 subjects who would be likely to do this by random guessing. Thumin thus felt that his research ". . . clearly demonstrated that certain brands of cola can be identified on the basis of taste."[2] (Thumin, 1962, p. 359.) While this conclusion is justified from a statistical standpoint, it is interesting to note that many subjects were able to make correct identifications *less than* three out of four times. For example, 60 out of 79 subjects were *not* able to identify Coca Cola more than twice out of four possible tries when this beverage was paired with another, and 13 people were not able to identify Coca Cola *at all*. In view of these findings, the conclusion reached earlier in the case of cigarettes seems to be equally appropriate for cola beverages; that is, the ability to discriminate among the various brands of cola may technically exist, but the magnitude is quite small and is unlikely to be of great value in the marketplace.

(As an aside, it is surprising how few adults can *consistently* distinguish among cola, ginger ale, and 7-Up in informal "blind" taste tests. This is an amusing parlor trick for an evening's entertainment with friends.)

Discrimination among beer products has been studied by a number of investigators. The Institute for Research in Mass Motivation found that 81 per cent of 379 subjects were unable to distinguish among different brands of beer in "blind" taste tests. In another proprietary study, when one of the leading nationally distributed brands of beer suffered a decline in its share of the market in the late 1950's, they conducted a taste test comparing their brand with another national brand which had not suffered a decline in sales. Results from 300 in-home taste tests showed that identifications were no more accurate than if the respondents had simply guessed without even tasting the two beers presented for comparison. Even respondents who regularly drank one brand and "couldn't stand" the other were unable to distinguish between the two when identifying labels were removed. (As a result of this study, the brewer was able to con-

---

[2] It is interesting to note that subjects were no better at identifying their "favorite" cola than they were at identifying other brands.

centrate his efforts on the real problem — his label and advertising — rather than wasting time in reformulating his product.)

Lack of sensory discrimination has also been found for other types of consumer products. In one study, it was found that 60 per cent of the adults interviewed could not distinguish between current models of two popular cars when the cars were pictured without any identifying marks. Another study showed that regular and buffered aspirin did not differ in effectiveness if the subjects did not know which one they had taken. One wonders if motorists would be able to distinguish between the performance characteristics of different brands of the same type gasoline or if consumers could properly identify different ice creams or wines. Many studies of this type remain to be done. Yet the evidence to date points clearly to the essential interchangeability of different brands of many products. Differences which do exist are often so small as to be beyond our powers of sensory discrimination.

The implications of the above evidence are numerous. Since many types of consumer products are nearly or wholly indistinguishable on the basis of sensory processes, they must be distinguished on the basis of something else. The consumer must have something to hang his perceptual hat on. The "something else" which serves to distinguish such products is often the product image that is created by the manufacturer: "Coca Cola — the pause that refreshes!" "It's Pepsi — for those who think young!" and the like. (On the other hand, because the consumer likes to *believe* he can discriminate among brands, advertising encourages him with themes that stress "the difference you can *taste!*" This keeps everyone happy — manufacturer *and* consumer.)

Does this mean that sensory processes and physical product characteristics are of negligible importance in consumer marketing? Not at all. There are a great many types of products for which noticeable differences between brands do exist, and these differences form at least part of the basis for consumer choice. But more importantly, one of the greatest challenges of any consumer marketer today is to explore new sensations which *are* noticeably different from those already on the market, especially in product lines which have many similar brands. Products of this type contribute something really new and help to expand the base of available offerings to consumers. They help to keep vitality in the consumer spending portion of our economy.

Gestalt Psychology

Thus far, we have focused primarily upon *stimulus* factors (color, sound, texture, taste, etc.) which affect perception. There is a tendency to come to regard these factors as inert, with no active properties; that is, the stimulus is what it is and will produce the same perceptual reaction in a given individual no matter how it is presented. Gestalt psychologists strongly reject this view, which was held by many earlier psychologists. Gestalt psychologists argue that perception is a dynamic process which often results in something quite different from what would be expected if each element of the stimulus situation were considered separately.

Can perception occur even when there is *no* physical stimulation of one of the senses? Yes, even something as extreme as this can happen. This phenomenon was noticed in the early 1800's by experimenters using a stroboscope, a device for illuminating a moving object with intermittent light. An object is seen only in stationary positions at discrete intervals when the light goes on; but if the time between flashes is short enough, the total effect is that of a moving object despite the fact that no movement is *actually* seen. "The psychological study of this effect . . . received a great impetus from Wertheimer's paper of 1912. He called it the Phi phenomenon and attached theoretical importance to it as a sensory configuration that had more in it than was present in the series of stimuli. In fact, this research of his led to the founding of Gestalt psychology." (Woodworth & Schlosberg, 1960, p. 512.) It also led to the development of the motion picture, a series of *discrete snapshots* which are displayed in rapid sequence to produce the sensation of motion even though this motion is *not present in the film itself*.

Gestalt is a German word for which there is no adequate English equivalent. Roughly, it means the "whole" or "total configuration." In defining Gestalt psychology Wertheimer said, "There are wholes, the behavior of which is not determined by that of their individual elements, but where the part-processes are themselves determined by the intrinsic nature of the whole. It is the hope of Gestalt theory to determine the nature of such wholes." (Wertheimer, 1944, p. 2.)

When we look out the window, we do not see 175 objects, brightnesses, colors, etc. We see the sky, houses, and trees. The scene has unifying *field* properties, external to the observer, which determine what is perceived. For this reason, Gestalt psychology is often called "field" psychology. For example, the dots

. . .

. . .

. . .

are perceived as a square, as three vertical units, or as three horizontal units, but almost never as nine separate dots. Similarly,

is perceived as four columns rather than as eight vertical lines. The lines nearer one another spontaneously come together. (Koffka, 1935.) We thus engage in a *silent organization* of the separate stimulus elements to produce a more meaningful whole.

GESTALT PRINCIPLES

Gestalt psychologists have developed many principles which reflect the manner in which the *field properties* of stimulus objects affect our perception of them. These principles include the following:

Closure. We tend to produce a complete figure. The Kellogg Company utilized this principle in a series of billboard advertisements showing the name "Kellogg" at the far right-hand side of the ad, with the last "g" cut off by the right boundary of the billboard. No matter; we simply add the final "g" to produce the whole (paying greater attention to the ad in the process, of course). This company in particular has used many Gestalt principles in its advertisements, such as substituting a banana for the letter "l" and a quarter for the letter "o" in its name.

Closure is a dangerous device to use in advertising, however. People differ widely in their ability to supply missing elements and achieve closure. An advertisement which is overly subtle, for instance, may cause many people to feel frustrated by their inability to see its point. The person who *does* catch the point is delighted, of course, by his perceptiveness. This functions as an extra "reward" which might attract him strongly to the product being advertised. Experienced advertising men thinking of the general market, however, often reject ads which seem too "cute." This may lead less experienced advertising men to feel that their superiors lack humor and creativity. Ads relying on the principle of closure for their effectiveness should be thoroughly tested in advance. Figures and brand logo-types that are well known tend to help the closure process.

Context. The setting or situation in which a stimulus is perceived greatly affects its meaning. One major aircraft company announced a 10% reduction in pay by means of individual letters to its employees signed by the president. The immediate effect was the opposite of what was expected. Employees greeted the message with amusement rather than consternation. It was only after official verification that the true meaning was established, for the letter had arrived at each employee's desk on April Fool's Day!

Fads and fashions in advertising often become popular because a context has been created in which they can be understood. Outrageous fantasy has been used a great deal in detergent and cleanser advertising. Examples are the Ajax knight who is "stronger than dirt," the washer that is "ten feet tall," and the "giant in your washer." Any one of these by itself would seem foolish, and too many of them would eventually cause boredom. For a time, however, they provide a context for one another and tend to be mutually supporting. In the same way, "pop" art has provided a context for certain women's fashions — skirts with giant fake zippers, for example, or shifts overprinted with reproductions of Campbell's soup labels.

Expectation or Set. What we perceive often depends greatly upon what we are looking for. The page you are now reading would be perceived differently by a copyreader looking for typesetting errors, a student reading for understanding and memorizing for later testing, and a knowledgeable professor looking for errors in substantive content. Each person has a different "set" or expectation.

People approach products in exactly the same way. Kleenex, for instance, was used for years almost entirely as a cleansing tissue to remove cold cream. Both the consumer and the manufacturer saw the product as a substitute for the "towel on the bathroom door." Then the idea of using Kleenex as a handkerchief ("Don't put a cold in your pocket.") revolutionized the tissue business and enlarged the market enormously.

One psychological test for measuring creativity asks people to think of different uses for common items such as a brick or a shoe. Manufacturers should occasionally go through the same exercise to be sure that their mental "sets" are not causing them to overlook major new markets for their products.

Outstandingness. In a large number of homogeneous or very similar items, certain ones will "stand out" and be more noticeable than others, not because they are different but because they have certain locational properties. For example, the extreme left-hand and right-hand columns of a row of columns will appear to "stand out" from the others simply because of their position. The great Greek architects, Iktinos and Kallikrates, knew this when they designed one of the world's architectural masterpieces, the Parthenon on the Acropolis in Athens. The corner columns of this building are slightly larger than the others to make them *appear* equal in size. If the corner columns were actually equal in size to the others, they would appear slightly smaller, partly because of their "outstanding" properties and partly because they are seen against the sky. The corner columns are also closer to their adjacent columns than are the interior columns, since equal spacing would have made the corner columns "stand out" away from their neighbors.

In viewing a shopping gondola (grocery shelves) in a supermarket, a housewife's attention goes first to items at eye level, then toward the middle or left. This places such a premium on shelf position that large consumer-products manufacturers assign a considerable amount of salesman time to simply going from store to store moving their products into more "outstanding" shelf locations and trying to increase total shelf exposure, at the expense of competitors' products, of course.[3] (Gestalt psychologists would contend that the upper left-hand corner of a printed page produces more attention because of its "outstanding" properties.)

Another shelf-space tactic is the use of "flankers" to make a product stand out from other similar products. Campbell's has four kinds of pork and beans, for example — regular, barbecued, with beef, and with weiners. Campbell's regular pork and beans are thus surrounded by "flankers," and competitive brands of pork and beans are kept some distance away. Toiletry manufacturers use the same tactic and "flank" their major products with other products. Of course, these techniques also produce greater "total exposure" of the brand, as do packages with larger frontal areas.

Recency and Primacy. The order in which stimuli are presented affects our perceptions of them. One experimenter assembled a group of subjects and read them two lists of traits (e.g., envious, stubborn, critical, impulsive, industrious, intelligent), one of which allegedly characterized one group of people and the other, another group. The two lists were *actually the same*, but the order was reversed. The audience gave markedly different descriptions of the two groups on the basis of the "different" lists, suggesting that perception of traits *later* in the list was affected to a considerable extent by those heard first. (Asch, 1946.) This seems to support what every salesman knows: that his first impressions upon a prospective customer are of critical importance. Weakness here often leads to the total rejection of an otherwise effective sales pitch.

Figure and Ground. In any perceptual situation, some parts present meaningful patterns and others do not. Gestalt psychologists call the meaningful patterns "figure" and the background "ground." What determines which parts of the total perceptual situation are perceived as figure? In visual studies, figure is most

[3] A recent study suggests that increased frontal shelf space may *not* be effective in increasing sales, at least for certain types of food products. (Cox, 1961.)

often produced by items or components which are physically *near* each other, are of a similar *type* or *size*, have a "*common fate*" (i.e., move simultaneously in the same direction), and produce a "*good figure*" (i.e., something symmetrical or meaningful). Enclos*ed* elements are usually seen as figure and enclos*ing* elements as ground. A circle inside a square, for example, is seen as figure, but the perception is reversed if the square is put inside a circle. Expectation or set also determines which parts are perceived as figure. (Woodworth & Schlosberg, 1960.)

In hearing, the spoken word is normally perceived as figure and background noise as ground. However, sports fans can tell from the roar of the crowd that their team has scored even before the announcer can clarify the situation. What was ground may become figure. Similarly, a *person* who delivers a message in an emotional situation or the *manner* of delivery in terms of tone, poise, assurance, etc. may be far more important than the message itself. President Eisenhower's appearance on television to outline our missile development program, immediately after the launching of Sputnik, undoubtedly reassured many Americans even though most of us were unable to evaluate the plans he proposed.

Simplicity. People tend to follow a principle of "parsimony" in their perception. We organize what we see into the simplest possible patterns. The eight dots below, for example, are seen as a circle, not as two intersecting squares.

Simplicity of structure is important in advertising, with respect to both *layout* and *message content*. Features of a design which do not "fit" the simple pattern perceived tend to drop out of consciousness.

In all of this there is a common thread. Our perception of a situation depends upon far more than the stimulus elements which make up that situation. We try to produce order and sense out of the deluge of stimuli which reach us. Combs and Snygg point out, "If perceptions were not organized, we would be at the mercy of every momentary shift of attention. Our fields would make no sense without organization. We would be so continuously distracted by the myriad changes in the external environment . . . as to make it almost impossible for us ever to accomplish anything." (Combs & Snygg, 1959, p. 169.)

What we perceive is a product of the *total situation*. Gestalt psychologists would say, for example, that Weber's Law holds only when other things are equal. In an interesting study which supports this notion, identical or nearly identical advertisements were placed in two magazines of very different size: *The Readers' Digest*, which is small, and *Life, Look* or *The Saturday Evening Post*, all of which are large. On the basis of Weber's Law (or the square root law) the ads in the larger magazines should have attracted more attention, but, on the contrary, the results of this study showed that "in general, the *absolute* size of an ad has little to do with the number of readers who perceive and recall it. A single page ad appearing in a smaller magazine is perceived and recalled by the same proportion of readers as a single page ad appearing in a larger magazine (provided it is essentially identical in both advertising and editorial content)." (Ulin, 1962, p. 49.) Consumers apparently "adjust" their perceptions to fit the total situation.

The literature of Gestalt psychology is rich with studies which support Gestalt views of perceptual phenomena. Gestalt psychologists have shown, also, the importance of "field" principles in many other areas of human behavior, including learning, memory, motivation, and personality.

Applications

There are many applications of Gestalt principles to consumer marketing in addition to those already mentioned. For example, the following lists of shopping items were shown to 100 housewives:

List #1	List #2
Pound and a half of hamburger	Pound and a half of hamburger
2 loaves Wonder bread	2 loaves Wonder bread
bunch carrots	bunch carrots
1 can Rumford's Baking Powder	1 can Rumford's Baking Powder
Nescafé instant coffee	1 lb. Maxwell House coffee (Drip Grind)
2 cans Del Monte peaches	2 cans Del Monte peaches
5 lbs. potatoes	5 lbs. potatoes

The two lists are identical, of course, except for the coffee entries. Half of the women were shown list #1, and half list #2. Each respondent was asked to write a brief description of the personality and character of the woman who bought the groceries. Results were most interesting "Forty-eight per cent of the people described the woman who bought Nescafé (instant) as lazy; 4 per cent described the woman who bought Maxwell House (regular) as lazy . . .; 48 per cent of the people described the woman who bought Nescafé as failing to plan household purchases and schedules well; 12 per cent described the woman who bought Maxwell House this way." The small difference in coffee purchase (instant versus drip) had such a great effect on perception of the whole or the total configuration that, even though all other entries were identical, they could not override the difference in perception induced by the coffee entries. (Haire, 1950, p. 650.)

A company who can do so has a certain advantage in employing the concept of "family brands," e.g., Heinz "57," Post cereals, the entire line of General Electric household appliances. Introduction of a new product by these companies is perceived as fitting in with the existing product line — it "makes sense." Also, price must be seen as being in harmony with the quality of a product — it must fit the consumer's expectations. (Oxenfeldt et al., 1961, p. 79 ff.)

Sometimes companies display only *portions* of an ad on outdoor billboards, leaving the remaining space blank. As we struggle to effect *closure* and make something meaningful out of the portion or portions shown, attention is produced.

All of these marketing practices draw upon one or more Gestalt principles.

The basic shapes and forms that people perceive in packages and products can be tested by a tachistoscope or blurring device. Sometimes the shape *seen* is not the shape intended. An arrowhead or a wedge, for example, usually suggests motion, going from the wide end toward the point. An automobile manufacturer tried to use exaggerated rear fins to create such an effect. When the design was flashed on a tachistoscope (a device for exposing a picture for a fraction of a second), people saw not an arrowhead but two rectangles, one more nearly square than the other, and had an impression of rest rather than motion. Figure 1.2 illustrates:

Figure 1.2

Actual Shape   Intended Gestalt   Perceived Gestalt

One ingenious study showed the importance of context by showing that the *same advertisement* can produce different results in different settings. For this study, the investigators selected a page in the Des Moines Register, a daily newspaper. The page contained four ads in addition to a column or so of editorial copy. In each of three special runs of the press, one of the ads was deleted and the resulting space was left blank. In a fourth special run *all* ads were deleted, leaving nearly the entire page blank. Interviews were conducted among subscribers to determine how many had noticed each of the blank spaces. In general, the more space that was left blank, the more people there were who noticed "something unusual" about the paper. Then the investigators determined how many subscribers had noticed one particular ad (for a bank) when other ads on the page had been deleted. The results are shown in Table 1.2.

Thus, when the bank ad was deleted and the space left blank, 22 per cent of subscribers noticed the blank space. When the

Table 1.2

RECALL OF BANK AD OR EQUIVALENT
BLANK SPACE, IN FOUR CONTENTS

Ad Left Blank	% Recall of Bank Ad
None (all ads appeared)	20
Dishware ad	31
Color-TV ad	14
	% Recall of Blank Space
Bank ad	22

bank ad was left in on a full page with no spaces, 20 per cent noticed the ad, or about as many as noticed the blank space. However, when the dishware ad was deleted, 31 per cent of subscribers were able to recall the bank ad — an increase of nearly 50 per cent over recall when all ads were left in. The authors concluded:

> Taking out the dishware ad so changed the page that it received, as a whole, less attention from women and more from men. . . . In effect, each blank space so changed the configuration of the page as to alter its meaning and appeal to different readers. This suggests that the page rather than the individual advertisement represents the appropriate unit for measuring the reader's exposure to newspaper advertising (or editorial content, for that matter), since awareness of any element depends on what is seen as a whole. (Bogart & Tolley, 1964, p. 27.)

Winick provided additional evidence on the importance of context in printed advertising. He showed a portfolio of four ads to two similar groups of adults in New York City. Both groups were shown the same ads, but one group was told that one of the four ads (Ad "A") appeared in magazine "X" and the other was told it appeared in magazine "Y." (The magazines were actually named in the test). Table 1.3 shows the great difference in the preference and recall *ranks* assigned to Ad "A," depending on which magazine it was attributed to. (Winick, 1962, p. 29.)

Context, then, does have a significant effect on the way in which a stimulus object is perceived.

Table 1.3

FREQUENCIES OF RANKS OF AD "A" WHEN
ATTRIBUTED TO MAGAZINES "X" AND "Y"

	Most Liked				Most Believable				Recall			
	1	2	3	4	1	2	3	4	1	2	3	4
Magazine "X"	141	131	161	138	227	181	61	102	216	191	120	44
Magazine "Y"	112	81	182	196	171	95	112	193	163	114	149	145

CORPORATE IMAGE

The problem of communicating with consumers presents an interesting illustration of Gestalt principles. In the past, it was too often assumed by the manufacturer that each of his products or messages would "stand on its own feet," that each separate contact would be evaluated on its own merits in a more or less objective fashion by consumers. This, of course, is not in keeping with "field" principles, which suggest that the consumer perceives within a total situation. In other words, we consider the source of a product or message as well as other factors.

Just as each of the shopping lists in the Haire study produced an image of the person it purported to represent, companies may possess "images" which differentiate them from each other within the same product field. As one writer put it: "Who wants to be associated with just another firm that seeks only to survive? American mores place a premium on being on a winning team, or at least being above average. Firms, like individuals, seek to differentiate or distinguish themselves in some respect." (White, 1960, p. 190.) These differentiations may be real or largely imaginary, but consumers *respond* to them to build an image of a company or of a product. Thus, Purex bleach may be perceived as coming from a company who "keeps the housewife in mind" in developing products. A good company image should *predispose* the consumer toward favorable experience in using the product.

Measurement of the corporate image assumed great importance in the 1950's and interest continues unabated today. Hundreds of studies have been done by business firms in many types of industries to determine what sort of impressions are in the minds of consumers; that is, what people think of when the name of the company or the brand name is mentioned, what its strong points are and what its weaknesses are, what the ideal company should be like according to the consumer, and so on. Only after information of this type becomes available can a particular company see where it now stands in relation to its long range public relations objectives and in what context and against what background the consumer will perceive its products and advertising.

Corporate image is measured by various rating devices called psychological scaling techniques. These are not too different from those used in the merit rating of employees within a firm, except that in this case a *consumer* is evaluating a *company*. One image-scaling device is shown in Fig. 1.3. The respondent places an "A" in the appropriate box to represent his feelings about Company A, a "B" for Company B, etc. Often he is also asked to place an "I" in a box to show where he feels the ideal company would be in terms of some aspect such as its sheer size. (A very large company, for example, is not necessarily ideal in a consumer's mind.) There are many other types of image-scaling techniques which are useful for specific problem situations. (Winick, 1960.)

No matter what kind of rating scale is used, the result of image-scaling is generally some kind of profile. The profiles shown in Fig. 1.4 are those of five household cleaning-products companies as seen through the eyes of their distributors. Company A is considered creative, aggressive, successful, and the like, but high-priced and inconsiderate. Company E, on the other hand, is generally seen as the reverse, while other companies are seen as somewhere in between. (Hill, 1961.) Information of this kind helps a company to undertake correctional programs.

Why is corporate image so important? Gestalt psychology provides an answer. When a company directs communications of any kind to consumers or places a new product on the market, consumers evaluate what they see or hear against their image of the company. If the image is neutral, it becomes relatively unmeaningful "ground" in the total situation; if the image is *very* favorable or unfavorable, it becomes "figure" and the message, package design, or product itself may produce little impact. Extensive studies on communications show that the "credibility

Figure 1.3

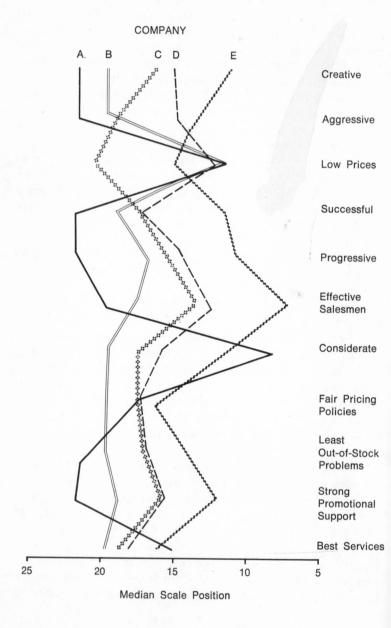

COMPANY

A   B   C   D   E

Creative

Aggressive

Low Prices

Successful

Progressive

Effective
Salesmen

Considerate

Fair Pricing
Policies

Least
Out-of-Stock
Problems

Strong
Promotional
Support

Best Services

25   20   15   10   5

Median Scale Position

Figure 1.4

This company is the *most considerate.*

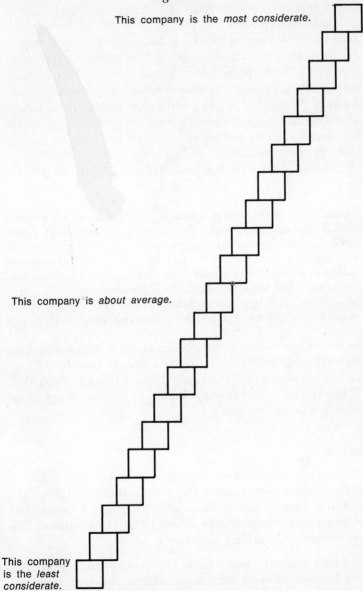

This company is *about average.*

This company
is the *least
considerate.*

Source: Human Factors Research, Inc., Los Angeles, California

of the communicator" is a critical factor in determining audience reaction to a message. In this sense, "credibility" and "image" are almost synonymous.

One hardware company found in the early 1950's that even its own distributors considered it among the newer, smaller companies in the field. In actuality, it had consistently sold more household locks and door handles than any other company since the end of World War II! As a result of its finding, the company initiated an ambitious dealer-education program to correct the misconception which was interfering with the accurate perception of its communications.

A concept similar to company image is *brand* or *product* image:

> Sometimes a specific use is associated so strongly with a product that it dominates its image. For instance, the makers of Jell-O tried unsuccessfully to get consumers to think of this product as an elegant dessert. Consumers had been so used to thinking of Jell-O as a 'shirtsleeves dessert' that they could not modify their impressions and begin to regard it as a luxury product. 'If I have to spend so much time making a dessert,' they said, 'I might as well make a fancy dessert, not Jell-O.' (Oxenfeldt, et al., 1961, p. 82.)

The laboratory studies discussed earlier have shown that consumers are either partly or completely unable to identify different brands of cigarettes, colas, and beer. Given evidence of this kind, it is easy to see why company, brand, or product image often assumes the paramount role.

Illusions

We all know that our eyes play tricks on us, but it has remained for the psychologist to study this phenomenon carefully. The Geometric visual illusions have been investigated thoroughly, and several theories have been advanced to explain them. Illusions are generally divided into two types:

Contrast illusions. Small items look even smaller than they are by contrast with some larger object, and vice versa.

Confluxion or assimilation illusions. Small items look larger than they are by virtue of similarity with larger objects.

Whether contrast or confluxion takes place depends upon many situational factors. In each case, however, something is being compared with something else.

One of the best known is the Müller-Lyer illusion:

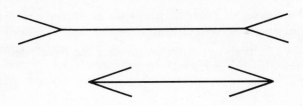

The lower line looks shorter in *contrast* with the upper line. Actually, both lines are the same length.

Illusions are frequently utilized in package design. An irregular shape, for example, that makes a package taller (but thinner) than competitive products may make it *appear*, by contrast, to hold more. A manufacturer wishing to promote sales of his higher priced tires or gasoline may establish a new top-priced line. His lowest priced products will seem so cheap by contrast that consumers will be more likely to move up to a "middle" price range. The sales success of American economy cars in the late 1950's may well have been due in part to their contrast in size with the standard models. The size differences appeared so large as to suggest that the price differentials were greater than they actually were.

QUESTIONS
FOR REVIEW

1. Increased advertising expenditures sometimes show diminishing returns. Is this an instance of Weber's Law? Does Weber's Law have any application to copyright and trademark infringement litigation?

2. Some people find it easier to achieve closure than others when exposed to an incomplete perceptual structure, such as an advertisement with missing elements. What problems does this pose for the advertiser who uses closure to obtain consumer participation in his ads?

3. Is subliminal advertising related to any of the principles of Gestalt psychology?

4. What factors determine which elements in a point-of-purchase display are perceived as figure and which are perceived as ground?

5. Give examples of how the principles of illusion are used in various aspects of consumer marketing.

6. Should a firm always strive to produce the most "desirable" corporate image possible? Discuss.

2

Learning, Memory, and Cognition

"MOST AMERICAN PSYCHOLOGISTS, especially those of an experimental bent, regard learning as the fundamental process in the understanding of human behavior." (Berelson & Steiner, 1964, p. 133.) This is not surprising since psychologists define learning as any *change in behavior* which comes about from experience or practice in that general area of behavior. Learning does not include changes in behavior which occur from fatigue, normal maturation process, drugs or alcohol, radical changes in motivation, illness, and so on. Generally the changed or "new" behavior is in some way superior to the old, at least in terms of the individual's goals or objectives.

There are many forms of learning, reflecting the various processes through which individuals seek to improve their adjustment to or control over their environment. We are interested here primarily in how these various learning processes relate to consumer behavior.

What do consumers learn?

- A man learns of a new stereophonic sound system for passenger automobiles.

- A housewife learns to select better lettuce, oranges, and other produce in a market by observing features such as firmness and color before purchasing and by relating these to satisfaction in later use of the produce.

- A family learns which new clothing styles are acceptable (and indeed expected) among their friends.

- A housewife learns to associate the name Birdseye on a package of frozen foods with a quality product.

- A teenager learns how to get more performance out of his hot-rod.

These are only a few of the many ways in which learning is related to buying behavior.

If learning is one of the fundamental processes of human behavior, it is certainly a basic part of consumer behavior in the market place. Both the initial establishment of a buying pattern and any subsequent change in this pattern are based upon learning processes. Before relating learning principles to the marketing context, it is well to review the basic processes themselves to provide a better understanding of this complex phenomenon. Examples can then be drawn from the buying situation to illustrate practical marketing applications of knowledge about learning.

Forms of Learning. One form of learning involves the *acquisition of information.* All normal human beings are constantly in the process of absorbing new information and consumers, being human, are no exception. The housewife learns of a new product or of additional uses for an old product; the teenager learns different techniques of applying cosmetics or the name of a new recording artist. The fact that there are so many things to *be* learned means that consumers must necessarily be selective in what they *do* learn, and this is a major problem in informing consumers of new products or services. Nevertheless, a vast reservoir of interest does exist for most products, and consumers *in the aggregate* are always open to new ideas or information.

Learning also involves the formation of *associations*, either between stimulus objects (e.g., a baseball belongs with a bat or a fielder's glove) or between an action and the results of that action (a soft drink reduces thirst). When associations of the latter type develop from frequent repetition of an action, they may lead to the formation of *habits*, which are more or less automatic responses to familiar situations or encounters. A man out of cigarettes buys Winstons without giving the matter any thought; most housewives, relying on habit to ease their shopping burdens, buy the same brand of coffee, margarine, or canned peaches that they bought last time. (Imagine a shopper giving critical thought to each of the many items she puts in her shopping cart!)

In a buying situation, action based upon associations previously formed is often triggered by *cues*, another key concept in some theories of learning. Cues are sensory stimuli of almost any kind (size, color, pattern, sound) which arouse some kind of response simply because they have in the past been associated with that particular response. In other words, what has been learned is the cue-response association. The housewife passing a shelf of cereals will reach for a package of Cream of Wheat, the package being the cue for a particular action which has long since become a habit.

Another form of learning is *thinking*. Thinking is a mental process of applying the abstract, the conceptual, the symbolic to the solution of some problem. The decision by a college student to buy a Honda motorbike results from consideration of a great many factors such as cost of the motorbike, available competitive brands, cost of an automobile, parking fees, safety factors, expected weather conditions, and anticipated social life. He must evaluate these factors in relation to one another to produce an optimal solution for his personal situation.

While learning is generally thought of as applying primarily to information, objects, or events, other subject matter is often involved. For example, we learn certain *tastes*, such as a preference for Scotch whisky or jazz music. A preference may come by influence from others in our social context or it may come simply from familiarity over time. We also learn *perceptual discrimination*, the ability to distinguish between perceptual patterns of different types, some of which are desirable according to some standard while others are not. For example, the development of "good taste" in clothing, interior decoration, landscaping, or visual art forms is based primarily on one's ability to discriminate among various complex patterns and colors to find those which are socially acceptable or otherwise more desirable.

We even learn to *need or want* certain objects or events. If others in our neighborhood have color TV or a cleaning woman once a week, we tend to acquire a desire for the same thing. As our income goes up, we "learn" that we "need" certain labor-saving devices which we previously considered luxuries.

(Gestalt psychologists view learning in a different light. In keeping with their emphasis upon the search for meaning in diverse perceptual material, they hypothesize that learning involves the continuous organization and reorganization of one's perceptual systems into more meaningful patterns. As the individual gradually develops new meanings and perspectives for the same perceptual data, his behavior changes accordingly and we can say that he has learned.)

Learning, then, is a vast panorama and it impinges upon our buying behavior in a great many ways. All of the above concepts and illustrations involve learning in its fullest sense — a change in behavior to improve in some way upon earlier behavior in similar situations.

Although learning can be *defined* in a meaningful fashion, it is quite difficult to *measure*. We cannot directly observe the mental processes of learning but instead must piece the puzzle together from the outward signs and expressions (e.g., verbal reports, task performance, and behavior changes). One authority cautions, "Learning is always an inference, derived from changes in performance, and learning is not the only factor that can cause these changes" (Hilgard, 1951, p. 517). Because of this, our understanding of the learning process is far from complete. But a great deal of knowledge does exist, and much of it is relevant to many aspects of consumer behavior.

Building Associations

One of the simplest forms of learning involves the establishment of associations between two or more separate stimuli or between a stimulus and a response to that stimulus. One early school of psychology, Behaviorism, called the associations between stimuli and responses "S-R bonds" and contended that all forms of human behavior, no matter how complex, could be reduced ultimately to these elementary associations. Whether these bonds are established simply by repeated exposure or whether they demand some form of reward or reinforcement in order to be formed is still a subject of controversy among psychologists.

Early psychologists were concerned mainly with associations between two or more separate stimuli. They found that associations were more likely to be produced between stimulus objects which were *similar* in form or meaning, located *near* one another, seen together *frequently*, seen or heard for a long *duration*, and so forth.

In consumer marketing, associations may be built by the simple repetition of a product slogan with the brand name; for example, "For faster relief, get Bayer aspirin." One cigarette brand, Newport, claimed to be the first to air a radio commercial which did not mention the brand name, certain that the distinctive background music would immediately bring the name of the cigarette to the listener's mind because this association had been built over many previous radio and television commercials. General Electric states, "Progress is our Most Important Product." DuPont claims, "Better Things for Better Living Through Chemistry." Pall Mall cigarettes are for "particular" people. All of these slogans attempt to build the associations which are so important to corporate or brand image.

In general, studies show that promotional efforts have been quite effective in building these associations. Consumers do indeed "learn."

It should be stressed that *meaningful* associations are more easily formed and are retained longer than those based upon mere repetition. Progress can be associated with General Electric but not with a buggy whip manufacturer. It is also true that *understanding* contributes far more to the learning process than simple repetition. One writer points out that a slogan such as "LS/MFT" can be put across, but only by an enormous expenditure of money. (Britt, 1955.) More meaningful slogans, conveying information which leads to better understanding, are likely to be more easily absorbed; for example, "Preparation H shrinks hemorrhoids without surgery."

Pavlovian or classical conditioning is one means of establishing associations. In the conditioning process, a bell is rung every time food is given to a dog. After a time, the dog salivates whenever the bell rings, even though he is not given any food. This shows the power of *associating* the bell with food over so many occasions that such an intrinsically meaningless noise can produce the same response (saliva) as food itself. But this is just a laboratory experiment which has nothing to do with the way consumers behave in the marketplace. Or does it? Consider such common sales promotion devices as price discounts, free recipe booklets, and attached or enclosed premiums which can stimulate a housewife to try a new brand for the first, second, or third time. Eventually, an association is established between the intrinsically desirable "unconditioned stimulus" (price reduction, recipe book) and the "conditioned stimulus" (product brand). If the latter is of comparable quality and performance to competing products, the association initially established may persist and develop into the form of a *habit*, so that the conditioned brand is selected with no accompanying sales promotion.

In a similar manner, classical conditioning applies to many aspects of our lives. Children are conditioned to respond to a raised eyebrow, a frown, or other sign of parental disapproval. The young college graduate entering a business firm is conditioned to respond to subtle cues from his superiors indicating what is expected of him. The salesman is conditioned to respond to small changes in a buyer's voice or facial expression in planning his next course of attack. It is no wonder that the Russian scientist, Pavlov, was in great favor with Stalin for his discovery of classical conditioning principles. Stalin saw these as a powerful means of controlling the minds of the Russian people and, indeed, used classical conditioning extensively.

Another form of conditioning involves the accomplishment of some goal or objective. As an illustration, an individual in serious financial trouble will cast about for some source of funds. He may not be successful with friends, the minister, banks, or members of his family, but he may secure his funds from a personal loan company. This is a form of instrumental conditioning. The finance company is an *instrument* by means of which the individual meets his immediate needs. He becomes conditioned to turn to the same company the next time he is in financial difficulty. In a similar manner, we become conditioned to use Excedrin for headaches, Enden shampoo for dandruff, and Johnson's Wax for floor protection. Each solves a particular problem, which tends to establish for us an association between the act of buying the product and the solution of the problem. In each of these examples, some form of reward or reinforcement is present and facilitates the learning process.

Applications to Consumer Marketing

The phenomenon of association is of great importance in consumer marketing in many ways. One objective, of course, is to form an association between some disorder, problem, or need and the product or service which will provide the solution or satisfaction. Every consumer-product manufacturer tries to do this.

But beyond this, there are the more subtle associations which result in consumers seeing *more* in a product than is warranted by either the physical features or the performance characteristics of that product. One writer observes:

> The things people buy are seen to have personal or social meanings in addition to their functions. Modern goods are recognized as psychological things, as symbolic of personal attributes and goals, as symbolic of social patterns and strivings. In this sense, all commercial objects have a symbolic character, and making a purchase involves an assessment — implicit or explicit — of this symbolism, to decide whether or not it fits. (Levy, 1959, p. 410.)

This writer states that years of research have shown that darker colors are symbolic of more "respectable" products; pastel colors mean softness, youthfulness, femininity; the word "science" implies an interest in quality and technical merits rather than enjoyment; theatrical references imply glamour and the "suspension of staid criteria."

Other investigators have found that the *usage* of certain products is associated with people of certain characteristics. For example, the use of hot cereal is associated with children, farmers, athletes, poor people, and elderly people, but not as much with movie stars, rich people, or teenage girls. Males are thought to eat more hot cereal than females. (Westfall, Boyd, & Campbell, 1957). Associations of this type are not readily apparent and the foundations for them may be vague or even nonexistent. Nevertheless, these associations exist in the consumer's mind and from a purchasing standpoint their accuracy is largely irrelevant. The important fact is that they can and do influence buying decisions.

To show the different kinds of associations that are formed, Brink and Kelley replicated an interesting study by Dale Houghton of New York University. College students were given a list of common "irritations": headache, indigestion, sleeplessness, offensive breath, etc. For each of these, the student was asked to write down the first "remedy or product" which came to mind after reading the irritation. He was also asked to indicate what brand, if any, he *actually used* for the irritation. They comment:

> One would expect a high degree of brand associations for these highly advertised medicines (proprietary drugs) . . . There was such an association; a trademarked item was associated with needs in nearly 50 per cent of all cases . . . A generic term (e.g., aspirin) was given 38.6 per cent of the time, probably because there was little experience with certain needs (in the case of some students not suffering from the irritation). Although the trademark remedy was mentioned in about one half the cases, the respondents indicated they actually used the associated brand in only 25.7 per cent of the total . . . In 17.9 per cent of these cases the respondents indicated they had no use for the item first associated; the remainder had had a bad experience with the associated brand . . . There is a lesson in this: the mere establishment of a need-brand association is not enough; subsequent experience with the brand must be favorable, or the consumer will countermand the initial association. (Brink & Kelley, 1963, p. 128.)

Research studies sometimes turn up what can only be called false associations. It is not uncommon for consumers to associate a company's slogan with its competitor, especially if the competitor is a giant who dominates the industry. Most of us, for example, if shown a soup slogan, would automatically name Campbell's as the originating company. The false association would be the result of a somewhat logical assumption that a soup slogan is more likely to come from Campbell's than from any other firm. A false association may well affect buying behavior.

It is likely, for example, that all soup advertising helps Campbell's, since a quick reader would note that a magazine ad is for soup, associate it with Campbell's, and go on to the next page.

Associations unintended by an advertiser may also be formed. One child came to the conclusion, on the basis of television commercials, that nasal congestion was a remedy for colds and urged his mother to buy a bottle of "Nasal Congestion" for his stuffy nose!

It is important to remember that associations are not uniform from person to person. A manufacturer may try to build associations which seem clear to him but which remain invincibly obscure to many of his potential customers. The design of the Edsel is a case in point. The car had a free-standing vertical grille which was highly admired by people within the automobile industry. The grille was compared to the classic cars of the 1930's, the Pierce-Arrow and the LaSalle, and to sports cars such as the Bugatti and Alfa Romeo. These associations were unmistakable to the industry's knowledgeable designers and executives, but few people in the general market remembered the LaSalle and even fewer were familiar with the Bugatti. To most people, the front end of the car was simply incomprehensible.

Similarly, an attempt was once made to promote dark green as an automobile color. Since a dark, almost black green is the official British color in continental Grand Prix racing, people in the industry enthusiastically associated the color with the glamour of Grand Prix racing. To the general public, however, the color was no more than an exceptionally dark green and was not widely ordered (although it became popular ten years later, in the middle 1960's).

One national brewer found by an intensive marketing research study that a decline in his sales during the late 1950's was due largely to masculine associations among the general public toward his beer. The red label with the spread-wing eagle, the team of horses used for publicity purposes, and the lack of women in ads all contributed to the unusually strong masculine associations for this beer. It was about this time that beer was beginning to be sold in supermarkets, where it was bought mostly by women. Their avoidance of such a masculine-appearing product forced the brewer to redesign both his can and his advertising to appeal more to women buyers.

SIGN-EXPECTANCIES

A closely related topic of current interest to marketers of consumer goods is *sign-expectancies*. Consumers look for signs in a product, package, or advertisement which lead them to *expect* a certain quality or performance from the product or service. We try to associate certain signs or product characteristics with the results which will be realized from later use. For example, we learn from experience that cloth which feels soft will normally not wear as well as harder fabrics such as worsteds or sharkskins for men's suits. To shorten this learning process, the producer tells us what to look for in making a purchase: "Knock on the wall — demand genuine lath and plaster," or "None genuine without my signature." These signs become associated by constant repetition with satisfaction (if the product is good), and satisfaction is the objective of the consumer. The next time he sees the same or a similar sign, the favorable association is evoked.

Consumers look for many types of signs. Although it is not usually thought of in this way, *price* may be a very important sign in some purchasing situations. We normally expect a higher quality item to cost more and, therefore, we may expect higher priced items to be of higher quality and, hence, more desirable. This may be true particularly in the case of products which are perceived by consumers to have *large differences in quality* among brands. When a buyer is faced with a choice in this type of situation, he may be more likely to look for signs to help him select a brand. Price would certainly be one of the signs, and the buyer should tend to choose a higher priced over a lower priced item.

To test this, one investigator asked a sample of adults to "choose" (i.e., tell what brand they think they would buy) one of two hypothetical brands in each of four product categories. Two of these product categories were felt by subjects to have *large* differences in quality among brands (razor blades and floor wax) and two were felt to have *small* differences in quality (cooking sherry and moth flakes). The subjects showed a slight tendency to select the higher priced brands of the "large-quality-difference" product categories, but not of the "small-quality-difference" products, suggesting that better quality was imputed to higher priced items. (Leavitt, 1954.)

To verify these results, another team of investigators conducted a similar study using another four product categories, two of which were considered very similar from brand to brand (table salt and aspirin) and two of which were considered quite different from brand to brand (liquid shampoo and floor wax). Three hypothetical brands, randomly labeled with letters of the alphabet, were used for each product category. Subjects were asked to play the role of family shopper and to assume that the brand they would usually buy was out of stock when they went to make a purchase. Each subject was given a low, medium, or high *reference* price (the assumed price of the brand "you usually buy"). They were then asked to choose one of the three hypothetical brands in each product category using only price to guide their choice.

Results showed that regardless of which reference price the subjects were given, there was more of a tendency to choose high-priced brands in product categories which were thought to have large differences in quality among brands than in product categories in which quality differences were thought to be small. In other words, when subjects had to choose among brands of supposedly similar quality, their choices tended to follow the shape of the traditional demand curve; that is, as price increased, there were fewer choices for that brand. However, in product categories with brands of dissimilar quality, many more subjects indicated a preference for higher-priced brands. In this experiment, price became an important *sign* from which the quality or desirability of a brand was inferred. (Tull, Boring, & Gonsior, 1964.)

Along a similar line, one of the writers once asked 400 men and women what word they associated with the word "expensive." A few gave negative responses such as "ostentatious," and a third of them gave rational responses such as "dear" and "costly." But two-thirds associated "expensive" with high quality: "best," or "superior."

Another sign used by consumers is that of color. Different colors lead buyers to expect differences in quality or performance. One study determined the effects of color newspaper ads upon readers' perceptions of the merchandise being advertised and upon the image of the store itself. Coats advertised in color were preferred to those not in color; but more importantly, 70 per cent of the respondents attributed the color ads to high-status stores. They used color as a sign to infer quality of the sponsoring store. (Gardner & Cohen, 1964.)

Another study showed that consumers use the type of wrapping paper as a sign of the freshness of a loaf of bread. Equally fresh loaves, one wrapped in cellophane and another wrapped in waxed paper, were presented to housewives so that they could feel but not see each loaf. The women were asked to tell which loaf was the fresher. In this situation, "They perceived fresh bread of equal freshness to be fresher when wrapped in cellophane than when wrapped in wax." (Brown, 1958, p. 260.) (This was true for one- and two-day-old bread as well.) Note that the sign in this case came from the tactual sense only. The loaves were not visible to the housewives.

The cosmetics and beauty-aids industries in particular have grasped the importance of sign-expectancies. They know that women of all ages are anxious to preserve (and increase) their own natural beauty features and that many women simply do not like to pay too little for their cosmetics. Why? Undoubtedly these women are subconsciously or even consciously using price as a sign to impute the quality of a product or brand. Low price tags on beauty aids and cosmetic preparations seem to be a sign of low quality products. Use of inexpensive products suggests to a woman that she is not doing the most possible for her face or figure. Consequently, products of this type may even have a "reverse" demand curve, so that higher prices sell *more* products of a given type or brand than lower prices. Although no published studies are available to support this hypothesis, it is well known that profits in these industries are quite high. One shampoo manufacturer, Alberto-Culver, reported spending *60 per cent of gross sales* on television advertising in one year. This would hardly be possible without rather substantial gross margins on these shampoos.

One could also argue that high-priced drugs "cure" better than low-priced drugs, especially in the case of disorders of a psychogenic nature.

"Signs" of various kinds are used constantly by consumers to make inferences about products. It is interesting to note that there is an amazing uniformity among people when they are asked whether a design is conservative or advanced, masculine or feminine, strong or delicate. The reason for this uniformity is that people have learned to "read" the signs built into the design of products offered for sale. These signs give the consumer information about the product itself. A man buying a suit will feel the material, check the label, and count the number of buttons on the sleeves. For years, four buttons meant a quality suit, three buttons a lower-priced suit, and two buttons a flashy suit, especially if the buttons were smooth rather than embossed.

PROBLEM SOLVING

There have been many studies of problem solving using both animals and human beings. As compared with rote memory and simple goal-seeking behavior, problem solving is a complex phenomenon. Ruch makes the point: "Problem solving, on the one hand, utilizes the products of previous learning experiences and, on the other, is a learning experience itself. Higher mental processes may also be called into play — reasoning, forming concepts, making and testing hypotheses, and so on." (Ruch, 1958, p. 308.) On the basis of intensive review of various formulations, he suggests that the following steps characterize the problem-solving process:

1. Becoming concerned about or interested in a problem.
2. Assembling the materials with which to work, including physical tools and/or available knowledge.
3. Deriving a number of possible solutions which can occur by insight (the sudden arrival at the solution), by more or less random trial and error behavior, or by various reasoning processes.
4. Evaluating the possible solutions before actually testing them, by recalling any information pertinent to the problem and using this information to check each hypothesis under consideration.
5. Objectively testing and revising the solution to see if it "works."

Our primary concern here is with the extent to which problem solving enters into the consumer buying situation. Is problem solving an important aspect of the purchasing process? Some writers think so, pointing out the "problems" of the housewife in running her home — "deciding" what to have for dinner, and so on. But other observers argue that real problem solving in the form of decision making is not characteristic of the consumer buying process. Katona states:

> Problem solving behavior is a relatively rare occurrence . . . The main alternative to problem solving behavior is not whimsical or impulsive behavior (which was considered the major example of 'irrational' behavior by nineteenth century philosophers). When genuine decision making does *not* take place, habitual behavior is the most usual occurrence: people act as they have acted before under similar circumstances, without deliberating and choosing. (Katona, 1953, p. 310.)

His point is that habitual behavior may well be and usually is *rational* behavior and that we cannot say that a consumer is irrational just because he does not engage in problem-solving, decision-making behavior each time he makes a purchase. In contrast, some writers distinguish between habitual behavior and rational behavior, considering the latter as the kind of behavior exhibited when the consumer chooses among products on the basis of such factors as price or convenience. (Cf. Woods, 1960.)

Even though observers differ in their definitions of buying motivations, they tend to agree that the problem-solving, decision-making type of purchasing behavior is not as prevalent as habitual behavior, shown when the consumer repeatedly buys the same products or brands without giving much thought to the matter. However, in those relatively rare situations in which consumers are presented with really *new* products. or when some problem arises in connection with the use of some *present* product, or when the consumer is contemplating a major change in his mode of living, problem-solving behavior may be brought into play.

THE LEARNING OF TASTES

Thus far we have dealt primarily with the learning of *cognitive* material: the acquisition of knowledge, the reasoning processes, conceptual thinking. What about such *affective* materials as feelings, emotions, and tastes? Are these also *learned*?

It is obvious that some affective material has a strong social component (i.e., an individual is greatly influenced by the feelings and tastes of those around him), but we are interested here in means of learning affective material, particularly preferences and tastes, which may not depend exclusively upon the social context.

An early study involved 15 students who met for two hours a day, ten days in a row. These students were exposed to a wide variety of tasks such as viewing paintings of well-known artists, writing down the names of Russian women, and copying from a book sentences that contained certain key words. In the later sessions, students were asked without warning to make a judgment of personal preference or were offered something different. For example, they were shown 15 matched pairs of paintings by the same artists whose work they had viewed earlier. One painting in each pair was the one they had seen during the early part of the experiment. There was a tendency for the students to prefer the more familiar painting in each pair, while another group of students *without* previous exposure split their preferences equally between the pictures in each pair. Similar preferences were shown for the Russian women's names the students were familiar with and for a familiar rather than a "new" method of copying sentences and marking tests. The overall results clearly showed a tendency for these students to choose the familiar, i.e., what they had been exposed to. (Maslow, 1937.)

Krugman, in a later study, played swing music to three students who were extremely interested in classical music and never listened to swing. At the same time, he played classical music to three students who were extremely pro-swing and to three who were indifferent to it. The records to be played to each student were selected by playing a number of records until three were found which the student neither liked nor disliked. From then on these same three records were played once a week for eight weeks. Preference ratings were made by students each week, and these ratings showed a steady increase in liking for at least two of the three selections over a period of six weeks. After that, the increase in preference tended to level off. At the end, *all* students agreed that they could get to like some of the selections in the music category to which they had previously expressed a strong aversion. (Krugman, 1943.)

A more complex study involved the relationship between familiarity with an item and the liking for both this item and the *category* in which the item belonged (e.g., Oriental, floral, modern, landscape, or portrait paintings). Krugman and Hartley summarized the results of this and other studies as follows:

> It may be said that Maslow demonstrated that familiarity with items created liking for some *items* but not for others; Krugman demonstrated that when familiarity with items created liking for the items, then some combination of familiarity and liking could create liking for the *category;* Hartley showed that familiarity with items created familiarity with the category, but that this might not create liking for the category depending upon a number of different factors. . . . The . . . above may be used to conduct research on products, brands, tastes, styles, or ideas. It matters less what is actually studied than the fact that a real gap in our knowledge is represented here, a gap that should be of concern to both the social scientist and the businessman. (Krugman and Hartley, 1960, p. 631.)

If consumers can learn tastes and preferences for aesthetic items of many types, how and where do they learn them? The real significance of the experimental work cited above is in suggesting that people can learn to like things simply by being exposed to them; that is, by seeing them around frequently, quite aside from their initial preferences, from social influences, and so on. It follows, then, that the marketer can exert some amount of *direct influence* upon the taste preferences of the consumer through the design and characteristics of the products and services he offers.

Fashions in clothing readily come to mind. Clothes designers exert a very considerable influence upon how women will look and how they will *want* to look. An interesting article by Burck traces the influence of business on tastes in many other product lines including furniture, appliances, and homes. He points out:

> Precisely because businessmen are so often at a loss to know just how public taste is going to shift, they tend to let their corporate and personal self-esteem line them up on the side of good, or at least professional, design. And for their part, even the most mercenary practitioners of the "We'll design you any damn thing

you want" school would rather turn out something they regard as good than something pandering to bad taste. Most good designers, indeed, take the view that the public's frequent uncertainty about its taste offers the opportunity of turning out something better than they might if the public knew exactly what it wanted. (Burck, 1949.)

Burck feels, in summary, that the business forces changing American tastes are changing them for the better. He concludes, "Business will still be able to sell junk to a lot of Americans. But it surely will be able to make more money operating on the assumption that people want something "better," not only functionally but aesthetically."

Factors Affecting Learning

Through laboratory and field research, we know a great deal about various factors which affect the learning process. Those which are more appropriate to the consumer learning situation than others will be stressed here.

REINFORCEMENT OR REWARD

Reinforcement is a central concept in many learning theories. Thorndike's Law of Effect states, "Of the responses made to a situation, those which satisfy the organism's needs tend to be retained, while those which fail to satisfy these needs tend to be eliminated." (Thorndike, 1911, p. 224.) Hull substituted *drive reduction* for reward and stated that any stimulus-response sequence that is followed by a reduction in strength of a drive will be reinforced. (Hull, 1943.) Thus, a shampoo which reduces scalp-itch the most and for the longest time will reinforce the association between this brand and our scalp problem. A corollary principle is that the *greater* the reward or reinforcement, the stronger is the association or learning. Being extremely satisfied on only one occasion with an item of clothing, for example, strongly predisposes the consumer to return to the store where that item was purchased. Also, the *strength or importance* of the need must be considered. Learning is more likely to occur when the objective or problem is of great importance, as in the purchase of a house, a car, or medical services.

The learning process can be characterized by either partial or total reinforcement. In *total reinforcement*, the appropriate behavior is rewarded every time it occurs. The chicken that pecks at the red button gets a kernel of corn as a reward for each peck. In *partial reinforcement*, the behavior is rewarded only some of the time, usually on a random schedule. The chicken does not always get his kernel of corn.

Learning is much faster when there is total reinforcement, but the learned behavior is harder to extinguish and is better retained when it is the result of partial reinforcement. It is easy to see why this is the case. The chicken who is accustomed to receiving a kernel of corn every time he performs some act will notice that something is wrong when the corn is suddenly no longer forthcoming. The chicken who has been rewarded with corn some of the time, but not all of the time, will not be surprised if corn is not forthcoming for a time. He will continue to peck for a much longer time in the absence of a reward. Berelson and Steiner point out, "Extremely tenacious behavior is created by schedules with variable intervals — where reinforcement may be delivered one time after five minutes, the next time after twelve, then after two, and so on." (Berelson and Steiner, 1964, p. 155.) These writers suggest that this may explain the great attraction slot machines have for some people. The variability of the reinforcement produces great interest. The same might certainly be said for speculating in the stock market.

The strength of partial reinforcement is one reason that it is extremely difficult to change brand images, most of which are formed on the basis of partial rather than total reinforcement. If the consumer has "learned" on the basis of a few unfortunate experiences that a brand of appliance is not reliable, he will be able to resist successfully a great deal of evidence that the brand is, in fact, highly reliable. If a neighbor reports good experience with this brand, he will assume most likely that the neighbor was simply lucky. His original opinion will not be shaken that easily. Similarly, a consumer who has learned that a brand of automobile is well made can accept a "lemon," or even a series of "lemons," with equanimity and remain convinced that the brand is generally of high quality.

These principles and examples illustrate the significance of reinforcement or reward in the buying context. Clearly, the happier a consumer is with a product or service he has purchased, the greater is the reinforcement, and the stronger is the learning which takes place. Sometimes the principles of reinforcement work for the marketer, sometimes against. In either case, they help to explain why buying behavior often follows paths which seem capricious to the rational observer.

Massed versus Distributed Exposure

One of the important factors affecting the speed of learning is the *pattern or frequency of our exposure* to the learning situation. Given the same total amount of exposure time, do we learn more from continuous exposure (massed practice) or from intermittent exposure over a longer period of time (distributed practice)? Many research studies, covering everything from the learning of motor skills (e.g., writing or typing) to rote memorization and even the development of symbolic skills, show the *general superiority of distributed practice,* provided, of course, that the intervals between exposure are not so long that a great deal of forgetting occurs between exposures. There may be several reasons for this finding. Continuous or even closely spaced application to a task is likely to produce boredom and fatigue. Our "physical plant" needs time to recover. Further, intervals between exposure permit some beneficial forgetting such as eliminating inappropriate or erroneous learning. They also provide time for building more durable associations and relationships, while massed practice relies solely on immediate memory, which fades more rapidly.

On the other hand, there is evidence that as the task becomes more meaningful or ideational, the superiority of distributed practice tends to decline and may even be reversed. For example, in certain kinds of logical-reasoning problems, massed effort has been shown to be generally superior to distributed effort. Ruch states: ". . . Motor learning and ideational learning are quite different with regard to the distribution of practice. In the former, distributed practice followed by massed practice gives the best results; in the latter, the formula is reversed." (Ruch, 1958, p. 334.)

Manufacturers of consumer products are often faced with a very real problem. Given a fixed budget to cover all radio or television advertising for the coming year, is it better to shoot the works in one or two "blitz" campaigns or to distribute the expenditure evenly during the year? If it is better to spread it out, what is the ideal interval for maximum impact? The manufacturer's proper course of action depends upon the type of product, the message he wishes to convey, the stage in the life cycle of the product, and other factors. If his objective is simply to inform the consumer, to build associations, to develop rote memory — ignoring for the moment the critical dimension of motivation — he would normally choose to advertise at intervals to take advantage of the principles of distributed practice. However, if his product or service is new or different and demands some thought on the part of the consumer before purchasing, a few heavy exposures might be better. Generally, *continuity* of advertising is sought in the case of established products, *impact* in the case of new products.

The Starch Readership Service provides some information relative to the best *frequency* of advertisements for established brands of firms who use "spaced" advertising. For the five-year period from 1956 to 1960, Starch related the amount of advertising to the purchase rate for 103 brands in product categories including cake mixes, cigarettes, coffee, cold cereals, gasoline, and soft drinks. Table 2.1 shows the relationship between the number of pages of advertising per year in magazine M and the gain or loss in purchases.

Table 2.1

PAGES OF ADVERTISING PER BRAND PER YEAR IN RELATION
TO INCREASE OR DECREASE IN BRAND PURCHASES

No. of Brands	Pages per brand per year in Magazine M	Increase or decrease in purchases per year
5	13	6.8%
17	8	5.5%
12	5	1.2%
29	1	−3.7%
40	0	−6.0%

Starch concluded:

> The important indication is that the cross-over point from decrease to increase in purchases is at four pages a year. In a competitive market, apparently four pages a year are necessary to hold brand purchase even. Another significant finding is that very old brands used for several decades declined much less when there was no advertising, but they did decline two or three percentage points a year, whereas newer brands, those in the market only a few years, declined much more without advertising, as much as 14 per cent or 15 per cent a year. (Starch, 1961, p. 45.)

The finding that older brands declined less with no advertising is a very interesting commercial illustration of a well-known principle of forgetting, Jost's Law: If two associations are of equal strength but of different ages, the older one will lose strength more slowly than the newer one with the further passage of time. It would thus be expected that, other things being equal, older brands would require less frequent advertising to hold their share of the market than newer brands, exactly as Starch found. This suggests a definite edge for early brands in a particular product category, since the early brand should get by with less advertising after the market becomes crowded with many brands. Funds are thus freed for the promotion of early brands in *other* product categories served by the manufacturer. Stage in the life cycle of a product therefore has an important bearing on the allocation of advertising funds.

SERIAL POSITION.

The order of items also affects the ease and rapidity with which they can be learned. In the case of a series of words, one presented immediately after the other, learning is greatest for those at the *beginning* and at the *end* of the list. The more toward the middle a word is located, the less well will it be learned. This is found in both massed and distributed practice. (Gestalt psychologists would suggest that this occurs because words at the beginning and end of a series possess "outstanding" properties in much the same way as do objects in a perceptual situation.)

As an illustration, Figure 2.1 shows how serial position affects the learning of two types of items, nonsense syllables and familiar

Figure 2.1

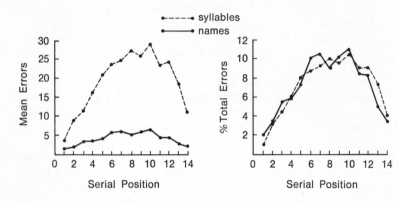

names. The left-hand graph shows the *absolute* number of errors, which, as would be expected, are much lower for familiar names than for nonsense syllables. However, when errors in each serial position are expressed as *percentages* of the total number of errors for each entire list separately, as shown on the right-hand graph, the two curves look almost identical. For both types of material, errors in the middle items are three to five times as great as those in the beginning and end. (McCrary & Hunter, 1953.)

The implication is obvious. In relaying a sizeable amount of information to a consumer, the really important parts should be located at the beginning or at the end of the message. The advertiser who feels that all portions of his message are equally critical must face the fact that certain parts, most likely those near the beginning and the end of the commercial, will be learned better than others. (This ignores, of course, variations in the basic consumer interest in the different portions of the message and the forcefulness or cleverness with which a particular portion might be presented. (Cf. Chapter 8.)

STIMULUS GENERALIZATION

Stimulus generalization, or generalization gradient, has come into some importance in recent marketing literature. The basic principle is this: If a person has learned to associate some stimulus (e.g., aspirin) with some response or result (relief of headache), a very similar stimulus (buffered aspirin) will be more easily associated with the same result (relief of headache). The more similar the second stimulus is to the original stimulus which produced the association, the more likely it is that the consumer will respond to the second stimulus. The attributes of the original stimulus are *generalized* to the similar stimulus, and the latter may be expected to produce a result similar to that of the original.

One goal-object (brand A, perhaps), because of its associated expectancies, can be assumed to have maximum appeal within the set of alternative goal-objects. The alternates can then be ordered in terms of how their associated expectancies approximate those of brand A.

Brand A		Brand A
Brand B		
	or	Brand B
Brand C		Brand C

These differences in ordering and psychological distance are referred to as generalization gradients. In the first case, the expectancies associated with brand B are quite similar to those for brand A, but are not quite as powerful in appeal. Brand C has relatively little of this. In the second case, the generalization gradient is of a different form, showing that brand B offers relatively little psychological competition to brand A. (Bayton, 1958, p. 287.)

This is precisely the phenomenon that helps a smaller business firm obtain a share of the market for some consumer good from the larger firms who have pioneered in the introduction of a relatively new product. For example, General Electric introduced the electric blanket, but many other firms were able to "ride the coattails" by offering a product similar in every major respect to the G.E. blanket. There was extensive stimulus generalization to competing brands. The same may happen with soaps, cosmetics, television sets, or major automobile styling and performance features. Stimulus generalization thus makes possible the successful entry of many new brands in the "growth" and "early maturity" phases of a new product life cycle.

A company selling quality merchandise sometimes uses a family brand in an attempt to influence consumers to generalize its quality image to a lower priced line. The danger in this is that stimulus generalization can work both ways. Packard's introduction of a low-priced car, for example, caused the reputation of its higher-priced car to suffer. (Consider the probable effects of a "compact" Cadillac!)

Manufacturers have some choice in the way they use the principle of stimulus generalization. General Electric, for example, in the case of its electric blankets, would certainly try to establish a generalization gradient along the *brand* dimension covering its blankets and its other highly respected products. A less well-known manufacturer would try to establish a generalization gradient along the *product* dimension covering his blankets and those of General Electric. As outlined in Figure 2.2, General Electric would try to form the generalization A-B, other manufacturers to form the Generalization A-C.

Figure 2.2

| | PRODUCTS | |
Brands	*Blankets*	*Other*
General Electric	A	B
Other	C	

Participation in the Learning Process

A fundamental and thoroughly verified principle of learning is that active participation in the learning process increases the speed and amount of learning. The more an individual enters into the learning process in some way, the better he learns. This is a primary reason that the lecture-only classroom approach has been largely superseded or supplemented by the lecture-discussion, the case method, and business games in better schools of business administration. Students simply do not learn as much in a passive role.

In the marketing context, this principle has long been known and has been utilized whenever feasible by vendors of many types of consumer products. Automobile salesmen urge prospective new-car buyers to take a test drive. Electric razors are offered on a 10-day trial basis. Life insurance salesmen first ask customers to estimate their *own* insurance needs and then proceed to build a program to fit those needs — a technique that has been successful in increasing sales, since the customer usually submits greater needs than he can afford to pay for and the initial needs have to be scaled down to fit a reasonable budget. Note, however, that these illustrative applications occur primarily *after* the customer has initiated or allowed the sales contact, and that they are restricted to products which happen to lend themselves to this approach.

Marketers of many other types of consumer products are not so fortunate. Products that move through supermarkets get no personal selling effort, and about the only way a housewife can "participate" in the learning process is to take the product home and try it. For this reason, free samples are sometimes offered, but this strategy tends to be quite expensive and, again, is restricted to certain types of products. Television commercials which show housewives preparing foods or putting up their hair attempt to encourage the viewer to participate in a vicarious fashion. Generally, these efforts are weak approximations that do not really get the viewer involved.

Are there other ways for a consumer to participate in the learning process? One writer suggests that this can be done by utilizing an important Gestalt principle in conjunction with media advertising, the principle of *closure*. We have already learned how closure can produce greater *attention*. Let us see if it can also produce greater *learning*.

As pointed out earlier, closure is the Gestalt term for efforts to *complete a perceptual situation* in a meaningful way. Heller suggests how this principle can be put to use in the learning situation:

> The principle of closure states that in any situation where the whole is perceived as incomplete, tension results, and there is aroused a drive to complete the perception. That is, behavior is directed toward an end situation that brings closure with it. With closure the tension is reduced. The reduction of tension is a reward and thus the phenomenon of closure is an aid to learning. (Heller, 1956, p. 248.)

To test this, Heller designed a study which compared two kinds of advertising copy: product slogans in their original form and the same slogans with every seventh letter omitted (for example, busine_s is goo_ but adv_rtisin_ makes i_ better). One group of students saw the incomplete slogans, the other group saw the slogans in their normal form. Later testing showed that the experimental group (incomplete slogans) remembered an average of 20.9 slogans as against 18.3 remembered by the control group. This is a rather small but statistically reliable difference. In a similar experiment, students were given a series of 15 complete and 15 incomplete slogans, but this time the *same* students saw both types of slogans. An average of 9.1 incomplete slogans were remembered as against 7.0 complete slogans. This again is a small but statistically reliable difference. Heller concludes:

> This study does not mean to imply that future advertisements should consist of mutilated or incomplete words. This study does reaffirm the theory that memory is a function (in part) of the degree of active participation, the degree of self-involvement, and the degree of reward in the material which is to be recognized and that the closure phenomenon can bring about each of the above (depending on one's theoretical interpretation of the phenomenon). To develop advertisements that had every nth letter omitted would be both crude and, once other advertisers followed suit, rather obvious. (Heller, 1956, p. 253.)

He then suggests a number of ways in which copy and layout might be arranged to accomplish the desired objective in a less obvious fashion. The main value of this study would seem to be in opening our eyes to the possibility of more subtle means of encouraging the consumer to participate in some way in the learning process. Hopefully, this would increase the efficiency of our promotional efforts. There are many ways in which increased participation can be developed, some of which are suggested by Heller.

INDIVIDUAL DIFFERENCES IN LEARNING ABILITY

It is well known that individuals differ widely in their ability to learn. Remember the concept of I.Q. and how the normal, or bellshaped, curve describes the way in which general intelligence is distributed in the total population (Figure 2.3). (The term "general intelligence" as used here refers to scored intelligence using a composite mental abilities test.)

To say that there are differences in individuals' ability to learn is, at best, a great understatement. A common hope among parents is that their child will be above average in intelligence. ("Everyone should be above average.") Yet for each person with an I.Q. score of 120, the average score of college graduates, there inevitably must be another person with an I.Q. of 80 who has only a 50-50 chance of reaching high school. (Cronbach, 1960.) We are not, then, dealing with *a* consumer market but with many *market segments*, based on individual consumers' abilities to build associations, to commit advertising claims to memory — in short, to learn.

The complexity of the problem increases alarmingly when it is realized that there is really no such thing as "general intelligence." Rather, intelligence has been found to have a great many components, each somewhat separate and unrelated (although individuals high in one are also a little more likely to be high in others). Thus, we have verbal comprehension, numerical reasoning, spatial visualization, word fluency, general reasoning, creativity, and many others. One investigator feels we may ultimately find as many as 120 separate components of the intellect. (Guilford, 1966.) Add differences in personality, interest, and immediate environment, and we can easily see how each individual is unique. All of these factors — separately and in combination — determine what a consumer can and will learn. (Person-

Figure 2.3

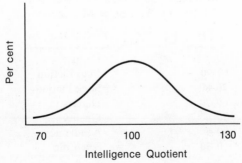

Per cent

Intelligence Quotient

ality and interest are related more closely to what a person *will* learn and properly belong in the discussion of motivation in Chapter 3.)

Many scholars are critical and even scornful of current American advertising. They consider it "in poor taste," "unimaginative," "hackneyed." Admitting for the moment that there is ample room for improvement, let us remember, that approximately one-quarter of the people whom advertising tries to reach have an I.Q. *below* 90! Yet these people may buy as much (or more) soda pop, shaving lotion, or detergent as those with I.Q.s over 110. What is conceptually uncomplicated to the scholar and well-educated consumer is simply beyond the comprehension of a great many other consumers. Hence, television "shows" how each tablet of Roll-Aids absorbs 47 times its own weight in stomach acid and how Contac tablets shrink membranes to produce better breathing.

One useful scale for measuring the difficulty of a message directed to consumers is the *Flesch count*. This readability formula — there are many others — scores the number of words in a sentence (the less words, the higher the score), the number of prefixes and suffixes per 100 words (the more affixes the lower the score), and the number of personal references (e.g., you, he, she) per 100 words (the more personal references, the higher the score). The result is a single score which indicates the general ease or level of readability for the message. Table 2.2 shows Flesch counts for several types of American magazines (Flesch, 1949, p. 150).

Table 2.2

READING EASE SCORES FOR SELECTED
TYPES OF AMERICAN MAGAZINES

Score	*Typical Magazine*
90–100	Comics
80–90	Pulp Fiction
70–80	Slick Fiction
60–70	Digests
50–60	Quality
30–50	Academic
0–30	Scientific

Advertising agencies use this scale and others to obtain a rough, objective measure of the readability of a piece of copy in terms of the intelligence level at which they are aiming.

Memory

After learning has been accomplished, there remains the important matter of *remembering* the information or process which has been learned. Some schools of clinical thought hold that nothing is ever really forgotten but that the material in question is simply inaccessible to the conscious mind under normal conditions. Results from hypnosis and psychoanalysis tend to support this view, and certainly many things that are not readily accessible to the conscious mind may influence us subconsciously, that is, without our being aware of it. The question of memory, then, depends upon the criterion which is used for deciding what has been remembered. It also depends upon the method used to measure memory, since different methods of measuring produce very different results, as will be seen later.

We are not interested at this point in the matter of emotional feelings and problems which can affect our adjustment to the everyday world. We are concerned primarily with *information* which has been learned to some criterion of adequacy, that is, information which at some time can be repeated accurately. What sort of evidence is available relative to the process of forgetting? There has been a great deal of laboratory work on this important topic, and some of the more relevant findings will be reviewed briefly to provide a better background for understanding the process and role of forgetting in consumer marketing.

MEASURING RETENTION

One way to determine how much learning has taken place among consumers is to measure retention (memory) sometime after the material to be learned has been presented. There are three major approaches to measuring retention which are feasible in the commercial situation:

Unaided recall. The consumer is given no cues at all, but is simply asked to tell what advertising of any kind she has seen recently. Prompting, even in a general product category (e.g., cereals), would produce greater awareness, with a resulting tendency to remember more advertisements in that product category. For this reason, no prompting is used.

Aided recall. The consumer is given some prompting, usually in the form of questions about ads in a specific product category. Or she might be given a list showing names or trademarks of advertisers which appeared in a particular magazine issue along with names or trademarks which did not appear in the issue. The principle is similar to that of the multiple-choice question in a college examination and the police line-up where the suspect is put in a line along with other vagrants (and even plain-clothed policemen) not connected with the crime in any way.

Recognition. The consumer is actually shown an advertisement and is asked whether or not she remembers seeing it. Of course, she may not have seen the particular ad or product in question but might have seen a similar one which would lead to a "false recognition" response.

As one might expect, there is a definite increase in retention as measured by the different approaches — from a low using "unaided recall" to a high using "recognition." Figure 2.4 shows the results of measuring the retention of nonsense syllables by different methods (Luh, 1922, taken from Woodworth & Schlosberg, 1960, p. 724.) (This investigator used some methods of measuring retention that we have not discussed specifically, but written reproduction and anticipation are merely variations of the recall methods discussed earlier. In any event, Figure 2.4 is quite satisfactory as an illustration.)

There are several points of interest in these results. Notice that retention as measured by the recognition method is much greater than retention as measured by the recall methods (lowest two curves): three to four times as great after 24 hours. Clearly, the "memory" obtained from an individual will depend upon the method used to measure this memory. Also notice the similarity of the shapes of the different curves. We find a similar *pattern of forgetting* after the first day or two no matter how we

Figure 2.4

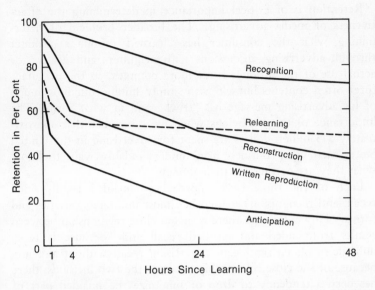

measure retention. The only major difference is that the great drop which occurs in recall scores after the first day or two is not matched by a corresponding drop in recognition scores. All of this shows the importance of specifying the method of measurement when talking about the amount of remembering.

Can't we simplify this problem? What is *the accurate method* of measuring retention? Unfortunately, no one knows. The best we can do is to realize that recognition scores yield a much higher estimate of memory for a particular advertisement or product than do recall scores. Unaided recall, in particular, is likely to greatly underestimate the amount remembered. The reader can easily verify this by trying to recall every text he used in high school or college, then going to his bookshelf for visual inspection. He will "recognize" a number of books he was unable to "recall." The reader might also try to recall each of the fifty states — a difficult task by unaided recall, but extremely simple by recognition. (It is easy to recall forty or forty-five states, but the balance is very difficult.)

Measuring Advertising Effectiveness

Retention is of critical importance in determining the effectiveness of media advertising. The broader problem of determining what the consumer has "learned" about a product through advertising, discussions with neighbors and dealers, or actual use of the product is far more complex, so the manufacturer often contents himself with simply finding out how much of his advertising message has "stuck" and in what form. The importance of this is obvious when we remember that approximately $15 billion dollars are spent for advertising in the United States each year. Business firms understandably want to know what they are getting for their money.

Each of the three basic approaches (unaided recall, aided recall, and recognition) is used in almost unlimited varieties and forms.[1] However, since there is such a close relationship between results from aided and unaided recall and "because it is so difficult to obtain significant advertising recall without aids and because of the close relationship between the two methods, there has been a tendency to drop or minimize the unaided part of recall surveys." (Lucas & Britt, 1963, p. 95.) This leaves aided recall and recognition as the principal means of measuring retention of advertising and other forms of promotion. Our discussion will focus primarily on these techniques.

There are two commercial services which provide subscribers with advertising retention information on a regular basis. One employs the recognition method and the other a form of aided recall to measure retention of advertisements *after* they have appeared in national magazines. Many variations of these approaches have been developed by the larger advertising agencies and by consumer-products companies for their own use; however, the services described below will illustrate the principles involved.

Starch Readership Service. This firm periodically selects issues of national consumer and business publications (e.g. *Saturday Evening Post, Business Week*) for audit. For each issue, a sample

---

[1] The reader may refer to the text, *Measuring Advertising Effectiveness*, by Lucas and Britt, for illustrations of many approaches in actual use.

of 150 men and 150 women (or either sex only, as determined by the nature of the publication) is selected throughout the United States, using only individuals who can "qualify" themselves as readers by telling something of the content of the magazine. Each qualified respondent is then asked to go completely through the magazine page by page, giving the following information about each advertisement:

"Noted" — the reader remembers having seen the advertisement

"Seen/associated" — the reader has seen or read any part of the advertisement that clearly indicates the name of the product or advertiser

"Read most" — the reader has read *more than half* of all written material in the ad

The above results are presented for each advertisement for men and women separately, and each of the above scores for each ad is also related to the cost of the space in the magazine, to get a measure of the "efficiency" of the ad (readership per dollar spent). Clearly, this is a *recognition* method, since respondents are shown the magazine copy and simply asked if they remember seeing or reading it. There are two sources of error here; 1) false recognition (the individual has not actually seen a particular ad but thinks he has because of similarity with other ads he has seen, or wishes to convey the impression that he has seen the ad to "look good" to the interviewer), 2) actual forgetting or repression (the individual actually forgets or else is reluctant to indicate that he has seen an ad as, for example, in the case of personal hygiene or sanitation products). To what extent one of these types of error tends to offset the other is almost impossible to determine for any particular advertisement.

In spite of these limitations, the Starch Readership Service is a widely used means of getting feedback on advertising copy and layout. This firm instructs users not to interpret results on an *absolute* basis, that is, not to infer the actual number of people nationwide who have "noted," "seen/associated," or "read most" of the ad. There are simply too many errors of measurement to justify interpretations of this kind. Rather, the Starch Service recommends attention to *relative* scores (such as comparisons of a firm's present campaign scores with scores from earlier campaigns), trends in readership over time, and comparisons with rival firms in the same product category. The same errors of measurement presumably operate in each survey (whatever these errors may be) so that comparisons of the type recommended should be meaningful.

Even though the recognition method can easily produce overestimates due to false recognition, the percentage of respondents who claim to have even "noted" an ad seldom exceeds 70 per cent even for the more popular and interesting product categories (e.g., cars, food products, and baby-care products), while many categories show less than 40 per cent (e.g., insurance, finance, and pharmaceuticals).

Gallup and Robinson, Inc. This service uses the (aided) recall method to measure the "impact" of a magazine advertisement. As in the case of the Starch Readership Service, "qualified" readers are located. Then each reader is asked to tell what he can remember about the advertisements in the issue *with covers closed.* He is aided in this by being shown names or logotypes of both advertisers in the issue and nonadvertisers of the same general product category. For every ad the respondent mentions, probing questions are asked: "What did the advertisement look like?" "What did the advertiser say?" The emphasis is upon eliciting as much information as the respondent can remember to determine what ads or parts of ads made any "impact" upon him.

While the Gallup-Robinson recall method produces a much lower readership rating than the Starch method and is an underestimate of the true amount of retention, it has the advantage that the advertiser is at least reasonably certain of the percentage of readers who were able to *prove* readership. Comments from respondents are also quite helpful in revealing to copywriters what message really got across; i.e., comprehension. With the sharp drop in retention which occurs immediately as measured by recall, it is imperative that interviews be conducted very soon after readers have viewed the magazine and that all readers are interviewed at approximately the same time after exposure to the issue.

Otherwise, results from different interviews and from different issues will not be comparable. Gallup-Robinson is well aware of this and conducts its interviews accordingly.

In addition to the services which measure retention of national *magazine* advertisements, at least one advertising agency does the same type of thing in connection with *television* advertising. Immediately after an ad has appeared on television, a survey is made among a sample of viewers to determine retention, impressions, and other factors.

There are also a great many tests which are run on magazine, radio, and television ads *before* they appear in the national media. Portfolio tests of magazine ads before they appear are quite common. The respondent is shown a portfolio containing many ads, among which are those to be tested. After going through all the ads, the respondent is asked to tell as much as possible about selected ads with the portfolio closed. Relatively unaided recall is used first, then successive degrees of aid. This gives the agency an idea of the impression left by each ad format, and changes can be made to improve upon weak features which were not anticipated. In a case of this kind, of course, we are closer to measuring *learning* than *retention* since testing is done almost immediately after the advertisement is seen or heard.

Problems. The measurement of advertising retention is an extremely complicated issue because each measurement reflects the influence of a number of factors:

- Immediate attention value of the ad (perceptual factors)
- Effectiveness of theme and message
- Intrinsic product interest by the consumer
- Method of measurement used
- Concurrent competitive advertising

Problems and pitfalls in the measurement of advertising retention are almost endless. A tremendous amount of time and money has been expended over the years to improve our understanding in this area, and the end is still not in sight. Each new contribution brings greater insight into the problem, but it also raises additional problems and adds complexity to the situation. It is fair to say that no one approach or service now has "the answer" to the problem of evaluating advertising effectiveness simply because there is no single answer. Advertising has many objectives — to inform, to create a long-term image, to stimulate short-term sales — and the effectiveness of any particular advertisement must be judged against the objective of that ad. (Colley, 1961.) Failure to recognize this has added a great deal of confusion to an already complicated problem.

Beyond the difficulties of measuring retention, there is the greater problem of determining what advertising really causes people to *do* — what changes in behavior result from promotional efforts of various kinds. Problems of this sort require experimental studies and even complex mathematical models. It will be some time before the problem has been traced in all its ramifications, but in the meantime we can benefit from the intelligent use of the tools now available for measuring retention if the limitations of these tools are understood.

Changes in Cognitive Material

What happens to information that is learned? Does it stay as it was when originally committed to memory or do *changes* occur in some way? We have already discussed the fact that a great deal of forgetting takes place and that this is rapid at first, then more gradual. But what determines which part of the originally acquired information will be forgotten? Are there systematic changes in the retained material and, if so, what are the basic processes involved?

There are at least three forces which operate continuously on the information we acquire:

Leveling is akin to the forgetting which is found when retention is measured. What is retained always tends to become shorter, more concise, more easily grasped, although this process never reaches the point where the memory is obliterated.

Sharpening is the reverse of leveling. If much of the original is forgotten, what remains is "sharpened" in our mind. It carries greater importance and stands out above all the information acquired about a particular topic.

Assimilation is the key process that leads to the elimination of some of the details (leveling) and the pointing up of others (sharpening). It is the *selection* of material to be remembered, based upon the habits, interests and attitudes of the individual. It depends partly on the individual's own goals and experiences and partly on what he learns from social contacts with others. Stereotypes are important in assimilation. If the subject matter involves a person, group, or race with which we are familiar in some way, what is assimilated tends to conform very closely to our prior conceptions and expectations regardless of the objective 'evidence or facts. (Allport & Postman, 1958, pp. 58–61.)

The old parlor game of passing a message around the room by whispering from one person to another demonstrates these principles. A clear, understandable message of any length at all is leveled (shortened), sharpened (certain points emphasized), and assimilated in a very confused way, since many individuals are involved in the process and the selection of the portions to be retained takes place in a very unsystematic way. The message transmitted to the last person often bears little relationship to that whispered to the first person in line.

Some writers refer to the leveling and sharpening process as *selective retention* to parallel the more commonly used *input* term, *selective perception* (which will be discussed in Chapter 4). These terms emphasize that neither input nor retention takes place in an accurate, objective way, but proceeds harmoniously with what the individual *wants* to perceive or remember from any given situation. This process simply compounds the problem of transmitting information to the consumer public. Even if the perception is accurate, later systematic changes in the retained material can dilute or even obliterate the ideas or portions which are considered most important by the vendor. In the advertising context, Maloney points out:

The advertising message may be distorted by being *leveled* or *sharpened*. An advertising message is *leveled* when people distort the meaning, by overlooking something in the advertising message which is out of phase with pre-existing beliefs. A message is most likely to be leveled when it presents information which is generally in accord with what the reader, listener, or viewer would expect, but when at the same time it contains information just a little out of the ordinary. Under these circumstances the person quickly characterizes the advertisement as something quite familiar ('something I already know all about') and overlooks the new details in the message. . . . The advertising message is *sharpened* when people 'read into the message' additional or unintended meanings in order to make the message conform to pre-existing beliefs. The message is quite likely to be sharpened if it represents a departure from long-standing advertising themes for the product. Thus, out of any 100 respondents to an advertisement for a product of the Campbell Soup Company, a few respondents may be expected to report that the advertisement contained pictures of the Campbell Kids, whether or not the Campbell Kids were pictured. Because of many repeated past experiences, many people have come to expect Campbell advertisements to picture the Campbell Kids. (Maloney, 1963, p. 4.)

A more extreme example of sharpening comes from a recent nationwide survey of magazine readership made by S. E. Gill Associates in New York. This survey showed that nine per cent of all qualified respondents in this survey asserted they currently read *Collier's*, and seven per cent said that if they could only have one magazine regularly it would be *Collier's*. "It takes a truly loyal reader to think he still reads a magazine that has been out of business since January of 1957!" (Business News, 1965, p. 4.)

The changes which occur in retained material are not random. We are constantly shaping this material, working it over to produce a better "fit" in our minds in accordance with our past experiences, goals, and attitudes. The forgetting which inevitably occurs tends to follow this pattern. While this process is inadequate and inaccurate from a strict information-retrieval standpoint, it is quite understandable from the Gestalt viewpoint which stresses the importance of meaningful "wholes" and relationships in our cognitive world.

The nature and relevance of information given to the consumer are obviously important. Engineers refer to the feeding in of useless or inaccurate information to a computer as GIGO

— Garbage In, Garbage Out. This is a good term for the advertiser to keep in mind.

The two important factors to be remembered from a study of memory are that the consumer does not remember much of what he sees or hears, and that what is remembered tends to be based more upon *subjective* factors in the consumer than upon *objective* factors in the object or message. These points will be discussed in detail in later chapters about the subjective factors which influence or regulate what the consumer will remember.

COGNITIVE DISSONANCE

Another interesting change which may occur in material stored in our memory is referred to as *cognitive dissonance*.

> This theory centers around the idea that if a person knows various things that are not psychologically consistent with one another, he will, in variety of ways, try to make them more consistent. Two items of information that psychologically do not fit together are said to be in a dissonant relationship to each other. The items of information may be about behavior, feelings, opinions, things in the environment, and so on. (Festinger, 1962, p. 93.)

A great deal of experimental work has been done at Stanford University by Festinger and his colleagues to determine the conditions under which cognitive dissonance occurs. Festinger reports an experiment by one of his associates in which high school girls were asked to rate the attractiveness and desirability of 12 "hit" records. Then each girl was given a choice between two of the records which she herself had rated as being only moderately attractive (and thus of approximately equal desirability). According to dissonance theory, the rated desirability of the record chosen should *increase*, to be consistent with the girl's knowledge that she had chosen to keep this record rather than the other one. Results clearly indicated such a change. Other girls were asked which of the two records they preferred, but were given *both* to keep. As would be expected, they showed no change in rating the desirability of the chosen record since there was no apparent inconsistency or dissonance between the choice and the possession. Girls who were given only one record apparently felt compelled to change their attitudes toward the chosen record in order to reassure themselves of the wisdom of their choice.

The theory of cognitive dissonance has been supported by many studies of this type which tend to show that some form of systematic processing goes on in the mind to change initial impressions so as to reduce any major discrepancies. Berelson and Steiner report: "When the real world and the motives of the subject are at odds, behavior is first designed to bring the real world into line with the motives. But when this is impossible, for external or internal reasons, the discrepancy (or dissonance, as it is now called) can be reduced by appropriate changes in the perception of reality." (Berelson and Steiner, 1964, p. 266.) (Evidence of this type tends to support the Gestalt view that there is a constant process of mental reorganization going on to produce more "sense" with respect to a given topic.)

Does cognitive dissonance normally accompany a consumer's free choice among products which are equally attractive? This has been a subject of some discussion and research in very recent years. One investigator postulated the theory that a new-car purchaser might feel apprehensive after making such a large purchase. There might be dissonance caused by the knowledge that he has made his choice and the feeling that he might have gotten a better deal elsewhere; that the Plymouth, for example, might really be a better automobile than the Chevrolet he chose. In such a situation, he might seek reassurance by especially noticing advertisements which point out the superiority of his car's features. Engel interviewed individuals who had recently purchased a Chevrolet. Using several measures of retention and opinion of a Chevrolet ad in the local newspaper, he was unable to find dissonant consumers among his sample. (Engel, 1963.)

However, in another study, 125 male residents of Minneapolis were interviewed to determine the extent to which they selectively exposed themselves to information about the cars they owned. Sixty-five were new-car owners, and the rest owned cars three or more years old. Results showed that, as dissonance theory would predict, new-car owners recalled reading significantly more advertisements of their own car than did old car owners. When offered information about different makes of cars, a few more new-car owners than old-car owners elected to read about their own make. The difference was not statistically reliable but was in the expected direction. (Erlich, Guttman, & Schonbach, 1957.)

Studies of this type are suggestive but are inconclusive in any event, since we would have to be sure that the buyer noticed more ads for his chosen brand *after* the purchase than before in order to show that dissonance was actually operating. Dissonance cannot be demonstrated adequately in single-shot, "cross-sectional" study designs.

From a broader point of view, there is no reason that dissonance should exist only in the "cognitive" mind. *Conative* (motivational) *dissonance* is often present. Caught between the desire for recreation and the demands of an assignment of some sort, a student often *rationalizes* that recreation will enable him to study harder later in the day. *Perceptual dissonance* is often present also. Anything which is out of harmony with other objects or sounds in a perceptual field or with one's expectations based upon experience can be changed to fit the Gestalt of a more meaningful total configuration. Examples of this were given in Chapter 1.

Whether or not *cognitive* dissonance occurs in the buying situation is still uncertain and will continue to be until we develop better means of measuring this phenomenon.

QUESTIONS
FOR REVIEW

1. What is the relationship, if any, between "signs" and "cues"? Between "cues" and "classical conditioning"?

2. Are there any buying circumstances under which learning would be of little importance?

3. How might a retailer make use of the stimulus-generalization concept?

4. What relationship, if any, is there between the learning principles discussed in this chapter and the principles of perception discussed in the previous chapter? Which would be the more useful to a consumer products manufacturer?

5. Review the various means a vendor has of reinforcing information he wishes a consumer to learn.

6. In what way are the phenomena of discrimination and generalization relevant in the development of the brand policy of a multiple-product firm?

7. Is cognitive dissonance related to any principle of Gestalt psychology?

8. How might a manufacturer use sign-expectancies in package or product design?

3

Motivation and Emotion

THE TOPICS OF MOTIVATION and
emotion provide a transition from the psychology of the individual to social processes and the psychology of the group.
Motives are one point at which an individual's own needs and
resources converge with those of his group and of society as a
whole. Without considering social processes, we cannot explain
individual behavior in any but the simplest of situations.

In our earlier discussions of learning, motivation was not considered as an integral part of the learning situation. Yet we know
that an individual's motivations will determine at least to some
extent what he learns from a given situation and, indeed, whether
or not he will learn anything. It is even possible to argue that
every single act of behavior is the direct outgrowth of a motivational state of some kind in the individual, although some psychologists have disagreed with this proposition (see Hunt, 1965.)

Psychologists often think in terms of three principal components of the individual: cognition, conation, and affection i.e., intellect, will, and emotion or, in more common terms, thought, action, and feeling.

> In [this] psychological trichotomy, cognition, on the one hand, has been viewed as a realm governed by verbalized rationality, while affection, on the other, has been viewed as a very chaotic, though often pleasant, place where inarticulate irrationality is in command. Conation, the middle category which deals with behavior or determination to act, has been caught between the other two, sometimes believed to be swayed by the rationality of the cognitive mind but at other times suspected of having a secret allegiance to the whimsical irrationality of feeling and emotion. (Kelly, 1964, p. 36.)

The present chapter will consider the roles of motivational and emotional forces and the interplay between these forces in consumer behavior.

Understanding Human Motivation

The field of motivation seems to contain more semantic confusion than most other behavioral areas. Some writers insist that *motives* are different from *drives* and use the latter term primarily to characterize the basic physiological "tissue" needs (e.g., hunger, thirst, shelter, sex). Others distinguish between *needs* and *wants,* stating that needs are the basic motivating forces which translate themselves into more immediate wants which satisfy these needs (e.g., hunger *needs* give rise to *wanting* a good steak dinner). The discussion in this book will not consider the finer points of distinction among these various terms, but will be based upon the following definition: [Motives are] all those inner striving conditions variously described as wishes, desires, needs, drives, and the like. . . . Formally, then, a motive is an inner state that energizes, activates, or moves (hence 'motivation'), and that directs or channels behavior toward goals. (Berelson & Steiner, 1964, p. 239.)

Early psychologists did not even consider the matter of motivation in their work on learning and other forms of behavior.

Motivation was artificially generated or simply assumed to exist. It remained for Freud, in his work with abnormal psychology, and McDougall, in his research into social psychology, to point out that some of the extreme forms of human behavior (outside of the laboratory) could not be explained adequately without reference to purposes, goals, urges, and the like. Experimental psychologists gradually absorbed this orientation, but they view motivation in a very different way. At the present time, "Some psychologists regard motivation theory as indissociable from learning theory and place them both within 'behavior theory.' Others would be more inclined to annex motivation theory to 'personality theory.' Motivation theory consists of an area of inquiry and, although it would be hard to obtain agreement on where precisely its boundaries lie, its territory is demarcated by questions rather than by answers." (Berlyne, 1964, p. 447.)

The subject of motivation has received more thought and effort, with less in the way of tangible returns, than perhaps any other area of psychology. There is still great disagreement among psychologists about the basic nature of the driving forces within us and the relative importance of these various forces. One writer comments:

> Theorists who conceive of behavior as primarily motivated by benign and socially approved motives may be paired with theorists who see the chief impellants of behavior as primitive and unacceptable urges. For those who believe learned or socially acquired motives are of predominant importance there is opposition in the form of theorists convinced that the physiologically grounded and largely innate drives are of primary importance. Some have emphasized the abstract or logical status of motivational constructs, while others have stressed the physical reality and concrete existence of motives. The conceptual nature of motivational variables has remained so murky that even the clear distinction of these variables from other classes of concepts employed in psychological theory is yet to be accomplished. (Lindzey, 1964, p. 4.)

One authority wants to do away with the concept of motivation entirely and to substitute for it the idea that man is *active* simply because he is *alive*. This generalized activity is then *directed* in ways which are seen by the individual as better extending and defining his own *system*, that is, his own way of looking at the world and his objectives in traveling the road of life. (Kelly, 1964.)

PROBLEMS IN UNDERSTANDING MOTIVATION

The reasons for such divergence of opinion among authorities involve the many problems one encounters in trying to assess or measure motivational variables. To begin with, are we looking primarily for conscious or for unconscious motives? And, in either case, how do we actually *measure* the motive? Can it be measured directly or only indirectly through some intermediate psychological process? For example, individuals with the same basic motivation express this motivation in different ways. To satisfy the urge for social approval, one individual joins many social groups while another shuts himself up in a library to write a book or practices some athletic activity which he hopes will later make him more popular with his peers. Each individual has a different "style" of expressing his basic motivations, and it is necessary to get behind the style somehow in order to measure the more basic drive.

The matter of environment must also be considered. Both the psychological and cultural aspects of an individual's environment impose restrictions or standards upon acceptable means of expressing basic drives or motivations. As one writer points out, there are usually various cultural paths to the same goal and therefore conscious, specific, local-cultural desires are not as fundamental as the more basic, pervasive, unconscious goals which cut across cultural lines. (Maslow, 1943.) In our materialistic culture, we Americans express our needs for social approval and status quite differently from the way people in many other cultures do.

There are other more immediate, more specific "field" forces which structure the manner in which a given motivation will be expressed. Thus the need for social approval will be expressed quite differently in a church group than in a motorcycle or hot-rod club. Musical interest will be displayed differently on a dance floor than in a record shop or book store. Any given environment presents only a limited number of ways in which a given motivation or desire can be expressed.

Maslow also points out that any given act usually has *more than one motivation* and that the problems involved in distinguishing among the various motives for the same act are often profound. For example, a man selects a particular life-long occupation for any number of possible reasons — income potential, status considerations, aptitude for the work, personal friendships, etc.

For all of these reasons, the nature and direction of motivational forces are not clearly understood at the present time. Problems of measurement are at least as great here as in any other aspect of human behavior.

LEWIN'S TOPOLOGICAL AND VECTOR PSYCHOLOGY

One of the major attempts to provide a suitable theoretical framework for understanding human motivation was provided by Kurt Lewin in the 1930's. Lewin saw the individual — at any given point in time — as occupying a space within an *environment* of physical, psychological, social, and other factors, and this environment ultimately determines what the individual will do at that point in time. The environment is characterized by:

- *Topology*. It has boundaries, barriers, and spaces of different sizes and accessibility, and can be depicted graphically.
- *Vectors*. These are *forces* of many types, both internal and external, which impinge upon the individual and motivate him to action.

Whether the vectors or forces will produce any effects, and also what effects they will produce, depend upon the strength and direction of the forces as well as the "topological environment" in which the person exists at a particular point in time. There may be barriers which prevent the desired or indicated action; these barriers may be physical, they may involve social restrictions (e.g., a girl does not normally call a boy for a date) or perhaps certain psychological problems (e.g., extreme shyness or lack of intellectual or athletic ability).

Each individual responds to his environment and the forces in it in his own unique way. Lewin coined the term *life-space* to indicate "the totality of facts which determine the behavior of an individual at a certain moment." (Lewin, 1936, p. 12.)

To show the various ways in which different vectors or forces could interact in a given situation, Lewin chose the case of *conflict* because of its particular significance in human behavior. He posits the following three types of conflict:

Conflict between two positive forces. The individual is forced to choose between two desirable alternatives such as spending a bonus check on a new car or on a trip to Mexico. This is depicted topologically by

In this type of conflict situation, the decision is usually relatively painless. The greater-attraction force wins, at least in the oversimplified situation where only *one* person is making the decision.[1]

Conflict between two negative forces. The choice is between two undesirable alternatives such as buying a second car versus continuing to ride public transportation when other family members need the first car. This can also be depicted topologically.

Conflict between one positive and one negative force. Consumers who want a color television set must commit several hundred dollars from their present or near-future savings. Conflict results.

The latter form of conflict has been studied extensively in laboratory experiments using animals. When a chicken pecks at a particular button he might receive a kernel of corn and *at the same time* be given a mild electric shock. The corn will cause him to approach the button; the shock will cause him to avoid it. Conjoined positive and negative reinforcement thus lead to what has been called the *approach-avoidance* reaction. The approach component in this reaction is not affected by distance,

---

[1] Curiously, Lewin notes that after the choice is made, the goal chosen often seems *inferior* and oscillation occurs. (Lewin, 1935, p. 89.) This would seem to contradict the principles of cognitive dissonance. (Cf. Chapter 2.)

but the avoidance component becomes stronger as the thing to be avoided is approached. The chicken who has been conditioned in this manner is consequently hesitant. Hungry, he will approach the button that gives him corn but will slow down noticeably as he comes closer to it. Depending on the strength of the avoidance component, he may stop his approach just before he reaches his goal. This behavior can be repeated indefinitely until his growing hunger strengthens the approach component sufficiently to overcome the avoidance component.

Consumers exhibit the same behavior in major purchasing decisions. They want a color television set, which sets up an approach reaction. To get the set, they must lay out several hundred dollars from their savings, a reason to avoid the purchase. The closer they come to the actual purchase, the more important this outlay becomes. Some observers feel that many consumers enter into a state of virtual panic before making the final decision on an expensive item. They consequently may "almost" buy a color television set on several occasions before they finally take the plunge. Salesmen are very familiar with the customer who is enthusiastic at first but cools down when he is at the point of signing on the dotted line. Closing techniques have been developed to overcome this "terminal horror." "No cash down" and "Fly now, pay later" are examples. (If the customer's black-and-white television set breaks down, of course, his need for some kind of set will tend to overwhelm his resistance to final decision. Many people, for instance, finally buy a contemplated car only when they face the need for major repairs on their present car.)

March and Simon use a somewhat amplified Lewinian model to describe decision processes in conflict situations. They posit three types of decision-making situations:

1. *Uncertainty*, in which the individual involved lacks sufficient information to evaluate his alternatives.

2. *Incomparability*, in which there is little or no basis for choice among the alternatives offered. All might be equally good or equally bad, for example.

3. *Unacceptability*, in which none of the alternatives is considered acceptable by the decision maker.

In the March-Simon model, uncertainty would lead to a *search for clarification*. The decision maker would attempt to acquire more information about his alternatives in order to be able to make a more intelligent decision. The uncertain consumer would perhaps read advertising and cross-shop to reduce his uncertainty.

Under conditions of incomparability, in the absence of unacceptability, decisions would not ordinarily be difficult. The consumer in this kind of choice situation would be confronted with equally attractive alternatives. Simon and March say:

> Under such conditions, choice will depend on attention and the sequence in which alternatives are presented. Without arguing that individuals never assess marginal differences between alternatives, we think that the choice between several satisfactory alternatives depends more on attention cues and the order of presentation than it does on indifference curves. . . . The literature of market research, for example, is full of evidence susceptible to this interpretation. (Simon & March, 1958, pp. 116–117.)

Advertising is often aimed at nothing more than capturing the consumer's attention in the hope that his decision will favor the advertiser when the consumer is in conflict because of the incomparability of alternative products.

Finally, conflict due to the unacceptability of all the alternatives offered should lead the consumer to *search for new alternatives*. Repeated failure to find an acceptable alternative would lead to changes in the consumer's aspiration level and in his definition of "acceptable." Shoppers will sometimes reject a product, visit other stores to look at similar merchandise, and finally return to buy the product originally rejected.

CLASSIFICATION OF MOTIVES

The reader may wonder: "Why confuse me with all of this theory and controversy? All I need is some kind of a *list* of the basic consumer motivations which determine buying behavior, so I can better understand the real reasons people buy a certain type of product or service, or at least understand what is going on in their minds as they decide what to buy." We have tried to show that *a generally accepted list of motivations does not exist because not enough is known about basic human motivational forces and the expressions of these motivations in the total human experience,* much less in the marketplace. If there is one point about which most motivation theorists agree it is that a simple list of human motives will get us nowhere in promoting a real understanding of the reasons people behave as they do.

Scholars do, however, distinguish between the various motives in a number of useful ways, for example,

Biological. This includes "tissue" needs, including hunger, thirst, and sex.

Psychological-sociological. This includes desire for social approval, status, and other "psychic" satisfactions.

Another distinction, which does not directly overlap the above is:

Learned. Behavior or tastes based upon the norms or desires of one's social group are acquired or learned by the individual just as he learns cognitive material and tastes.

Instinctive. Common to nearly all human beings. This includes the biological motives and even such social motives as the desire to be with others or to excel.

Freud proposed a personality structure based upon three levels or components. These parts do not correspond directly to motives, as such, but different motives can emanate from each level:

Id. This encompasses the more basic drives and pleasurable urgings which are instinctive in nature. Since many, but not all, of these are "antisocial" (e.g., loud burping, open acts of hostility, promiscuous sex), it is necessary to have a censor in the form of the *ego*.

Ego. This is the rational side of our personality structure. It controls the id and guides our behavior in ways meaningful and acceptable in the everyday world (e.g., socially acceptable behavior in work, recreation, eating).

Superego. This is more or less the individual's "conscience," which upholds those ideas of moral right or wrong, especially in matters above and beyond the requirements of law or strict custom (e.g., caring for one's elderly parents rather than spending the same money on oneself).

The id and superego, according to Freud, are in constant conflict, and it falls to the ego to make peace by compromising with reality in some acceptable fashion. When the ego fails in this, the individual collapses into some form of neurosis. There are other theories of personality structure, but none so well articulated or widely used as Freud's.

An individual's *values* in life often form the basis on which some motivations are built. Once he adopts a value system of some sort (often based primarily upon family patterns and expectations), the individual is motivated to conform to these values and thus they furnish a driving force and direction for his actions. *Emotions* are yet another motivational source. Emotions are reactions to symbols or external stimuli of some sort which have significance to an individual. This reaction energizes him in some way, either toward or away from the source or to other more complex forms of behavior.

Motives, then, come from many sources and are expressed in a great many ways.

Despite the fact that attempts to produce a single meaningful classification system for human motives have failed, we will suggest some psychological-sociological motivating forces for which there is some evidence and which seem to be particularly useful for understanding consumer behavior in the marketplace. We have not tried to be exhaustive. Some writers would insist on further breakdowns for many of the motives presented and others would condense these into fewer needs. Biological motives such as hunger, thirst and sex are omitted because they are fairly obvious. While the motives listed here are by no means definitive, they will perhaps furnish some landmarks through the motivational forests and provide a better perspective on the diversity of forces which affect consumer purchasing decisions:

Social approval. The desire to be accepted by others whom one values, to belong to a group, to conform to social and cultural standards, to behave and dress in a socially acceptable way.

Status. To rise above others by gaining a measure of recognition or of power, to attract attention in a desirable way, to occupy a strategic position in one's group or in the community or nation at large, to gain possessions of a prestige nature.

Security. To protect oneself against either physical or psychological harm, to avoid accidents or painful bodily sensations, to provide a measure of financial reserve against future need.

Personal interest. To amuse or enjoy oneself by seeking entertainment, playing or observing games, or following hobbies.

Curiosity. To ask questions, to adopt an inquiring attitude toward what is going on around one, to solve problems or puzzles, to read and seek knowledge. (There is some evidence that consumers sometimes switch brands simply because they are "curious" about another brand and are bored with buying the old brand.)

Self-realization. To achieve for personal rather than social satisfaction (completing a level of education not required for one's job; or losing weight).

Affection. To give love or affection to one's fellow man or to animals in the spirit of giving, of generosity.

There are other motives the reader can think of which do not fall neatly into these categories. For example, what about the desire for maturity among young people, simple hedonism (seeking pleasure, avoiding pain), recognition of a Supreme Being? Do these fit somewhere into our list or are they separate motives? And there is another general class of motives not mentioned — *instrumental* needs, which help to get a job done, as in the case of a washing machine, lawn mower, or wrist watch.

Implications and examples of the various motives in terms of consumer buying behavior will not be undertaken here. Some are obvious and need no further discussion, others will be discussed at length in later chapters. The reader can exercise his own imagination.

Even if we could clearly distinguish among all of the various motives, it would be difficult to fit the purchase of each product or service neatly into a single category. For example, a man buys an expensive Omega wristwatch for a combination of instrumental and status needs; a couple joins a country club for both social approval and personal interest (swimming, golf); a girl joins a "Great Books" discussion group for personal interest, social approval (her friends have joined), and perhaps self-realization. A Winchester rifle would satisfy primarily the personal interest and instrumental needs of a man who hunted game to reduce his food bills, but the same rifle would satisfy primarily the social approval or status needs of another man who did not want to be left behind by his friends during hunting season.

It is clear that a major problem in applying motivation theory to marketing is the "matching" of motivations and behavior. Different motivations can lead to identical behaviors and, conversely, the most disparate behaviors can sometimes be traced back to identical motivations. Thus a woman anxious to establish herself as a dedicated housewife might buy a cake mix, a bowl of flowers, or some different type of object altogether. She can express her motive, so to speak, in any of several ways. On the other hand, cake mixes and flowers are bought for many reasons besides the desire to be a good wife and mother. A working-girl with a sweet tooth might buy a cake mix mainly because of its convenience, and her boy friend might buy flowers as an act of courtship.

There is thus no simple one-to-one relationship between motives and buying behavior. Taking two lists, one of motives and the other of products or brands, any item on one of the two lists might be matched with any item on the other. *The relationship between motives and brands can consequently be shown only in matrix form.* Each of the cells in Figure 3.1 shows the percentage of people influenced by motives 1, 2, 3, 4, and 5 in the purchase of brands A, B, C, D, and E. If people were to fall only in the cells along the diagonal (A-1, B-2, C-3, etc.) and the other cells were empty, the relationship would be one-to-one. This is rarely the case. Economy, for example, which is an instrumental motivation, is a factor in almost every purchase.

A related problem is that people often lack the information needed to make "rational" choices. It is often found in research that people buying Brand A rather than Brand B give economy as the reason and that those buying Brand B also cite economy as the reason for their choice. In some cases, the two groups of people may have different concepts of economy. One may

Figure 3.1

RELATIONSHIP BETWEEN MOTIVES AND BRANDS
Motives

Brands	1	2	3	4	5
A	x	x	x	x	x
B	x	x	x	x	x
C	x	x	x	x	x
D	x	x	x	x	x
E	x	x	x	x	x

think in terms of low initial price, for example, and the other in terms of operating expenses. Often, however, one of the two groups is simply misinformed.

In practical terms, the foregoing means that motivations cannot be inferred directly from behavior and that behavior cannot be predicted in a simple way from motivations. Does this mean that motivation theory is inapplicable to marketing? Not at all. The task of the marketer is to establish an emotional or affective connection (*cathexis*) between his product and a reasonable number of consumers. Usually, certain motives can be attached to his product more easily than others or are more powerful in evoking buying behavior. These are the motives to which he should appeal in his advertising. He should relieve himself, however, of the idea that people buy his product for one reason and his competitor's product for another.

CONTRIBUTIONS FROM PSYCHOANALYTIC THEORY

Harold D. Lasswell, a student of political propaganda, developed the concept of the *triple appeal* from Freudian theory. (Lasswell, 1935, 1948.) The concept appears applicable to advertising. A triple appeal is one which appeals simultaneously to all three of the principal components of personality — the id, the ego, and the superego. An appeal to any one of these components alone, according to Lasswell, is likely to be ineffective.

- An *id* appeal activates superego defenses and, thus, may be rejected out of hand as immoral and antisocial. The advertiser may even find himself in difficulties with the Federal Trade Commission or some other regulatory body. Consequently, an appeal to the id almost always has to be veiled.

- The *superego* is mainly negative and tends to restrain behavior rather than to produce it. Since buying is often a self-indulgent act, the problem of the marketer is usually to placate the superego rather than to activate it.

- Appeals to the *ego* are instrumental and "rational" and, therefore, not likely to sweep a consumer off his feet.

Lasswell suggests that an effective appeal takes all three components of the personality into account. Good advertising would try to arouse id impulses toward sexuality or hostility, to placate the superego by suggesting that the id impulses are justified in some way, and to reach the ego by emphasizing the rationality of the proposed buying action. Clairol advertising has used the triple-appeal principle successfully for some time. "Does she or doesn't she?" is a frankly sexual theme, but the art accompanying the copy always shows a young housewife with a small child. The ad wins the approval of the superego by associating sex and marriage.

Cadillac has also used the principle successfully. Emphasis on the status and prestige afforded by the Cadillac in effect urges the consumer to gratify his hostilities and aggressions by ostentatious display. Since most people repress their hostilities, they would find a naked appeal to be a "big shot" totally unacceptable. "You deserve a Cadillac" is consequently a second theme used in Cadillac advertisements. The superego of the prospective buyer is reminded that he has worked hard and deserves the good things of life. In addition, Cadillac ads often enlist the support of the ego by mentioning the high trade-in value of the car, its low maintenance cost, or its surprisingly good gas mileage.

[The noted semanticist, Hayakawa, related the views of Freudian scholars toward men and their automobiles: "The seven-year-old cuts box tops from cereal packages and gets himself a space helmet to act out his fantasies. The thirty-five-year-old buys a Plymouth Fury." (Hayakawa, 1957.)]

It has been suggested that the superego — partly because of more permissive methods of child-rearing — is becoming less important in purchase decisions. One writer uses consumer credit to illustrate the subtle shifts which occur in buying motivations over time. In previous years, he postulates, our views toward the use of credit were controlled largely by Freud's superego. Debt was immoral, something to feel guilty about, to avoid, to hide. The ideal form of rational behavior (ego) was to save, to invest. Now, for some reason rooted in basic cultural changes, credit is more under the control of the ego and may be used freely up to the point of financial danger. (Bayton, 1958, p. 285.) (Rational fears of inflation may also be involved: we borrow today and pay back in "cheaper" dollars over the months and years ahead.)

Betty Crocker cake mixes, when first introduced, allegedly ran into some resistance on the grounds that they were *too* convenient and women felt guilty using them. (Guilt is, of course, a function of the superego.) The strategy used to overcome this was to have the housewife add a fresh egg to the mix. Making this gesture was presumably enough of a contribution to override the guilt stemming from the ease of preparation. Many mixes do not require the addition of an egg and are nevertheless popular, probably because relatively few women feel guilty nowadays about using convenience products.

Dichter has concluded that guilt and other superego appeals are not effective with "young moderns." (Dichter, 1962.) Riesman has made almost the same point in his discussion of inner-directed and other-directed persons. In effect, the *inner-directed* person controls his behavior by reference to internalized norms of his own value system, while the *other-directed* person controls his behavior essentially by reference to the expectations of others. (Riesman, 1950.) The latter refrains from certain kinds of behavior not because of guilt, but because of the expectation of social disapproval. (As we have noted, it is difficult to infer motives from behavior. Inner-directed and other-directed persons may behave in much the same way; one might support his aged mother because he sees it as his duty, for example, and the other because it is expected of him by his social groups.) Riesman sees a growing tendency toward "other-directedness" in our society.[2]

To the extent that inferences about the decay of the superego and the rise of the other-directed person are correct, current marketing efforts should appeal less to the superego and more to the desire for social approval. Instead of saying, "You deserve a Cadillac," the marketer might say, "People expect a man in your position to drive a Cadillac." Clairol might begin to appeal more openly to the single girl's desire to be sexually attractive. Clairol does ask, "Is it true blondes have more fun?" but continues to hedge its bet by implying that marriage rather than "fun" is the aim of sexual attractiveness.

Another concept from psychoanalytic theory is *rationalization:* strictly speaking, a defense mechanism to protect repressed motives. A person wishing to engage in some kind of behavior, but who finds his reasons for doing so unacceptable, may search for some acceptable reason. Once he finds it, he will cling tenaciously to this other reason as the "truth." During psychoanalytic therapy, for example, a patient might say he liked his father better than his mother and cite as a reason some event that occurred in his teens such as his father's having been more willing to increase his allowance. This would almost certainly be a rationalization since attitudes toward parents are formed much earlier in life. Rationalizations are extremely meaningful since they cause the therapist to wonder what the patient is hiding and help him to form hypotheses to test against later information. One obvious question in this illustrative case would be: Is the patient concealing hostility toward his father?

Clever advertising and astute salesmen can provide consumers with ready-made rationalizations. A young lawyer hesitating at the purchase of an expensive suit because his wife is doing without new clothes may be told: "You have to impress your clients. This suit is really an investment." In this particular instance, it should be noted, the rationalization is probably reasonable. Young lawyers do have to impress clients, and their wives

[2] An interesting study by Kassarjian showed that other-directed people tend to prefer advertising copy which includes pictures of and references to *several people*, while inner-directed individuals prefer copy slanted toward *solitary pursuits*. (Kassarjian, 1965.)

can wash and cook and even engage in social activities while wearing older dresses. Rationalizations are often "true" in this sense, but nevertheless do not represent "real" motives. (A soldier who deserts his platoon when it faces certain extinction may be correct in reasoning that his decision will not affect the outcome and that he should not throw away his life uselessly, yet these are likely to be rationalizations of his real motive, fear.)

Rationalization is thus an enormous help to the marketer. The wife who wants to redo her living room to keep the esteem of her friends can either muster reasons herself for redecorating or find reasons in advertisements. The husband who wants to own a motorbike looks for any convenient rationalization to help overcome resistance from his wife. Advertising should help in supplying these reasons.

A distinction should be made between *suppression* and *repression*. A person may be fully aware of one of his motives but suppresses the information and refuses to admit it because he knows it would be unacceptable to others. In repression, the motive would also be unacceptable to the person himself, which leads him to *repress* it into his unconscious. In the case of suppression, the information is fully accessible in the conscious mind of the person, although he might lie or refuse to talk about it. In the case of repression, the information is inaccessible even to the person himself.

Suppressed materials lie at the surface of the mind and bringing them into the open is almost a game of wits between an interviewer and a respondent. It has been alleged, for instance, that mail surveys are more effective than personal interviews in getting at suppressed materials. In filling out privately and anonymously a mail questionnaire, a person will admit the usage of certain products (e.g., suppositories for hemorrhoids or birth control devices) which he would hesitate to admit to an interviewer on a face-to-face basis. The "many people" device is also used extensively: "Many people suffer from hemorrhoids. . . . Which of these products. . . ?" People try to hide ignorance and sometimes pretend to have information. Gallup once found a surprising number of people who claimed to have read *Gone with the Wind* in reply to direct question. When he rephrased his question to, "Do you plan to read. . . ?" those who had read the book told the interviewer that they had and others (still pretending) said that they planned to read it. Persons skilled in questionnaire construction have developed many ingenious techniques for getting the truth about suppressed materials.

Repressed materials are another problem. Here the task is not to get the respondent to tell the truth about matters he consciously wishes to conceal; it is to bring out into the open matters repressed so deeply in his unconscious that they are no longer readily accessible even to himself. People normally need professional help to bring these materials to the level of awareness, and one of the aims of psychotherapy is to provide this help. Psychotherapists, many of whom are Freudian in their orientation, have developed two main approaches to the problem of uncovering repressed materials. One is the clinical psychoanalytic depth interview, and the other relies on the phenomenon of projection. Both have been borrowed by market researchers as motivation research tools, as discussed later in this chapter.

Over the years, Freudian psychology has been the subject of a vast amount of discussion and argument. In a single book of readings (Lindzey, 1964), we find such diverse views as the following:

> There is no need to underscore the point that Freud's intellectual contributions rank with the foremost scholars of our time. His impact upon the thinking world can be compared realistically only with Darwin and Marx among scholars of the past century. Indeed, it is difficult to find a field of human knowledge this side of the physical sciences that has not been influenced by Freud's formulations. (Lindzey, 1964, p. 8.)

Contrast this with:

> There was so much truth in what (Freud) said — so much truth. But like most theories of our times, psychoanalysis, as a theory, was conceived as an absolute truth, and, moreover, it was designed in such a manner that it tended to defy both logical examination and experimental validation. As the years go by, Freudianism, which deserves to be remembered as a brave outpost on the early frontier of early psychological thought, is condemned to end its days as a crumbling stockade of proprietary dogmatism. Thus, as with other farseeing claims to absolute truth, history will have

a difficult time deciding whether Freudianism did more to accelerate psychological progress during the first half of the twentieth century than it did to impede progress during the last half. (Kelly, 1964, p. 34.)

For the present, we can ignore the controversy and concentrate on some of the contributions of Freudian psychology to the understanding of consumer behavior. The principles and concepts of this theory are sometimes fruitful of hypotheses to explain why consumers behave as they do, although these hypotheses should always be (though seldom are) subject to objective, empirical validation in the marketplace prior to making important changes in marketing strategy.

Motivation and Consumer Buying Behavior

For most of the history of our country, we have had a *production* economy, characterized by an emphasis on producing the goods needed by individuals and families to live in a reasonably comfortable manner. Incomes were sufficient to provide necessities (e.g., food, shelter) but not many luxuries (e.g., household labor-saving devices, costly recreation, travel). After World War II, in the rush to meet pent-up consumer demand, we shifted to a *consumption* economy, where production problems were solved to the point that industry could turn out a surplus of goods of all types at lower costs. Consumers, with more discretionary income at their disposal, were able to choose from a wide variety of goods and services and to buy whatever suited them. Distribution problems became more important than production problems, and business found itself in the current "marketing generation."

During the production years, it might be said that biological and instrumental motives were paramount. The emphasis was upon "comfortable survival." In our consumption economy, psychological and social motives are often considered to have the greater importance for many products or services. The choice among products and/or brands is often based upon status, social approval, and personal interest motivations. Some observers go so far as to claim that we are no longer motivated to any appreciable extent by rational, economic objectives, but by our desires for social and psychological satisfactions. They cite study after study to show the capricious nature of consumer spending based upon motivations and images provided by Madison Avenue or by clever package design.

Traditional economic theory, on the other hand, holds to the "principle of rationality." The consumer, in considering alternative purchases, establishes an order of desirability of these purchases such that the most desirable will yield the greatest satisfaction per unit of cost, the next most desirable will yield lesser satisfaction, and so on. Faced with the same set of purchasing alternatives, the consumer will consistently make the same choice each time, and this consistency is a characteristic of "rational behavior" in an "integrated personality." (Arrow, 1951a, 1951b.) Katona, taking issue with this view, states:

> We may begin by characterizing the prevailing economic theory as a single-motive theory and contrast it with a theory of multiple motives. Even in case of a single decision of one individual, multiplicity of motives, . . . some reinforcing one another and some conflicting with one another, is the rule rather than the exception. The motivational patterns prevailing among different individuals making the same decisions need not be the same; the motives of the same individual who is in the same external situation at different times may likewise differ. This approach opens the way (a) for a study of the relation of different motives to different forms of behavior and (b) for an investigation of changes in motives. Both problems are disregarded by postulating a single-motive theory and by restricting empirical studies to attempts to confirm or contradict that theory. (Katona, 1953, pp. 313–14).

Most modern writers take an eclectic, middle stance. Alderson says: "While rational problem solving is believed to fill a central place in the behavior of the consumer buyer, the presence of irrational or nonrational factors cannot be ignored. Habit and impulse are often more in evidence than rational choice, and efficiency as a buyer is acquired only as the result of considerable experience. The concept of rational ends must be expanded beyond the acquisition and use of economic goods to include such objectives as the maintenance of a favorable self-image." (Alderson, 1957, p. 163.)

Morgan speculates that psychologists and economists may not

be so far apart with regard to motivation when the economists' *expected utility* is defined in terms which psychologists would accept. He observes:

> Finally, these three — the motivational dispositions, the probabilistic expectancies, and the incentive values — together produce something akin to the economists' idea of the expected utility of the object or outcome, which is compared with that of other alternatives in arriving at decisions. (Morgan, 1958, p. 106.)

RISK-TAKING ASPECTS OF PURCHASING BEHAVIOR

The University of Nebraska annually conducts a symposium on motivation, bringing together scholars from many disciplines to report and discuss advances in the knowledge and theory of motivation. Participants in these symposia have distinguished three ingredients or determinants of motivation:

Need or motive strength. This reflects the basic personality and social structures of the individual.

Expected outcome. A subjective probability or estimate that a certain course of action will lead to a particular outcome.

Incentive value. The desirability of a particular object or outcome to *a person in a particular situation.*

The work of Atkinson and others has shown, for example, that persons with *high basic need for achievement* tend to work harder on tasks with *low probabilities of success.* This demonstrates some of the interrelationships among motivational ingredients and suggests, for example, why businessmen often prefer a risky investment with a low *expected* value of success — because a successful outcome would represent more of an achievement. (Atkinson) The extent to which these ingredients combine or relate in the purchase of consumer goods is not known, but it is interesting to speculate that early adopters of new products may do so for reasons of high immediate incentive value (based upon a desire for recognition within a social group), in spite of the lower expected value of success with the product (due to frequently higher costs of a new innovation and to the normally greater risks of mechanical failure in new models).

Along a similar line, Bauer views purchasing behavior as an aspect of risk-taking and points out that risk-taking "is an integral part of many familiar phenomena of consumer behavior." He suggests that consumers normally adopt the kind of decisions which *minimize risk* in the purchasing situation. However — and this is very important — consumers do not always calculate risk probabilities or expected outcomes in the manner of a statistician intent upon determining the maximum probable dollar value for a given decision situation. Rather, consumers deal with "perceived risk," that is, risk as they see it *subjectively*. On this basis, factors other than dollar risk might be considered, for example, loss of face among family or friends for a "bad" choice, inconvenience of breakdown in product, or time required to return an item and purchase another (if this is possible). Of course, the economic magnitude of a risk would presumably be perceived differently by different income groups. The loss of $50 should seem less significant to an upper-income family than to a lower-income family.

With this perspective, it is easier to see why consumers exhibit widely different behavior in making a given purchasing decision. Perceived risk for any given purchase is very different for different people. It may also be different for various social classes. Bauer points out that a number of studies have shown that middle-class consumers tend to deliberate more over buying big-ticket durable goods than do lower-class consumers. This suggests to him that the middle-class group may "perceive" that they have a great investment in career, reputation, and personal property to risk, while lower-class consumers may not.[3] (Bauer, 1960.)

In the case of high perceived risk, consumers tend to cast about for support of some kind for their buying decision. This support may come from the reputation of the company itself (corporate image), the support of one's social group, assurances from "opinion leaders" who tend to be influential in product adoption, or other sources. It is interesting to note that Bauer's major premise is, essentially, that a consumer normally acts to

---

[3] Bauer is careful to point out that this difference may also be caused by less time for deliberation among lower-class consumers, since these people are more likely to wait until the product to be replaced has already broken down.

minimize risk, as he sees this risk. The possibility of consumers willingly *accepting* greater risk in order to satisfy other psycho-social objectives is not dealt with as clearly.

There are, then, three methods of dealing with risk in the buying situation:

1. The *optimization of some objective criterion of value* so that the net dollar expenditure over time will be the least for a given amount of utility (the traditional economic view). People who use this approach would often be among the five to ten per cent of the population who consult *Consumers Reports* and similar information services.

2. The *minimization of perceived risk*. This includes economic, temporal, social, and other factors which represent risk or uncertainty to the consumer.

3. The willing *acceptance of risk* in a purchasing situation, with the hope of satisfying basic "achievement needs": the desire to be first, to be best informed, to be a tastemaker, or even to "beat the odds" on some course of action.

There is no evidence as to which of these three is the most accurate model. Indeed, it is likely that an individual consumer uses each of these approaches on different occasions.

Cox and Rich found a definite relationship between the perceived risk of buying certain types of goods or products from a department store and the frequency with which these goods were ordered by telephone. Items with high perceived risk (curtains, small electric appliances, handbags, table linens, kitchen tables and chairs, etc.) were purchased by telephone far less often than items with low perceived risk (bed linens; women's underwear, stockings, and housedresses; men's sox and underwear; etc.). This was true in both metropolitan areas involved in this study, New York and Cleveland. Cox and Rich also suggest that housewives may have different "styles" or strategies for reducing uncertainty or risk in purchase decisions. One approach is to acquire information of a current nature (from newspapers, friends, etc.). Another is based upon past experience with the item, brand, or store in question (Cox and Rich, 1964.)

We have a long way to go before we determine the real nature of the relationship between perceived risk and purchasing decisions, but the evidence to date suggests that this is at least one important dimension of motivation in the buying situation.

TYPES OF CONSUMERS

Some attempts have been made to develop a classification system for consumers based upon *modes of buying behavior* or approaches to the buying situation. One writer sees six types of consumers:

Habit-determined, brand-loyal consumers who tend to be satisfied with the last purchased product or brand.

Cognitive consumers who are sensitive to rational claims and are only conditionally brand loyal.

Price-cognitive consumers who decide principally on the basis of price or economy comparisons.

Impulse consumers who buy on the basis of physical appeal and are relatively insensitive to brand names.

"Emotional" reactors who tend to be responsive to what products symbolize and who are heavily swayed by "images."

New consumers not yet stabilized with respect to the psychological dimensions of consumer behavior. (Woods, 1960, p. 17.)

This writer does not estimate the percentage of the total market in each of the categories, but reports that a study by Gedalecia suggests that cognitive (rational) behavior is found in about 20 per cent of the market. He also does not discuss the possibility that more than one form of buying behavior might characterize an individual consumer who might be a cognitive buyer for one product category and an impulse buyer for another. He does suggest:

No matter whether the consumer be 'habit determined,' 'cognitive,' or 'impulsive,' he will still acknowledge that Cadillacs do convey prestige connotations of some sort and that cosmetics do represent a means of conveying 'maturity.' Yet, while product variables and person variables represent two sets of variables, it is also true that interrelations do exist. The very nature of impulsiveness as a personality characteristic leads to greater susceptibility to products with hedonic appeal. Similarly, social needs will lead to association with products with status connotations. (Woods, 1960, p. 19.)

One study does offer some *evidence* about various types of consumer buying orientations. As part of a research project to study popular reactions to the establishment of a large chain department store, Stone interviewed housewives in a Chicago suburb to determine various aspects of their shopping behavior and their orientations toward stores in general. Respondents were asked if they would rather do business with local independent merchants or large chain stores and why. Follow-up questions were then asked to probe more intensively the initial responses to the open-end question, "Why would you rather do business with local independent merchants (or large chain stores)?" On the basis of their answers to these questions, he found it possible to classify the housewives in four categories to reflect their primary "orientation" toward stores and toward the shopping process:

The economic consumer. Here was the closest approximation to the "economic man" of traditional economic theory. This type of shopper expressed a sense of responsibility for her household purchasing duties. She was extremely sensitive to price, quality, and assortment of merchandise, all of which entered into the calculus of her behavior on the market. She was interested in shopping for values. Clerical personnel and the store itself were, for her, merely the "instruments" for her purchase of goods. Thus, the efficiency of sales personnel and the relative commensurateness of prices, quality, and selection of merchandise were decisive in leaving her with a pleasant or unpleasant impression of the store. The quality she demanded of a "good" clerk was efficiency.

The personalizing consumer. This type of consumer shopped "where they know my name." It was important that she shop at "her" store rather than "public" stores.[4] Strong personal

[4] The personal pronouns "I," "me," and "my" found their way frequently into the interviews, one indication of the extent to which these housewives built up strong identifications with the stores they patronized. Therefore, their relationships with store personnel are referred to as "primary" or

attachments were formed with store personnel, and this personal relationship, often approaching intimacy, was crucial to her patronage of a store. She was highly sensitive to her experiences on the market; obviously, they were an important part of her life. It followed that she was responsive to both pleasant and unpleasant experiences in stores. Her conception of a "good" clerk was one who treated her in a personal, relatively intimate manner.

The ethical consumer. This type of shopper shopped where she "ought to." She was willing to sacrifice the lower prices or wider selection of goods of the large store "to help the little guy out" or because "the chain store has no heart or soul." Consequently, strong attachments were sometimes formed with store personnel and owners or with "stores" in the abstract. These attachments mediated the impressions she had of stores, left pleasant impressions in her memory, and forced unpleasant impressions out. Since store personnel did not enter into her buying behavior primarily as instrumentalities, she had no clear conception of a "good" clerk.

The apathetic consumer. This type of consumer shopped because she "had" to. Shopping for her was an onerous task. She shopped "to get it over with." Convenient location, rather than price, quality of goods, relationships with store personnel, or ethics, was crucial to her selection of a store. She was not interested in shopping and therefore minimized her expenditure of effort in purchasing goods. Experiences in stores were not sufficiently important to leave any lasting impression on her. She knew few of the personnel and had no notion of a "good" clerk.

The relative frequencies of these various types in the sample is shown in Table 3.1.

"quasiprimary," for the store has become incorporated into the social self of the consumer. As Cooley, put it, "The social self is simply any idea, or system of ideas, drawn from the communicative life, that the mind cherishes as its own." Hence the store may be seen as a part of the social self of the personalizing type of consumer. (Cooley, 1902, p. 147.)

Table 3.1

DISTRIBUTION OF CONSUMER TYPES — RETAIL SHOPPING

Type of Consumer	Number	Per Cent
Economic	41	33
Personalizing	35	28
Ethical	22	18
Apathetic	21	17
Indeterminate	5	4
Total	124	100

Stone also determined the other characteristics of the housewives in each category. For example, economic consumers typically were younger, had higher aspirations, and were "on their way up" the success ladder, but had to be careful with money partly because of the cost of raising their children; personalizing consumers typically had lower social status, were newer in the community, had fewer children, and used their quasi-personal relationships with store personnel as a substitute for neighborhood ties they had not yet developed. (Stone, 1954.)

Another study, by the Housing Research Center at Cornell University, developed four types of consumers based upon their "value" systems, as given in Table 3.2.

Table 3.2

CONSUMER VALUE SYSTEMS

Type	Percentage[5]
Economic	30.3
Family	30.1
Personal	13.6
Not classified	26.0
Total	100.0

These investigators also recognized the existence of another value group, the "prestige" type, which was not found in their study. They then developed the implications of these classifica-

[5] Among 773 home-owning families.

tions in terms of a house-design appropriate for the living patterns and desires of each group. (Housing Research Center, 1954.) Notice the similarity of some of these classifications to those of Stone's study.

A study by the Survey Research Center of the University of Michigan reported two major categories of households — achievement-oriented and security-oriented — on the basis of answers to questions about satisfactions with job, income, and present living standards. Each category was further classified into two sub-categories according to whether the household appeared relatively *satisfied* or *dissatisfied* with past progress, income, and standard of living. Achievement-oriented households which were relatively satisfied were called "integrated achievers," and those not satisfied were called "other achievers." Table 3.3 shows the percentages of the various types among a nationwide sample of 572 households.

Table 3.3

FREQUENCY OF CONSUMER TYPES

Type	*Percentage*	
Achievement Oriented	38	
Integrated Achievers		25
Other Achievers		13
Security Oriented	62	
Satisfied Securers		30
Other Securers		32
Total	100%	

Differences were found among the various consumer types in terms of cash versus installment purchases, number of major durable-goods expenditures, and propensity to save. There may, however, be an overlap of these classifications with "stage in the life cycle" (see Chapter 7) since achievers tended to be in their middle thirties with preschool children while securers tended to be in their middle forties with school-age children. (Boulding, 1960.)

There are, then, a number of meaningful ways of classifying consumers according to their buying patterns. The implications of the first two studies in particular are very interesting. For one thing, they suggest why the small retailer has a place in the distribution structure and will probably continue to have one even though the trend is toward larger stores. Personalizing consumers tend to seek some measure of personal identification in a community, and the small retailer is more likely to provide this than are the larger chain stores. Also, ethical consumers are by nature unfavorably predisposed toward big business. Taken together, these two types form the largest percentage (46 per cent) of all shoppers in the Stone study, so it can be expected that their influence would be considerable.

On the other hand, it is not impossible for large stores, especially smaller branches of chain stores, to develop the sort of individual service necessary to attract the personalizing shopper, and many chains make a real attempt to do this. The significant number of apathetic buyers (17 per cent) suggests why convenience of location is important and also indicates why it is possible for an inefficient retailer to stay in business. It might caustically (and perhaps unfairly) be observed that these are the people — rather than the small merchants themselves — who are responsible for some of the inefficiencies in our distribution system today.[6]

MEASURING READINESS TO BUY

There is also a temporal aspect of motivated behavior. Not only is *why* we buy important, but also *when* we buy. How do we know at what point in time the consumer is ready to buy or, conversely, at what stage of "readiness to buy" a consumer is in at any given time? Bilkey formulates this problem in terms of psychic tensions. He refers to the theory of the psychologist Kurt Lewin, discussed earlier, who holds that consumer purchasing essentially involves a psychic conflict between a person's *desire* for the item in question and his inevitable *resistance* against its costs (dollars, time, etc.).

To test the usefulness of this concept in the buying situation, Bilkey asked 63 families in Connecticut to keep a diary of food

[6] Note that the Stone study was done in the early 1950's in only one city, Chicago. The patterns there may or may not be reflective of the situation in other large cities today.

purchases for one year. At intervals during this time, each family purchasing head was asked to indicate on a rating scale his or her strength of feeling about certain types of purchases:

a. How strong is your desire for the [item]?
b. How strong is your desire to avoid the expense which the [item] might entail?

Ratings could range from 0 to 100. One respondent, for example, had a "50" desire for a new car but a "75" desire to avoid the expense. (This particular respondent did *not* buy a car during the year.) The positive and negative expressions were averaged to produce a "net valence" for the item in question. Positive valences presumably showed that the respondent was favorable *on balance* toward the item, negative valences the opposite.

When these net valences or tensions for food expenditures were related to actual food expenditures, there was a fairly close correlation between the two ($r = .76$) for a period of one year. Bilkey states:

> The results of this study indicate that there is a quantitative relationship between people's stated psychic tensions regarding the purchase of particular items and their expenditures for those items. The further fact that these stated psychic tensions for food were found to relate to considerations (the interviewees' standard of living, their level of uncommitted cash balances, and price changes) which economists have found by independent analysis to have an influence on consumer buying indicates that the interviewees' stated psychic tensions tend to conform reasonably well with their actual psychic tensions — at least so far as food is concerned. (Bilkey, 1955, p. 255.)

Another investigator took a more direct approach to the measurement of buying readiness. This investigator asked respondents to indicate their own location on a "buying continuum" by selecting statements to describe how they felt about a particular product, as shown in Figure 3.2.

These buying-readiness indications were compared with actual purchases of the brand within four weeks after making the rating. Table 3.4 shows the results.

Figure 3.2

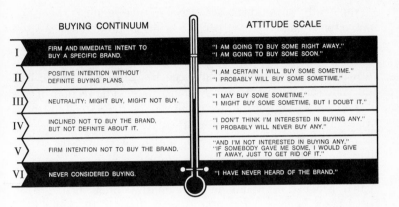

Table 3.4

Readiness and Purchasing Scores
for Two Household Items

	TOILET GOODS ITEM				GROCERY ITEM		
Brand	*Readiness Score**	*Purchasing Score***	*Purchasing/ Readiness****	*Brand*	*Readiness Score**	*Purchasing Score***	*Purchasing/ Readiness****
A	41%	23%	56%	A	37%	23%	62%
B	29	16	55	B	16	7	44
C	22	13	59	C	13	7	54
D	18	8	44	D	12	3	25
E	17	8	47	E	12	8	67
F	5	2	40				

* Readiness score: Per cent of respondents who chose one of top two readiness-to-buy scale statements about the brand.

** Purchasing score: Per cent of respondents who actually purchased the brand within four weeks after making rating.

*** Purchasing/readiness ratio: Per cent of respondents choosing one of top two statements who purchased the brand within four weeks. When this ratio is high, a large proportion of those with intent to buy have actually done so. When the ratio is low, something has interfered between predisposition and purchasing.

A definite relationship was found between purchasing readiness and actual purchasing, although this varied by brand and was affected by such factors as availability in the marketplace. (Wells, 1961.)

Apparently then, there are ways of determining a person's motivational state with respect to a given product at a given time. Note that we are referring to motive *strength*, *not* to the *identification* of the basic motivating force or forces. But information about motive strength can be useful even if we lack full understanding of the motivational state. The section of this chapter on motivation research will discuss the various methods of attempting to define *which* motives are operative with respect to a given product, service, retail outlet, advertisement, or the like.

Does all of this suggest that purchasing is directed to a particular product or brand on a thoughtful, premeditated basis, based upon some previous motivational states in the individual? Not necessarily. A great many studies have pointed to the increasing importance of impulse purchases in recent years. Estimates suggest that from 35 to 75 per cent of purchases are not specifically planned in advance. (This wide range results from different types of products and stores and different definitions of the term "impulse.") Some impulse buying is due to the simple unavailability of the particular brand initially sought, but a considerable amount is also due to eye-catching point-of-purchase displays, persuasion by sales personnel, or simply boredom with the usual brand and curiosity about another one. However, even impulse buying has motivational substance behind it. The difference between impulse buying and other buying is more temporal than substantive.

LEVEL OF ASPIRATION

As pointed out earlier, motivation is related to level of aspiration. Once our original motive is satisfied (e.g., we have joined the club or bought the car), we should, following motivation theory, experience a reduction in our urge to acquire similar things. This hypothesis is based upon what we know about the behavior of both animals and human beings after one of the biological drives has been satiated. Upon physical satisfaction, there follows a reduction in the drive.

Do we behave in a similar fashion with regard to psychological and sociological motivations? Katona, who has spent many years in studying consumer buying behavior at the Survey Research Center at the University of Michigan, points out that the answer to this question depends primarily upon an individual's level of aspiration, that is, what he ultimately hopes to attain. Based upon extensive work by himself and by Lewin, Katona formulates the following generalizations, which have been established in numerous studies of goal-striving behavior:

1. Aspirations are not static; they are not established once for all time.
2. Aspirations tend to *grow* with achievement and *decline* with failure.
3. Aspirations are influenced by the performance of other members of the group to which a person belongs and by that of reference groups.
4. Aspirations are reality oriented; most commonly they are slightly higher or slightly lower than the level of accomplishment rather than greatly different from it. Katona, 1960, p. 130.)

Citing numerous results from periodic surveys of consumer finances regarding the accumulation of liquid assets (savings, etc.), Katona shows that once a family has accumulated a certain amount of savings for some predetermined objective or purchase, the family typically continues saving at approximately the same rate even though the objective for which savings are accrued may change. He finds little evidence that the satisfaction of such a motivation (in the sense of reaching the original objective) leads directly to a state of saturation for that objective. He states:

> What the studies of liquid-asset holdings and of durable goods as well teach us is that it is possible for gratification of needs to result in raising our sights and aspiring for more assets or goods. But this need not happen, and good times are not necessarily self-perpetuating. Saturation, that is, a subjective feeling of having enough goods, may occur — under the impact of adverse attitudes. The feeling of saturation itself is an attitude closely likened to anxiety, insecurity, and a pessimistic evaluation of prospects as well as of prevailing conditions. (Katona, 1960, p. 137.)

Maslow points out that man is a perpetually "wanting" animal. He has a great many needs, which can be arranged in some sort of hierarchy of prepotency for a given person at a given time. Once the most important need is satisfied, the next most important takes over, and so on. (Maslow, 1943.) Aspirations furnish part of the basis for this ordering of needs in terms of prepotency.

Simon hypothesizes that people rarely attempt to optimize in their decision making. Confronted with several alternatives, they will tend, instead, to select any alternative that is satisfactory to them in terms of their present aspiration levels. A housewife looking for a new dress, for example, will not shop forever seeking absolutely the best dress for her money; she will simply examine several dresses and select the one which is most satisfactory. Suppose, however, that none of the alternatives offered is truly satisfactory. In this case, the housewife would engage in what Simon calls *search behavior*, that is, she would seek other alternatives. Shopping, of course, is pure search behavior, and the amount of search behavior that takes place depends on the original level of aspiration. If, after considerable search, no satisfactory alternative is found, what appears to happen is that *aspiration levels are lowered;* the housewife may go back to buy one of the dresses she passed over earlier. Simon has coined the term "satisficing" to describe this behavioral phenomenon. (Simon and March, 1958.)

The implications of our knowledge about aspirations and motivation are rather clear: The businessman need not be pessimistic about the overall outlook for consumer-goods purchases. There is always a reservoir of desire to be tapped; people are always "learning" and "acquiring" new needs. Walter Heller, former chairman of President Kennedy's Council of Economic Advisers, put it this way: "Consumer satiety is a myth!"

Motivation Research

In the 1950's, consumer-products companies of all types became seriously interested in the problem of how to determine why people buy one product or brand over another. With the large amount of discretionary income at consumers' disposal, and the fact that many products are virtually indistinguishable from others in terms of taste or major performance features (cf. Chapter 1), product characteristics become less important, image and attitudes become more important, and the manufacturer has greater difficulty in determining the basic motivations which cause the selection of one product over another.

For example, do most housewives regard desserts for their families as a nuisance and therefore look for quick solutions in the form of ready-made desserts (instrumental motive)? Or do they see desserts as an opportunity to demonstrate their superiority in the kitchen by cooking rich, tasty offerings (status, affection, or perhaps personal interest motive)? Do car owners regard their cars primarily as means of transportation (instrumental), or do they consider them almost as a "member of the family" and care for them accordingly (personal interest, affection)? Accurate knowledge of consumers' views toward product categories or brands can have a profound effect upon such factors as package design, promotion, and even channel of distribution. Thus, the knowledge that most clocks were bought as gifts (affection) rather than for the purchaser himself (instrumental) led Seth Thomas clocks to open up new channels of distribution through drug stores, hardware stores, and even supermarkets to augment its department store distribution.

If knowledge of consumer motivations is so important to the manufacturer or merchant, why not simply ask housewives *why* they buy a particular household cleaning product or *why* they don't buy a particular brand of hair shampoo? The concepts of suppression and repression discussed earlier explain the reluctance of many individuals to reveal some of their subtle feelings and motivations, especially to interviewers who are total strangers. For example, who wants to admit that he has bought his son an expensive 10-speed bicycle because the neighbor's boy has one and "I'm as successful as his dad"? What woman wants to tell a stranger that she buys only the most expensive cosmetics because her natural beauty requires the very best cremes and soaps? We all have a degree of reserve about our thoughts and motives — especially when these are related to status seeking, social approval, narcissism (self-love), and similar desires which are rather unacceptable to verbalize in our society.

The problem is a difficult one. How can these barriers

(Freud's ego?) be broken down in a very short time by unfamiliar interviewers so as to provide better insights into a person's real motives and emotions? Is it possible to provide a vehicle for expression which will allow the respondent to divulge innermost feelings without embarrassment or, perhaps, without his even knowing he has done so?

This is a problem which seems insoluble on the surface, but for many years clinical psychologists faced the same problem in probing for the deepest feelings and emotions of neurotic patients. Over the years they developed a body of techniques known as *projective tests*. The patient uses the test situation to "project" himself into someone else's shoes in a rather unstructured situation; without really knowing anything about the other person or the situation, the patient tells what the person is thinking. In such an arrangement, the reasoning goes, the patient unsuspectingly relates the only thing he really knows much about — his *own* feelings, attitudes, and motives.

A few diagnostic techniques which are in common use in motivation research studies today will be discussed briefly. Not all of these are truly projective techniques in which the individual projects himself into an ambiguous or unstructured situation; some (such as word association) simply call for the respondent to reply very quickly before his self-censor can begin to modify his initial thoughts or impressions, which are likely to reflect his true feelings. All of the approaches described below have in common the objective of finding out what the buyer is really thinking — what his real feelings and motives are with regard to the brand or product category in question.

Picture story (Thematic Apperception Test, or TAT). The respondent is shown a picture, usually involving a purchase situation. For example, the picure might show a woman pushing a shopping cart down a supermarket aisle alongside the frozen desserts cabinet. The respondent is asked to tell what the shopper is thinking as she passes by the frozen desserts. Now, of course, the respondent really has no idea as to what the shopper in the picture is thinking, since she has been given no information about this woman. Yet she finds no difficulty in telling a story about what she *thinks* the shopper is thinking. And since she has no information about the shopper, most of what she says must, presumably, reflect *her own feeling and thoughts*.

She might say of the shopper, "She is thinking that frozen desserts are just too expensive — not worth the money; only a lazy housewife will use a frozen pie when she should be baking her own and making a better pie at less cost." Or "She is thinking, 'Why shouldn't I buy a frozen pie? It's better than I can make." The respondent is "projecting" herself into the picture without realizing it. The question of whether she gives her own personal views or whether her story is a reflection of what she believes her friends and other housewives really think (which might be at variance with her own feelings) is simply unanswered in most motivation research studies. It is merely assumed that the technique reveals at least some feelings and motives which might not have been brought to the surface by direct questioning.

Word association. The respondent is read a list of words, one at a time, and asked to say the *first thing* that comes into her mind after hearing each word, for example, *beer* — "tickles" *shampoo* — "nuisance"; *washer* — "giant." The idea is that the rapid response indicates what the respondent is really thinking before she can marshal her powers of censorship to produce a more rational, acceptable answer. The Ford Motor Company used this technique to get reactions to possible names for the then-unnamed Edsel car. One proposed name produced interesting results while the name Edsel showed little promise, as shown in the following associations:

Corsair — "pirate," "swashbuckler," "princess."

Edsel — "diesel," "hard-sell," "pretzel." (Brooks, 1960, pp. 80, 82.)

With findings of this type, it is hard to understand the final choice of name for this car. The associations derived from this technique were originally formed, of course, in the manner discussed in Chapter 2. The word association technique helps to get at associations which are more emotional than rational.

Cartoon (Rosenzweig Picture Frustration). This is similar to the picture story technique, but there are usually two or more people talking with one another, as in cartoons or comic strips in the daily newspaper (hence the name, *cartoon*). For example, the respondent is shown a picture of two housewives talking in a living room or in a market. One says to the other, "Ethel and Joe just bought a color TV set; I wonder why they did that." The "balloon" above the other housewife is left blank for the respondent to fill in. She might write in, for example, "Oh, the people down the street just got one and Joe always has to show he can keep up — color TV isn't that good yet."

Incomplete sentences. The respondent is shown or read a partial sentence such as "People who buy home air conditioners ————." The respondent completes the sentence, perhaps by adding, ". . . are thoughtful of their family's comfort" or ". . . are just showing off; there's no need for it in this area." One study compared the results from incomplete-sentence tests with those from direct questioning in a survey for a firm which provides a building-maintenance service for large office buildings:

Interviewers told respondents that they would be asked about 'both pleasant and unpleasant things' in their experience with, or what they had heard about, the service . . . 'first, the pleasant ones.'

After discussing the pleasant points, respondents were asked about the 'unpleasant' ones. There were 42 per cent reporting something unpleasant, and the bulk of the criticisms fell about equally into two categories — one concerning general administrative arrangements (15 per cent), the other relating to the behavior of the client organization's personnel (18 per cent). The other 58 per cent reported nothing unpleasant. Interviewers then asked a question phrased as an incomplete sentence — a motivation research device in which the respondent is asked to finish the sentence when the interviewer stops in the middle. Here is the incomplete sentence: 'I know they are busy and have lots of people to take care of, but it seems to me that they could at least. . . .'

Over half of the 58 per cent who had reported nothing unpleasant now responded with criticisms, as did nearly all of those who had stated criticisms in the earlier question. The sentence completions of the former 'Don't know' people were remarkably similar in content to those given by the rest of the sample, and in both groups the criticisms relating to personnel now jumped to a ratio of four to one over criticisms relating to administrative arrangements. Furthermore, the personnel criticisms were given in much more vigorous language than appeared in the earlier request for criticisms. (Wiebe, 1958, p. 26.)

In this case, at least, the use of a motivation research tool was able to produce more information and, also, feelings of a different tone than would have been obtained from conventional consumer survey questions.

Another approach to the problem of eliciting hidden motives or attitudes is the so-called depth interview. Oversimplifying, there are three main characteristics of the depth interview as it is used in marketing. First, it is longer than the typical structured interview. A standard telephone interview is rarely longer than twenty minutes; a depth interview may run for two, three, or more hours (but not on the phone, of course!) Respondents must consequently be paid for participation, which runs up the cost per interview. (Commercial depth interviews, however, do not involve nearly as many hours as clinical diagnostic and therapeutic depth interviews; a psychoanalyst may spend three fifty-minute sessions a week with a patient over a period of three or four years, for a total of perhaps five hundred hours.) Second, depth interviews are open-end and permissive. Obviously the commercial researcher must try to keep the conversation on the problem under investigation, but the interviewer tries to get the respondent to talk freely and avoids making value judgments. Third, the interviewer — or the psychoanalyst back at the office — looks at his data in the light of Freudian or other psychological categories of personality. For example, a wedge of cheese shown standing on its base is seen as masculine; the same wedge lying flat on a plate is seen as feminine. These associations are easily understandable from what has been learned of sexual imagery from the study of dreams. (Psychoanalysts abjure the "Gypsy Dream Book" approach and insist that the symbols mean different things to different people and must be analyzed *in context*.)

Often, analysis of depth interviews can lead to product action or to changes in advertising messages. For example, compulsion neuroses in which people repeat ritualistic behavior (e.g., Lady Macbeth washing her hands) are fairly common, and most of us have a streak of compulsiveness in our make-up. Hypochondriacs tend to be compulsive, and it has been suggested that patent medicines sold to hypochondriacs should include directions such as "One pill after each meal and two at bedtime" instead of "One pill as needed." Hypochondriacs respond to ritualistic instructions. Many popular diets owe some of their success to the fact that they require people to follow regimens strictly. (An element of magic is involved here also. Failure to achieve the promised success can be ascribed to a failure to follow the ritual rather than to the diet or product itself.)

The advisability of using the above clinical techniques in the commercial situation has been seriously questioned by many psychologists and market researchers alike. Part of the problem is the need to secure thoroughly trained clinical psychologists to make the proper interpretations of "unstructured" survey results. It can safely be said that only a minority of the firms currently engaged in motivation research studies have professional psychologists with extensive clinical training. Even if they did, it is well known that clinical psychologists tend to differ in their interpretations of the same data depending upon the particular school of psychotherapy to which they are oriented. This tends to produce unreliable and inconsistent findings from motivation research studies.

For example, a household baking products manufacturer engaged two research firms to make recommendations about the image which it should strive to establish for the housewife whose name was a part of their trademark and brand name. One firm recommended a next-door-neighbor approach; the other felt that an authority-image — "Mother knows best" — would be most effective. Similarly conflicting recommendations have been made by separate motivation research firms in the case of a fruit juice beverage, a bacterial soap product, and other items. This has tended to reduce the confidence of businessmen and researchers alike in motivation research studies.

In addition, there is the question of whether the sophisticated, subtle motivation research tools provide any information that is not *more easily and perhaps more accurately obtainable through direct questioning.* The study by Wiebe using incomplete sentences suggests that they do, but one of the well-known industrial psychologists of our time, Mason Haire (whose work has been cited earlier), has a different view:

> I have seen some attempts to answer experimentally the question, 'Will projective techniques get anything that straight-forward questions won't?' I don't know of a conclusive proof that they will. I myself tried to demonstrate this and failed. (Evans, 1961a, p. 71.)

At the present time there is no sure knowledge as to the value of motivation research techniques. Wide differences of opinion still exist, with strong arguments from both sides. In defense of motivation research, it must be said that many manufacturers feel that studies of this type have provided them with valuable insights into their customers' minds, insights which they would not have been able to obtain in any other way. Because of this, motivation research studies continue to be widely used by consumer products manufacturers. Many researchers use motivation research techniques in the problem-formulation stage of a study, to produce hypotheses which can then be submitted to verification by rigorous experimental techniques.

Emotion

A product or service in the marketplace usually does not affect us so strongly that our reaction could be characterized by the terms normally used to describe emotional states: rage, fear, depression, elation, and so on. However, some products and advertisements produce in us a reaction strong enough to be called an *emotional response* in the sense that certain physiological changes take place in us when we view the object, think about it, or discuss it with others. Although these changes are very small, they do exist and can be measured by some of the more exotic instruments of the psychology laboratory.

GALVANIC SKIN RESPONSE

It has long been known that a sizable emotional reaction in a person causes him to perspire in the palm of his hand (as well as elsewhere). An electric current, passed by electrodes from the back of the hand through to the palm, flows more easily because of the increase in the galvanic properties of the saline perspiration moisture in the palm. This increase in conduction is referred to as a galvanic skin response (GSR) or a psychogalvanic response. (PGR). The process described by these interchangeable terms enables us to estimate changes in the emotional reaction of individuals to particular stimulus situations.

The GSR has long been used by police departments as part of their lie-detector test battery. Many other factors (e.g., rate of breathing, blood pressure, heart-beat rate) are also considered, but the GSR is a very critical portion of the entire lie detector process. Of course, we are in no position to give consumers lie detector tests, but it is possible to use the GSR to measure emotional reactions which an individual might have to a particular advertisement, a new product idea, a new label or package design, or similar stimuli.

This technique has been used for several years by one of the largest advertising agencies as part of the services rendered to its clients, and it is now used regularly by at least one firm which specializes in pretesting television commercials. The GSR is by no means in wide use, but it has been used, apparently successfully, for a number of years. It must be remembered, however, that the GSR is by no means a simple, reliable indicator of emotional activity; this measure requires very careful interpretation by a trained laboratory psychologist to determine what is a real emotional reaction and what is simply an artificial reaction produced by extraneous, irrelevant stimuli.

In one study, 60 male college students were exposed to advertisements for three products (nose tissue, ice cream, and air travel). Four different ad layouts were used for each product: Layouts A featured a picture of the product, Layouts B showed a picture of a single person using the product, Layouts C and D showed additional persons in the ads. The 12 advertisements were shown to subjects on a systematic basis to eliminate serial-position bias. Results showed that the GSR was sensitive enough to detect differences in the emotional reactions of individuals to the various ad layouts and to the various products. (Golin & Lyerly, 1950.)

Another study showed some differences in response among housewives to three different pancake-flour ads, and the differences were found to be related to later differences in actual purchase of the flour after the same ads were aired commercially. The ad format which produced the greatest GSR also resulted in 2.1 times as many sales as the other two ads. (Eckstrand & Gilliland, 1948.)

EYE PUPIL MEASUREMENT

Another measuring technique, even more exotic than the GSR, is the process of determining *changes in the diameter of the eye pupil* which accompany presentation of a stimulus object of any type. The original study using this technique found changes in the size of the eye pupils of subjects who viewed pictures of a baby, a mother and baby, a semi-nude male pin-up, a semi-nude female pin-up, and a landscape. Reactions of women viewers were much different from those of men viewers to each picture, as would be expected. (Hess & Polt, 1960.) (Some psychiatrists claim that this technique is an almost foolproof means of determining homosexual tendencies.)

To determine whether or not such a procedure would be useful in the marketplace, Krugman measured changes in pupil size in respondents while they viewed greeting cards and sterling silver patterns. There were definite overall differences in the percentage change in pupil response for different cards and for different silver patterns. Moreover, in the case of birthday cards and sterling silver patterns, the *change in pupil dilation* seemed to be related more closely to actual sales of the cards and patterns than were consumer *verbal responses* to questions about the desirability of each object. Krugman concludes:

> In general, the results of our experience with measurement of pupil response indicate that this is a sensitive and reliable technique with considerable promise for study of the interest-arousing characteristics of visual stimuli. The impact of the environment is often difficult to determine from conscious impressions verbally reported. For a variety of reasons, people may not be practiced or competent to accurately verbalize their feelings in certain areas of living. Pupil measurement seems to provide a powerful new tool for the study of these areas. (Krugman, 1964, p. 18.)

It should be remembered that both the GSR and changes in pupil size are *involuntary* responses to stimulus objects, that is, we do not normally consciously control the variation in our galvanic skin response or in the diameter of the pupils of our eyes. These responses are controlled by the autonomic nervous system and are beyond conscious manipulation by the individual under normal conditions. And, certainly, people would have little reason to falsify consciously their emotional reactions in the type of laboratory study done by advertising agencies to determine consumers' reactions to products or advertising.

Personality

The term *personality* has been a catchall for many years. Roughly speaking, personality refers to all the characteristics which make one individual different from another. Ruch distinguishes the following aspects of personality:

> The individual's external appearance and behavior, or social stimulus value;
>
> His inner awareness of self as a permanent organizing force in life; and
>
> His particular pattern or organization of measurable traits, both inner and outer. (Ruch, 1958, p. 65.)

We are interested primarily in the third aspect — the measurable traits of personality — and particularly in those traits which reflect the "temperament" of the individual: his friendliness, emotional stability, thoughtfulness, general activity, masculinity, etc.

Many psychologists have sought to classify the various dimensions of temperament in much the same manner as others have sought to classify motivations. Their problems have been similar. Hunt points out that the same temperamental characteristic manifests itself differently in different situations. His own research suggests that *situational* aspects may be many times more important than the basic temperament characteristics in determining the individual's response, that is, the situation he is in is more important than his own characteristics in determining how he responds. This leads Hunt to conclude that personality traits are *not* the major source of behavioral variance as they are thought to be by many other psychologists. (Hunt, 1965.) Nevertheless, they are *an* important source directing behavior, and we are interested in the extent to which temperament characteristics influence buying behavior.

With so many researchers at work on the problem, it was inevitable that many different classification systems would evolve. One widely used personality inventory, the Thurstone Temperament Schedule, provides scores on seven individual traits: activeness, vigor, impulsiveness, dominance, stability, sociability, and reflectiveness. Each of these traits is believed to reflect a relatively separate and distinct aspect of human personality. (Thurstone Temperament Schedule, 1953 ed.) Other investigators propose thirteen temperament characteristics based upon extensive statistical analyses of personality inventory items asking respondents about their habits, likes, and dislikes. (Guilford & Zimmerman, 1956.) (Note the overlap with Thurstone.)

General Activity
Ascendance vs. Submission
Masculinity vs. Femininity
Confidence vs. Inferiority
  Feelings
Calmness, Composure vs.
  Nervousness
Sociability
Reflectiveness
Depression
Emotionality
Restraint vs. Rhathymia
Objectivity
Agreeableness
Cooperativeness (Tolerance)

The Thurstone Temperament Schedule and the Guilford-Zimmerman list are but two of the personality inventories in common use today; there are dozens of others. As in the case of motives, there is no single classification system to which all scholars will subscribe, but there is enough overlap and similarity among various schema to indicate that most investigators are talking basically about the same aspects of behavior. In any event, we have a wealth of measuring devices to assist in answering questions about how some aspects of personality or temperament are related to buying decisions and shopping behavior.

In one study, Evans challenged the statements made by motivation researchers to the effect that the typical Ford owner was, in general, a different sort of person from the Chevrolet owner. Through heavy advertising investments, Ford had supposedly built an image of the Ford owner as independent, impulsive, masculine, alert to change, and self-confident, while Chevrolet owners were thought to be conservative, thrifty, prestige-conscious, less masculine, and wary of extremes. To test this, Evans measured approximately 70 Ford and 70 Chevrolet owners with the

Edwards Personal Preference Schedule, a personality inventory which provides scores on each of the following characteristics for each person:

Achievement: To do one's best, to accomplish something of great significance.

Deference: To find out what others think, to accept the leadership of others.

Exhibition: To say witty and clever things, to talk about personal achievements.

Autonomy: To be able to come and go as desired, to say what one thinks about things.

Affiliation: To be loyal to friends, to make as many friends as possible.

Intraception: To analyze one's motives and feelings, to analyze the behavior of others.

Dominance: To be a leader in the groups to which one belongs, to tell others how to do their jobs.

Abasement: To feel guilty when one does something wrong, to feel inferior to others in most respects.

Change: To do new and different things, to participate in new fads and fashions.

Aggression: To attack contrary points of view, to get revenge for insults.

Heterosexuality: To become sexually excited, to be in love with someone of the opposite sex. (Edwards, 1957, p. 14)

Evans also obtained extensive information about the personal history and background of each owner (his age, whether he owned or rented his home, his political inclinations, time at present job, income, and the like). With such an impressive array of information, it would seem that differences between Ford and Chevrolet owners surely could be found if, in fact, differences did exist. However, results were negative. Evans says:

Although respondents in this survey spanned wide ranges for most of the psychological and objective variables measured, none of these variables was systematically related to the brand of car owned for the two brands which constitute almost half the automobile market. The variables used here do not allow for further segmentation of this market. (Evans, 1959, p. 364.)

In a later study, Evans did find certain personality correlates of *shopping behavior* in connection with the purchase of an automobile. (Evans, 1962)

On the other hand, a proprietary study conducted in the early 1950's showed clear differences in the way in which Ford and Chevrolet owners were *perceived*. People were asked to check statements describing the kind of person who would drive a Ford or Chevrolet, and the Ford driver was seen as more masculine, more independent, more adventurous, younger, and more likely to have an occupation such as salesman rather than bank teller.

These data can be reconciled with Evans' findings in two ways. First, it is possible that the Ford owner is seen as more adventurous, but that the people who buy Fords are in fact not more adventurous. This would cast some doubt on the hypothesis that congruence of self-image and product image is important in buying behavior. Second, the discrepancy between the two studies may be due to *time*. Chevrolet introduced an eight-cylinder engine for the first time in 1954 and was more active than Ford in automobile racing in the late 1950's. Also, the 1958 Chevrolet was the first Chevrolet model that exhibited "high style." It is thus possible that, had the Evans study been done in the early 1950's, personality differences between Ford and Chevrolet owners would have been found. Among Ford marketing executives, the accepted explanation of Evans' data is that Chevrolet managed, by aggressive merchandising in the later 1950's, to capture Ford's reputation as a car for the adventurous, independent young man.

Another investigator tried to determine whether it was possible to distinguish between convertible and nonconvertible car owners on the basis of personality characteristics. This investigator stated. "Some of the early folklore of motivation research included a report that men who owned convertibles thought of their cars in the same way they might think of a mistress!" At the very least, convertible owners were supposed to have differed from non-owners by being more active, vigorous, and athletic. To see if this was true, Westfall compared personality characteristics of convertible owners with those of standard-size and compact car owners. He found:

> Differences in personality as measured by the Thurstone Temperament Schedule probably do exist between owners of convertible cars on the one hand and standard and compact car owners on the other. Compact and standard car owners do not seem to differ to any marked degree. The characteristics of active, impulsive, stable and sociable appear to have the greatest value as predictors of the type of car owned. . . . The fact that in this study, as in Evans', no personality differences were found between Ford and Chevrolet owners lends further weight to Evans' conclusion that personality differences do not exist between these groups. The fact that personality differences were found between the owners of two car *types* indicates that, at least in some cases, measurable personality differences do exist between owners of different products serving the same basic function. (Westfall, 1962, p. 39.)

Other studies also provide support for the proposition that some aspects of personality or temperament are related to product category purchase. An interesting study by Tucker and Painter showed that individuals who stated a preference for the standard makes and models of cars were more likely to show up higher on the "responsibility" scale of the Gordon Personal Profile than were those who preferred such sports cars as the Corvette or Thunderbird. This study also showed definite relationships between four personality traits (ascendance, responsibility, emotional stability, and sociability) and the use or non-use of such products as headache remedies, vitamins, cigarettes, alcoholic beverages, and mouthwash. (Tucker & Painter, 1961.)

Gottlieb found that individuals who are compulsive (i.e., like to schedule their activities, never throw things away, make decisions only after great thought, etc.) are much more likely to use antacid-analgesic products than are noncompulsive individuals. He also found that people with a punitive orientation (i.e., those who think people learn a great deal from suffering, who think discipline is most important in building children's character, etc.) tend to use *less* products of this type. Gottlieb suggests that there are two ways to use findings of this kind in building marketing strategies:

1. Find important *segments* of the market that are not now being operated effectively, and talk to these people in terms of their own interests.
2. Address advertising to the compulsive streak in all of us. (Gottlieb, 1949, p. 154.)

In considering this research, it must be kept in mind that the measures of temperament were *self-evaluations* based upon a standard personality measuring instrument. Results are only meaningful to the extent that the self-evaluations are accurate and that the measuring instrument measures what it purports to. If we can consider both of these assumptions to be within reason, it appears that there may be personality differences between users of product types when these products show relatively large differences in performance. When product differences are minor or are confined mainly to brand names, the personality differences among buyers postulated by motivation researchers and by Madison Avenue copywriters may not exist to any great degree or at least are not of primary importance in determining buying behavior.

QUESTIONS
FOR REVIEW

1. Would it be possible to determine the most important reasons (motives) why people buy stereophonic sound units? If so, how? Would it be of any value for us to do so? Why?

2. In what ways are the principles of learning (Chapter 2) related to human motivations? Illustrate how a manufacturer or retailer could draw upon this interrelationship.

3. Suppose you were a soft drink manufacturer. What is known about emotion and how to measure it that would be of any value to you?

4. As a retailer, how would knowledge about various types of consumers be of use to you? What specific action might you take on the basis of such knowledge?

5. Do consumers always buy the item representing the least *risk?* In what situations might we not do this? How is personality related to risk taking?

6. Do you think Evans might have found differences between Ford and Chevrolet owners if he had used motivation research techniques?

7. The electromyelograph is a device used by medical researchers to measure muscle tension, which presumably reflects the amount of stress a person is under. How might this device be used in marketing?

4

Social Factors
and Perception

SOCIAL PSYCHOLOGISTS are critical of the way in which experimental psychologists view behavior. In particular, they reject the notion that the beginnings of all behavior exist only *within the individual*. Experimental psychologists have tended to regard even complex forms of interaction and social behavior simply as an extension of the types of individual processes discussed in earlier chapters, whereas social psychologists focus upon the social setting in which behavior takes place and the various ways in which an individual is influenced by others around him. In their view, attempts to explain human behavior without reference to social forces are simply not meaningful.

Asch states the case for social psychology as follows: "The individual is always in a field of forces. His innermost properties are properties of interaction between him and the surroundings.

129

His identity and persistence are not threatened by the relation of dependence, but by faulty and inert ways of responding to the surroundings." (Asch, 1957, p. 45.) According to this view, social components of behavior are always present. Thus:

> Whether we are studying the behavior of a man in a laboratory, in a clinic, or in a crowd; whether we are studying his ability to memorize, his performance on an intelligence test, or his church-going, we are studying the behavior of a man as a participant in interpersonal behavior events. The effects of a man's past, present, and anticipated interpersonal behavior events influence each of his activities, no matter how simple or apparently remote. (Krech, Crutchfield, & Ballachey, 1962, p. 7.)

While it is easy to see how such a view holds for some of the aspects of behavior discussed earlier (e.g., motivation and even learning), its relevance to such other aspects as perception is perhaps less obvious. What evidence is there that social experiences and values affect even our basic perceptual processes?

The reader will remember that in the discussion of Gestalt principles (Chapter 1), reference was made to how momentary conditions of expectation or "set" determine what is perceived in a complex stimulus situation, for example, reading a page in this book. Bruner and Postman greatly expand this concept by stating, "The set which the individual brings to a perceptual situation is a function of his prevailing motives, needs, attitudes, and personality structure — all of which, in turn, are products of the interaction between the organism and his social environment." (Bruner & Postman, 1949, p. 71.) Our perception, even of inanimate objects, tends to be affected to at least some extent by our social experiences and environment.

Language, for example, is certainly a social phenomenon, and there is evidence that we see those things which we are able to put into established linguistic categories. Eskimos have dozens of words for snow which distinguish kinds of snow (dry, wet, packed, and so forth). Similarly, women in our culture have words for different kinds of coiffures which are meaningless to most men. (Can the male reader distinguish an English cut from a French twist, and does he know which — if either — is currently fashionable?) The socially-conditioned mental set that women bring to the perception of coiffures enables them to make much finer distinctions than men.

Influence of Social Factors Upon Perception

Mental sets are learned in large part from the social groups to which an individual belongs. One of the earliest proponents of this view was Sherif, who reported a series of experiments in which subjects estimated the movement of a small dot of light in surroundings of utter darkness. He found that under such novel and unstable conditions, each person tends to establish a range and a norm or standard within that range when performing the task *alone;* but when the individual is brought into a group of other subjects performing the same task, both his range and his norm tend to *converge* with those established by the group. When the individual *starts out* as part of a group, then afterwards faces the same perceptual task alone, he almost always sticks to the standards previously established by the group. (Sherif, 1935.)

Other investigators have shown that punishment and reward affect our perceptions of weight and even alter our perceptual organization processes; that matching a standard group of stamps or coins to a variable group depends in part upon the value of the coins or stamps in the standard or variable clusters; that our perception of words is related to our system of social values; and that the perception of ambiguous visual material (i.e., pictures presented out of focus) depends upon what the individual wants or expects to see, which, in turn, is based in part upon the social system in which he lives.

In a classic experiment, children were asked to adjust the size of a spot of light (using a knob on a projection apparatus) to equal the size of coins from a penny through a half-dollar when the coins were absent and when they were present. When the coins were used, some of the children were given the coins to hold in their hands while adjusting the light and others were given medium-grey cardboard discs identical in size to the coins. Results were as follows:

When coins and discs were used, coins (socially valued objects) were judged significantly larger in size than grey discs of identical size. Also, the greater the value of the coin, the greater the degree of overestimation of size, in general. . . . When no coins were present, both 'poor' children (from a Boston slum area) and 'rich' children (from well-to-do families) tended to judge the coins as larger than their actual size; however, poor children tended to judge these coins as being *much larger in size* than did 'rich' children. (Bruner & Goodman, 1947, p. 40.)[1]

An even more interesting study showed how deeply rooted in the social context our perceptual processes are. In this experiment, several groups of adults viewed a two and a half minute film showing three geometrical figures in motion: a large triangle, a smaller triangle, and a circle. These figures were moved about in various directions and at various speeds in a field containing a rectangle, one portion of which could be opened and closed, as in Figure 4.1. One group of observers was simply asked to tell what they saw; two other groups were asked to do the same except to consider the figures as human.

[1] A follow-up study did not confirm many of these conclusions but did support the view that poor children's judgment of coin size is influenced by their system of needs and values and that they tend to imagine coins to be larger than they are. (Carter & Schooler, 1949.)

Figure 4.1

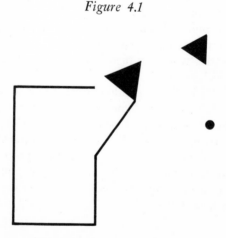

Although no actual human features were present since the entire field was geometrical in nature, nearly all subjects in the first group (no "human" instructions) reported that they saw *animated action* — in most cases, with human beings as actors and, in a few cases, with animals. Nineteen of 34 subjects reported some sort of connected story. For example, one subject said, "A man has planned to meet a girl and the girl comes along with another man; the first man tells the second to go . . ." (Heider & Simmel, 1944, p. 246.) None of the observers in the other two groups had any difficulty in reporting stories of human movement when asked to do so. Thus, the three inanimate forms in the rectangular field emerged as individuals who were interacting and reacting in a meaningful, motivated way. It is hard to think of a more convincing demonstration of our tendency to "read in" social meaning to an unstructured perceptual situation.

These studies and many others tend to support the view that social factors can influence an individual's perception of his environment and the objects in this environment in significant and predictable ways. Implications for the marketer are extensive.

SELECTIVE PERCEPTION

At this point we are ready to draw together several topics presented separately in earlier portions of this book — to synthesize our knowledge about various aspects of human behavior into a more meaningful view of the way in which an individual perceives the world about him.

Recall the following concepts:

- An individual's span of attention is low even under ideal conditions of concentration and interest.

- An individual tends to organize his perceptions and even his total knowledge in such a way as to "make sense" — to produce meaningful patterns and relationships among the separate elements. (Gestalt)

- What an individual *perceives* in many situations is determined not only by the intrinsic nature of the stimulus objects or sensations but also by his own system of values and needs, many of which are derived from the social context.

– What an individual *remembers* is determined by the process of assimilation, which in turn is based upon his habits, interests, and other factors which are developed in the process of interaction with others.

Because of the limitations of our basic sensory processes, we are forced to be selective, and this selectivity occurs in the manner which is most meaningful to us. Bruner uses the term *perceptual readiness* to describe our objective of *minimizing surprise* in any perceptual situation; we *anticipate* what there is for us to see and *select out* those portions which are likely to be most useful to us in pursuing our goals. Bruner summarizes with one of the most insightful comments in this or any other book relative to the nature of individual behavior:

> In conclusion, perceptual readiness reflects the dual requirements of coping with an environment — directedness with respect to goals, and efficiency with respect to the means by which the goals can be obtained. . . . What it suggests is that once a society has patterned a man's interests and trained him to expect what is likely in that society, it has gained a great measure of control not only on his thought processes *but also on the very material on which thought works* — the experienced data of perception.[2] (Bruner, 1958, p. 94.)

That is, an idea, object, or event tends *not even to enter* the conscious mental stream unless it conforms reasonably well, not only with the things we have come to expect in our culture and society, but also with our own personal interests, goals, and objectives of the moment. If it does not, it tends to be overlooked, ignored, forgotten immediately, or otherwise rejected; as far as our conscious mind is concerned, it simply doesn't exist.

Some humanists deplore the behavioristic view that man is irrational, biased, and inaccurate in his perception of the world. They consider "behavioral man" to be colorless and narrow, incapable of the full richness of human experience and the sublime heights to which individuals and societies are known to rise or aspire. To Bruner, however, the important question is not what the individual's social environment *is* so much as what it *means to him* in terms of his previous individual and social

[2] Our italics.

cosmos. How people *perceive* or *register* the various features of the social environment is crucial in determining how they will respond. This does not rule out high values and rich experiences in life; it merely suggests the limitations within which an individual responds initially to various aspects of the world about him.

This background helps us realize why it is often so very difficult to understand and predict consumer behavior in the marketplace. There is always the great (and often overwhelming) temptation to perceive and evaluate the consumer's buying situation in terms of *our own* conceptual framework, our own system of values, our own expectations. Ironically, this problem is most acute at the top management level, where the crucial decisions are made and survival of the firm is ultimately determined. For top management comprises men who are very different from the great majority of consumers in terms of psychological-sociological motives. How many top executives have average intelligence, live in modest houses, drive lower-priced cars, belong to "typical" social or recreational groups, and live on average incomes? Business management is simply not made up of such men. It is for this reason, perhaps more than any other, that most top executives today rely on market research departments to help them understand the consumer and on employee relations departments to help them understand the employee. Positions in these departments often go to psychologists and sociologists whose training can be of great value in bridging the gap between management and the consumer.

It should be pointed out, however, that upper-class people may have a better understanding of those in lower social classes than the converse. One study indicates that upper-class women can identify with considerable accuracy those products which have meaning and importance to lower-class women. They know, for example, that expensive clothes are less important than household appliances to working-class wives. Women in lower social classes do not understand upper-class women nearly as well. (Sommers, 1964.)

Nevertheless, executives may make serious errors in their estimates of what is important to consumers and employees. A common error used to be the exaggeration of the importance of status or achievement motives in marketing consumer products of all types. Preoccupied with achievement themselves, executives found it hard to understand that many assembly-line workers are not interested in competing for status and attach more importance to autonomy and group support. Even marketing executives took a long time to learn that "live better than your neighbor" has less appeal as a slogan to working class people than simply "live better." Most executives, in effect, tend to see the world selectively in terms of their own preoccupations with achievement.

A warning is in order. The term *selective perception* implies that a person gets out of the world less than there is to get. This is true in a sense, but it should be added that the perceiving person is able to contribute a great deal himself to the few impressions he selects or is given. One group of consumers was shown an advance model of a large, black, high-priced car with its brand identified. They were asked a series of approximately twenty "image" questions about the kind of person who would drive the car (banker, teenager, etc.), where it would be seen (opera, beach), and what it was like (elegant, fast). Another group of people was given only the words "big black car" and asked the same questions. The results obtained from both groups were nearly identical. What happened was that the people in the first group abstracted (or selectively perceived) the qualities "big" and "black" from the model shown and went on to make inferences from these few qualities. The second group "filled in" when given only these terms.

Bruner has observed:

> We have found it more meaningful to regard a concept as a network of sign-significate inferences by which one goes beyond a set of observed critical properties exhibited by an object or event to the class identity of the object or event in question, and thence to additional inferences about other unobserved properties of the object or event. We see an object that is red, shiny, and roundish and infer that it is an apple; we are then enabled to infer that if it is an apple, it is also edible, juicy, will rot if left unrefrigerated, etc. (Bruner, Goodnow, Austin, 1960, p. 244.)

In other words, it it not necessary to perceive an apple other than selectively. Indentations and subtle variations in size, color, and shape can safely be ignored unless one is actively attempting to select the best apples from a supermarket bin. In the same way, a company may need to get across only one or two simple ideas in its advertising and may depend upon consumers to take these ideas and construct inferentially a detailed picture of the company and its products. The company must be sure, however, that consumers will select the right ideas!

The process of *filling in* is related to the concept of stereotypes. We develop stereotypes of races, occupations, or even women drivers according to the way we expect people in these groups to behave. Scientists are expected to be "cold," entertainers are "high livers," and women drivers are "unpredictable." (One traffic authority has observed that when a woman driver puts her hand out the window of a car, we don't know if she is signalling a left turn, drying her fingernail polish, or waving to a friend.) A glance at a person's dress, or even the knowledge that he is in a particular occupational group, is sufficient to trigger the filling-in process whereby we infer a whole spectrum of behavior for that person (often quite inaccurately). Testimonial advertising is often based upon stereotypes. For example, an ad showing a doctor endorsing a particular brand of cigarettes immediately evokes the entire stereotype of the medical profession. French men and women who are completely unknown to the public often appear in ads of food and cosmetic products to evoke the proper stereotype.

Social Factors and Sensory Discrimination

Chapter 1 cited evidence that consumers are unable to discriminate among different brands of many products when labels are removed. What happens when labels ("social factors") are visible?

Two investigators furnished unlabeled six-packs of beer to 326 subjects previously identified as beer drinkers. Comparisons were made among five brands of beer: three national and two regional. After the unlabeled beer was tasted, each participant was given a six-pack with all five brands clearly identified with their usual labels, plus one extra brand to complete the six-pack. Ratings of each beer sample, marked and unmarked, were made on a ten-point poor-to-excellent scale for overall desirability and on a three-point scale for such specific qualities as lightness, aroma, foam, and after-taste. In the blind test, subjects apparently could not discriminate among the five brands; all beers received roughly equal ratings. But when the beers were identified by labels, the overall-desirability ratings increased a small but statistically reliable amount and the overall rating of one's "own brand" generally increased a great deal more than the ratings of the other brands. Ratings of beer characteristics were low in the blind test, but ratings of aroma, body, foam, and strength increased substantially when labels were used.

While a beer label is not as direct a "social force" as other individuals would be, it certainly has social overtones. Labels "added" desirability to the beer, both overall and in many taste characteristics. (Allison & Uhl, 1964.) Studies in other product categories have shown similar results.

Selective Perception and Consumer Behavior

Selective perception sheds considerable light upon the manufacturer's problem in getting consumers to try his product for the first time. He bombards the housewife with television and magazine advertising, sales promotion discounts and premiums, point-of-purchase displays and other promotion devices. Often these produce little change in sales. Follow-up research often shows that many consumers have no knowledge of the product or the promotion at all. Why? *Because this information simply never got through their "perceptual filters."* In the discussion about memory (Chapter 2), it was pointed out that for many product categories not more than 40 per cent of readers can later recognize ads in a magazine they have read. For many advertisements, recognition scores may even be less than 10 per cent.

In one instance, the executives of a large insurance company were in dispute with the advertising department. One side maintained that newspapers were better for local advertising; the other insisted that "spot" radio ads were more effective. A test city was selected and equal amounts of money were spent in both radio and newspaper advertising of virtually identical content for a period of one week. In follow-up telephone interviews, only three to four per cent of the households contacted reported that someone had read or heard *either message*, even when prompting was done (aided recall). These results under-standably led to re-evaluation of advertising efforts by top management.[3]

It is well known that advertisements are perceived selectively. A truism in the advertising business is that people suffering from headaches notice advertisements for headache remedies. People with clear heads either do not notice these ads or find their stridency offensive. In a sense, this is a boon for the advertiser. If his product meets a genuine and important need, market segments with that need will seek out his messages. Usually, however, selective perception creates a problem. An advertisement trying to induce people to switch brands ordinarily attracts fewer readers than are attracted by advertisements of the established brand it is attacking.

A recent study by the American Association of Advertising Agencies suggests that the average individual shuts out more than 1,400 daily ad pitches and reacts to only 13.

With such selectivity at work, it is easy to see how important it is for the manufacturer to obtain a "consumer franchise" for his product. Satisfied customers are not as likely to seek information about competing products and, even when it is forced upon them, are not as likely to allow it to pass through their perceptual filters. They simply "tune out" any information which is not in accord with their pre-existing beliefs and expectations. Even the use of a free sample of a new product is screened out by many consumers. They use the sample and then go back to their usual brand, following habits and tastes acquired over a long period.

BRAND SWITCHING

How, then, is change accomplished? Is there any hope of penetrating the perceptual filter of the consumer who is in the habit of using a certain brand of coffee or cigarettes?

[3] This is an instance of selective perception on the part of the executives concerned as well as on the part of the consumer audience. The executives were "sensitized" to notice their own advertising, partly because of emotional involvement and partly because of group pressures — they might be asked at lunch in the executive dining room if they caught the commercial on last night's television. They would consequently tend to be surprised that something which has so much impact on them can be treated by the public with such vast indifference.

To begin with, there is a hard core of people whose tendency to change is almost nil — whose attitudes or learned responses are too strong to allow new information to pass. This is true with respect to such diverse areas as political philosophies, religious beliefs, and education and child-training views, as well as choice of product or brand. These are the people who, as Tareyton cigarettes would like us to believe, "would rather fight than switch." (This slogan, incidentally, has induced many people to switch to Tareyton's.) Changing these people would be too costly in the short run if, indeed, it could be done at all.

At the other extreme are people who switch brands indiscriminately, responding to every new product, price discount, or promotional campaign in their search for something better, more economical, or simply "different." These are the best prospects for change, but is this change worthwhile to the marketer? One study to determine the characteristics of "deal prone" consumers found that these people tend to switch brands continuously, raising some doubt about the ability of a deal offering to attract new customers who will become loyal purchasers of the company's brand. (Webster, 1965.)

In between these extremes are the buyers who will switch for sufficient reason and, once having switched, will exhibit such a degree of product or brand loyalty that they can be held without continuing, expensive promotional effort. They become profitable customers for the manufacturer.[4]

While there is obviously a continuum running from the diehard through the occasional switcher to the compulsive switcher instead of three separate and distinct groups, there is proprietary evidence that some people exhibit *generalized* switching behavior. People who switch brands frequently may also show a tendency to switch jobs and are more likely to be divorced. Conversely, loyal buyers tend to exhibit rigid patterns in other departments of life. (Buyers of some minor brands of automobiles, for example, tend to score high on authoritarianism, which is usually taken as a sign of a rigid personality.)

As an aside, gasoline price wars — according to the trade — owe part of their momentum to the "loyal-switcher." At first

---

[4] Discussion here is based upon the commonly found oligopolistic situation in which there are several comparable brands of a given consumer product and no one brand has more than 50 per cent of the market.

glance, it might appear that a station owner can watch with equanimity while his customers desert to a competitor as long as he knows the competitor is losing money on every gallon he sells. The problem is that a certain percentage of his customers — either because they resent his high prices or because they come to know and like his competitor — will switch permanently. He is consequently forced to accept short-term losses to protect his long-run share of market.

What are the possible forces for change that can act upon the loyal-switcher group? Knowledge in this area is far from complete, but there are at least a few sources which seem to provide an impetus for change. Initially, of course, there are the forces of mass communication — the advertising media. While selective perception will screen out a great deal of advertising, it is possible to penetrate the veil by intelligent use of the knowledge we have about our perceptual process (cf. Chapter 1) and about the principles of effective communications (cf. Chapter 9). Faithful pursuit of these principles will result in more information "getting through." There are also the effects of pressures from the groups to which one belongs in setting norms or standards of behavior (cf. Chapter 6). Further, there is the rather considerable influence which emanates from a relatively few individuals, called opinion leaders or tastemakers, in setting trends in styles and in purchasing behavior (cf. Chapter 9). These forces, individually and in combination, are capable over a period of time of producing changes in buying behavior in all but the most recalcitrant consumer.

NEWNESS

One strategy for changing consumer purchase patterns is the claim of "new" and "improved" features for a product or service. DeGrazia, in his thoughtful *Of Time, Work, and Leisure,* has discussed the attractiveness to Americans of *newness* and the way this has been exploited by marketers. (DeGrazia, 1962.) People committed to Brand X may try Brand Y if they are convinced that Brand Y is "new and improved." This alters their previous frame of reference. Instead of a choice between X and Y, they are confronted with a choice between X and Y+. Ogilvy has offered this highly practical advice:

> Always try to inject news into your headlines, because the con-
> sumer is always on the lookout for new products, or new ways to
> use an old product, or new improvements in an old product. The
> two most powerful words you can use in a headline are FREE and
> NEW. You can seldom use FREE, but you can almost always
> use NEW — if you try hard enough. (Ogilvy, 1963, p. 131.)

It is rumored that one brand of cigarettes was introduced with
no intention of continuing it in production. The expectation
was that enough people, attracted by "newness," would try it
once to make it a profitable venture.

On the other hand, an ingenious bit of research by Whyte
(author of *The Organization Man*) suggests just the opposite.
After analyzing 60,000 words of advertising copy, Whyte isolated certain types of punctuation (hyphens, quotation marks,
exclamation points, etc.) and words ("more," "longer-lasting,"
"new," "easy," "exclusive," etc.) which tended to appear more
frequently in advertising copy than in ordinary writing. Table
4.1 shows the frequency of these characteristic constructions per
100 words of copy of consumer ads, editorial copy, and industrial
ads.

Whyte developed an index of "ad-iness" by totaling the number of hyphens, ellipsis points, italics, quotation marks, exclamation points, multiple adjectives, and clichés in an ad and
dividing by the total number of words in the ad. Thus, the
more of these characteristics there are in an ad, the higher is its
ad-iness score. To see how ad-iness pays off, he secured from
the Gallup-Robinson advertising-effectiveness service the 25 ads
which over a three-year period had ranked the highest in impact upon the public and the 30 ads which had ranked the
lowest. Although some high-cliché ads did have high impact,
the average ad-iness score of the high-impact ads was only 7.4
while the average for the low-impact ads was 10.8. With regard
to overused words, especially the word "new," Whyte concludes:

> Over the years a great number of the high-pulling headlines that
> made advertising history have contained the word 'new.' From
> this, many have deduced that the word 'new' itself is a high-
> pulling word. Is it? One of the reasons the great headlines scored
> was because they were advertising something that really was new.

But the word 'new' itself has little power independent of the context. When used to describe something not new or triflingly so, like a new picture on a cereal package, it has no punch; consistently, research has indicated that announcement-type ads of the 'new' or 'revolutionary' kind trail the quieter merchandising ads in audience interest. (Whyte, 1952, p. 100.)

Table 4.1

FREQUENCY OF CHARACTERISTIC AD CONSTRUCTIONS
(per 100 words of copy)

	Consumer ads in national magazines	*Editorial copy in same magazines*	*Industrial advertising*
Hyphens	1.1	.4	.43
3 dots (. . .)	.8	.05	.50
Italics or underscoring	1.0	.02	.46
Quote marks	.3	.05	.25
Exclamation points	1.3	.1	.53
Multiple adjectives	1.2	.3	.53
Stock expressions	2.3	—	.62
Total	8.0	.9	3.3

Hyphens: counted only when used to join words not commonly hyphenated, e.g., flavor-rich. *Italicizations:* counted only for words not customarily italicized. *Quote marks:* not counted when used to enclose quotations; counted only when used for emphasis or when advertisers quoted themselves, e.g., "No wonder people say it has famous 'feed-back' action." *Multiple adjectives:* two or more adjectives used in front of noun unseparated by "and," e.g., hearty, zestful, full-bodied flavor. *Stock expressions:* count made by checking copy against master list of expressions found to be most frequent in copy.

Characteristics have been charted by frequency per 100 words, since the figure is near the dimensions of the average ad. Stock expressions have been put in terms of 10,000 words chiefly to spare the reader too many decimal points.

Thus the "newness" strategy may or may not be influential, depending upon how and in what context it is used.

Heavy promotion outlays are often considered sufficient in themselves to produce major changes in the market share of a product brand. However, this is not in accord with most of the evidence we have. While such outlays almost always have a short-term effect, one authority argues that what may happen is that present sales are "borrowed" from future sales, that is, consumers simply accelerate their purchases slightly so that there is little net increase in sales in the long run. He feels that this is a rather typical pattern for consumer durable-goods spending and, possibly, for nondurable-goods spending as well. (Forrester, 1949, pp. 105–106.)

Sometimes the "valley" following the "peak" in sales produced by promotional efforts is deep enough to cause the net effect of the promotion to be negative. This can happen when, during a sales contest or heavy promotion, salesmen neglect their long-term sales development efforts and concentrate instead upon immediate, red-hot prospects. Automobile salesmen, for example, tend to hang around the showroom during a major promotion to take advantage of the sales represented by the "walk-ins" inspired by the promotion. The salesmen do not follow their normal "prospect locator and contact" routines and, consequently, sales decrease more than enough in the post-promotion period to cancel the accelerated sales produced by the promotion. The same happens in the life-insurance field when salesmen encourage prospects to buy early so that they, the salesmen, can qualify for "conference" trips to resort areas. Upon returning from the conferences, they often must begin almost anew the laborious and time-consuming process of developing new prospects for later sales.

It is important to keep in mind that changing consumer buyer behavior is not an instantaneous, all-or-none process. The consumer is not suddenly transformed from one state (nonbuyer) to another (buyer). From a behavioral standpoint, the consumer moves along a path or continuum ranging from complete unawareness of the new product to actual purchase (cf. Chapter 9). It is really only at the beginning of this path that selective perception poses a great problem for the manufacturer. Once his brand "breaks through" into the consumer's consciousness, selective perception will tend to work *for* the manufacturer by reducing the potential buyer's awareness of other, competing brands. The more the consumer considers a new or different product, the more he will seek information about it to the exclusion of possible alternative products.

Changing buying behavior is thus a very complex and difficult task. Still, the attempt must go on, both to attract new purchasers and to reinforce favorable impressions which already exist in the minds of satisfied customers. The many studies which have been done are nearly unanimous in the finding that when promotional effort ceases, brand market share declines. This is reminiscent of the statement attributed to John Wanamaker: "Half of my advertising money is wasted; the trouble is, I don't know which half!" It is important to note that, except in the case of new products, competitive pressures, or other unusual circumstances, big promotional pushes followed by lulls probably should be avoided.

QUESTIONS
FOR REVIEW

1. How might selective perception (attention, exposure, etc.) affect the organizational behavior of a marketing manager in his relationships with general management?

2. What are some feasible ways of overcoming the obstacle of selective perception for a product or company that is not well known?

3. In what way is selective perception an advantage in consumer marketing?

4. What does selective perception suggest about the effectiveness of subliminal advertising?

5. How does selective perception relate to learning principles? To motivation?

5

Consumer Attitudes

CONSUMER ATTITUDES are of extreme importance to the marketer. Attitudes directly affect purchase decisions and these, in turn, directly affect attitudes through experience in using the product or service selected. In a broad sense, purchase decisions are based almost solely upon attitudes existing at the time of purchase, however these attitudes might have been formed.

Attitudes may be *specific* (with respect to a kind of car or a particular recording artist) or *general* (as in the case of political inclinations or attitudes toward free enterprise). One writer refers to the more general attitudes as "belief systems, . . . an organized body of ideas, attitudes, and convictions centered around values or things regarded as important or precious to the group." He suggests, "Belief systems provide a larger frame of reference or background which tends to control the more specific thoughts or actions of individuals." (Young, 1956, p. 187.) These broad belief systems tend to have more of a *cognitive* basis (that is, we have given more conscious thought to them)

146

than do attitudes or opinions, which are often more *affective* in nature (based upon feelings or on immediate reactions). Thus, *belief systems form much of the basis for our selectivity in perception*, and they determine the manner in which we perceive and respond to external stimulation.

For purposes of the present discussion, all of these terms — opinions, attitudes, and beliefs — will be regarded as similar enough to be used interchangeably. They indicate some preference or inclination with respect to any object or idea in a person's total environment. Defined in this way, these terms are similar to, or even synonymous with, "tastes" for foods, clothing styles, music, and so on.

The word "attitude" — before it was adopted by social psychologists — meant something similar to "posture" and implied readiness for some kind of *action*. When we say a person has a particular attitude, we mean that certain behaviors are implied by the attitude and are more likely to occur than others. The action component suggests the relationship of attitudes to the motivational forces discussed earlier; there is often a motivational component of any given attitude. The tendency toward action, or behavioral element, in attitudes is not always given sufficient attention by marketers investigating consumer attitudes. The market researcher should continually ask himself: What kinds of *behavior* am I trying to predict by the questions I am asking? Sometimes, he finds that the answers he gets enable him to predict no more than verbal behavior, that is, how the person will reply to similar questions.

Another way of looking at attitudes is to consider them as a combination of emotional and cognitive factors. The emotional states of fear and excitement, for example, are physiologically equivalent; both involve the release of adrenaline, pounding of the heart, sweating of the palms, and so forth. Fear, however, is unpleasant and negatively evaluated, while excitement is pleasurable. Whether the person considers his physiological state unpleasant or pleasant depends, consequently, on whether he perceives his environment as threatening and fear-producing or whether he ascribes his feeling to excitement. The *cognition*, in effect, determines how the physiological state of intense emotion is evaluated. Almost all airline passengers, for example, experience some emotion as their plane takes off. Some passengers interpret this emotion as fear, others as pleasurable excitement, although their physiological states are identical. It has been suggested that airlines, instead of trying to overcome passengers' fear by playing soothing background music at take-off, try to convert the emotion to excitement by playing stirring martial music. (As far as we know, this has not been tried.)

The Formation of Attitudes

How are attitudes formed? This is a question the *social* psychologist is best equipped to answer, even though the formation of attitudes is basically a learning process as discussed in Chapter 2. While attitudes are developed in a number of ways and in reference to many different forces, both individual and social, one writer states: "The overwhelming evidence concerning the acquisition of emotional and intellectual attitudes supports the contention that these are learned in a process of interaction of the individual with others. In other words, social learning, in contrast with learning in general, occurs in a process of communication." (Curtis, 1960, p. 182.)

Attitudes develop and change in response to many factors. These are summarized briefly below:[1]

Biological motivations. It is inevitable that some attitudes are formed as the individual goes through the process of satisfying his most basic drives. He will tend to develop favorable attitudes toward people and objects which satisfy his needs and unfavorable attitudes toward those which block attainment. (At the extreme, just being alive is *good!*)

Information. Attitudes are based to some extent upon the kind and amount of information an individual receives and upon the nature of its source. Selective perception explains why there is not a perfect relationship between the information a person *receives* and what he incorporates into his belief system. Nevertheless, the importance of information must not be overlooked.

[1] This discussion is patterned after Chapter 6 in Krech, Crutchfield, and Ballachey (1962).

Group affiliations. Many of the attitudes held by an individual come either directly or indirectly from the groups of which he is a member (e.g., family, church, work, athletic, social). Groups are important not only in the *values* which they hold, but also in the amount and type of *information* which they transmit to an individual. They thus assume dual significance. Many authorities believe that "primary groups" (e.g., family and work groups) are a major force in determining attitude development.

Personality. There are aspects of personality which are too broad to be regarded as strictly a product of the individual's social environment, although many aspects of personality do have their roots in social processes. Personality factors of an individual nature (e.g., intelligence, appearance, activity levels, withdrawal tendencies, dominance) have some effect upon a person's attitudes.

Experience. Not to be overlooked are the results of actual experience with an object, event, or even something as broad as a philosophy of life. In the buying context, even if all previous factors predisposed us toward a favorable impression of a particular restaurant, just one occasion of dissatisfaction with the food or service might produce a negative reaction strong enough to prevent our return.

These factors are not listed in order of importance, primarily because the objects or concepts with which an individual must deal differ widely in their *attitudinal referent.* For example, we may not care at all what others think about our attitudes toward a certain brand of toothpaste, but most of us are sensitive to our friends' reactions to our views about a political party or a way of living. In the latter case, our attitudes or beliefs are usually formed in relation to group affiliation, while toothpaste selection tends to be based more upon information and experience.

As discussed earlier, there is an interrelationship between motivation and attitudes; each may affect the other. A strong basic motivation to succeed in business or in social life would normally lead us to adopt favorable attitudes toward those individuals, groups, or even products which we somehow associate with this goal. Conversely, we are not likely to be motivated to purchase a car or major appliance toward which we hold unfavorable attitudes (with respect to either the product category or a particular brand).

This apparent relationship between attitudes and motivation underlies much of the current emphasis on motivation research by large consumer-products firms. The term *motivation research* is sometimes misused, for instead of trying to determine directly what *motivates* people to buy as they do, research of this type often contents itself instead with the measurement of attitudes, opinions, associations, value judgments and perceptions which the consumer holds toward or about a given company, product category, or brand. (The measurement of corporate image, discussed in Chapter 1, is nothing more than the measurement of consumer attitude toward the firms in a given field.) It is almost axiomatic that buying *actions* will not greatly contradict buying *attitudes;* and even though favorable attitudes do not produce sales by themselves, they do predispose a consumer when he considers the possibility of a purchase of some kind.

Attitude Measurement

In view of the important of attitudes in the buying situation, let us turn briefly to methods which are currently used to measure consumer attitudes. There exists an almost inexhaustible variety of measurement techniques. The corporate-image scale in Chapter 1 is an illustration of an attitude scale constructed for a special purpose. Other scales have been used in such diverse areas as politics and voting behavior, social processes and institutions, religion, education, and, of course, consumer buying behavior. It is hard to think of an object, process, institution, value system, or concept toward which the public attitude has not been measured by some person or organization in recent years.

For more thorough discussions of the techniques and problems of attitude measurement, the interested reader may consult sources such as Guilford (1954) or Osgood, Suci, and Tannenbaum (1957). It will be sufficient here to illustrate a few commonly employed methods for quantifying those attitudes, beliefs, r feelings which the consumer is willing to express. Projective techniques and other motivation research tools described in Chapter 3 are also tools for uncovering attitudes, particularly attitudes which are fairly "basic", but most of these devices lack the precision necessary for them to be described as measuring or scaling devices. (This does not mean, of course, that deeper or more complex attitudes are unimportant, but only that their measurement is difficult in the commercial setting.)

Attitude scaling can be used to determine the position of *an individual* with respect to some topic or event, as in the case of a person's feelings about a given department store or food product. It can also be used to chart the *entire buying population* (or some portion of it) to determine the distribution or spread of opinion about some topic, for example, what per cent of all housewives are concerned with the cholesterol content of foods or what per cent of teenage boys are hi-fi enthusiasts. Information of this kind gives the manufacturer a "reading" on the market for his product that is expressed in quantitative terms, and quantification brings a great many benefits such as the ability to make statements of "better than" or "worse than" and "how much better or worse" and to compare figures on trends in attitudes over successive months or years.

Some of the most useful attitude scaling techniques are discussed below.

Continuum of Feeling. Nearly every attitude may be located along some continuum of feeling, agreement, or desirability. The respondent is asked to place a check or to call out a numerical rating along a continuum from high to low to indicate his or her feelings. For example, to determine attitudes toward cholesterol in foods, the question might be: "In your opinion, from the standpoint of health, how important is the amount of cholesterol in the food you feed your family?" (It must first be determined, of course, whether the respondent knows what cholesterol is.) A check is placed at the appropriate point on the scale:

Extremely Important	Very Important	Fairly Important	Of Little Importance	Of No Importance

Sometimes verbal scales (in which words are used to describe positions along the continuum of feeling) are supplemented by numerical scales to simplify tabulating and scoring. Thus, a person might be asked: "How did you enjoy the movie premiere you saw tonight? Would you say it was

Extremely bad	Very bad	Fairly bad	Neither good nor bad	Fairly good	Very good	Extremely good
−3	−2	−1	0	+1	+2	+3

Some studies go even further and determine the strength of feeling or certainty with which a given attitude is held. For example, if a housewife indicates that she feels the cholesterol content of butter is "very important," she may be asked, "How sure are you about this?"

- ☐ Extremely sure
- ☐ Very sure
- ☐ Fairly sure
- ☐ Not sure at all

The housewife might feel that the cholesterol content of food is important, but she might be only fairly sure or not sure at all that she is right. (There is even conflicting opinion among medical authorities about the effects of cholesterol.) Such an approach might be used to good effect in the current dispute over regular aspirin versus buffered aspirin. Many people may feel "extremely sure" that there is "no difference at all" in the effectiveness of the two types of products because of their own experiences plus reports of studies sponsored by the American Medical Association.

Paired Comparisons. Items, words, colors, or other materials are presented in pairs for comparison. For example, to determine tastes with respect to various designs for dinner plates, the manufacturer assembles a number of designs. The respondent is shown all possible pairs (i.e., two designs at a time) and asked which of the two she prefers. After all pairs have been judged by a group of women, their judgments are combined by statistical methods to produce for each design a "psychological scale

alue" which reflects the women's judgment of the desirability
f each design in relation to the others shown.

Rank Order. Rather than going through the laborious process
f presenting all possible pairs of plates, one pair at a time, the
investigator may show all designs at once and ask each respon-
ent to rank them in order of preference. Comparisons are also
made in this process, of course, but not in so rigorous a fashion
s in paired comparisons. Ranking is considered somewhat in-
erior to paired comparisons in certain technical aspects, but it
is much more economical and is adequate for many purposes.

One problem in ranking is that an item which is conspicuously
ifferent from the other items being tested may produce an er-
oneous impression of desirability. For instance, in a study of up-
olstery materials, the alternatives might include three cloth
abrics and one vinyl. People who liked cloth fabric would rank
he vinyl last and people who liked vinyl would rank it first, as
nown in Table 5.1. The fabrics would consequently appear
land, as if they were neither liked nor disliked strongly, while
he vinyl would appear controversial.

Table 5.1

	Fabric A	Fabric B	Fabric C	Vinyl
est liked	16%	17%	17%	50%
econd	33	33	34	—
hird	34	33	33	—
east liked	17	17	16	50

bviously, opposite results would have been obtained in this
ase if one cloth fabric had been compared with three vinyls.
he fabric would have appeared controversial and the vinyls
land.

Statement Selection or Sorting. Attitudes may be measured by
aving individuals respond to verbal expressions about a given
opic, for example, "Almost every advertisement is honest."
When a large number of such statements have been developed
or a given topic (in this case, government regulation of advertis-
g), several alternative approaches may be used:

Thurstone scaling. The statements are given to a number of judges who are asked to sort them into piles according to favorability of the statement. If there were eleven piles, for example, Pile 1 would represent the most *unfavorable* statement that could be made about a given topic in the eyes of the respondent, Pile 11 would represent the most *favorable* statement, and Pile 6 would be for neutral statements.

After each judge has sorted all statements, those statements which show the most consistency among judges (i.e., are placed in approximately the same piles by all judges) are selected for use in a final scale. Each statement so selected has a point value indicating the *average* degree of favorability as assigned by the previous judges (e.g., a value of 9.4 on a 10-point scale would indicate a very favorable statement). These statements are then shown to respondents in a consumer survey and each respondent is asked to select statements with which he or she agrees, without knowing the point value. The attitude score for each individual is calculated as the *median* of the point values for the statements she chose. Thus an individual's score of 2.8 for statements about advertising would reflect a generally unfavorable attitude toward advertising.

Likert scaling. Again, a number of statements are developed about a given topic, for example, "Home permanents are a mess." Then a scale indicating *strength of agreement* — agree very strongly, agree fairly strongly, etc. — is presented. Each respondent rates *each statement* to show how strongly she agrees or disagrees, and the score for each respondent is determined from both the direction and strength of her feeling toward the various statements. As in Thurstone scaling, the statements with which the respondent agrees or disagrees are often descriptions of *behavior*. A study of racial prejudice might ask a person: "Supposing a Negro family moved in next door to you, what do you think you would do?"

a. Visit them and welcome them to the neighborhood.

b. Be a good neighbor but not go out of your way to be friendly.

c. Have as little to do with them as possible.

These kinds of statements tap the "tendency to action" dimension in attitudes.

Stephenson Q-sort. In this technique, the statements about an object or topic are sorted into nine piles, with a specified number of statements forced into each pile so that the resulting distribution will be "normal" (i.e., bell-shaped). For example, in sorting 38 statements, the number of statements in each pile would be:

Score	9	8	7	6	5	4	3	2	1
Frequency	3	4	4	5	6	5	4	4	3

The resulting scores for each statement can then be compared among several groups and also subjected to rather sophisticated statistical analysis which requires normal distribution of variables.

These statement-sorting or grading techniques may be used to determine the attitude of one individual, the aggregate attitude of all housewives, or even the attitude of the general population with regard to a given topic or type of product.

Osgood Semantic Differential. This technique was presented in Chapter 1 to illustrate the measurement of corporate image. Basically, it involves pairs of words or statements of opposite meaning which might describe a product or company (e.g., sharp — bland, reliable — unreliable, modern — old-fashioned, clean — dirty). The respondent rates each of several products or companies on each dimension by placing a check or letter at the place on a line which indicates his feelings. The average of the checks of all respondents is plotted as a "profile" for each product, as shown in Figure 5.1.

Osgood's work with the semantic differential has shown that in one way attitudes are rather simple and in another way discouragingly complex. Responses obtained when a concept is rated on a large number of adjective scales seem to be governed by three main factors: good — bad, strong — weak, and active — passive. These three factors account for almost 50 per cent of the total "meaning" of concepts, almost regardless of the concept, the adjectives against which it is judged, or the people do-

Figure 5.1

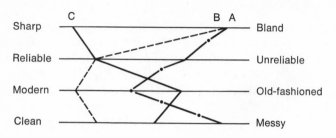

ing the judging. It is in this sense that attitudinal structures can be said to be simple; they are complex in the many opaque factors that are necessary to explain the remaining 50 per cent of the meaning.

Evaluation of Scaling Methods. There are many variations of the above scaling techniques, and each investigator must select the approach that best suits his needs. Fortunately, the available evidence suggests that overall results do not differ greatly from one technique to another; an individual with negative attitudes toward an item or topic will show this no matter which scaling method is used. Choice among the various alternatives often depends upon the objectives and the cost and time limitations of a study.

The well-known *halo effect* is one of the reasons that different scales and different scaling methods often tend to yield similar results. One manufacturer once compared his product with his principal competition in terms of over twenty different product characteristics. When the results of the survey were subjected to statistical analysis, it was found that one factor was sufficient to account for almost all the variance. That is, one question — "Which product do you like better?" — would have yielded as much information as the twenty-odd questions asked. The people who were interviewed apparently answered every question by generalizing "like" and "dislike."

Nevertheless, different kinds of scales sometimes produce significantly different results, and this can be embarrassing to the researcher since he is then confronted with the problem of

In a study of 465 housewives in the Chicago area, Banks analyzed the interrelationship of brand preference, purchase intentions, and actual purchases in seven product categories. He found:

> . . . Brand preference was almost identical with purchase intention; about 96 per cent of the panel included their most preferred brands in their purchase intentions.
>
> Preference for brands was a good predictor of purchases. . . . Last purchase made and statements of purchase intentions were even better predictors of relative brand purchase.
>
> Preference was a fairly good predictor of purchase for the individual panel member as well as for the entire group. Only 15 per cent of the group who stated brand purchase intentions bought brands entirely different from those mentioned. However, another 15 per cent performed only partially on their brand intentions. . . . (Banks, 1950.)

Banks also found that consumers did not predict accurately the *amount* of purchase for the products in question. On the whole, they bought 61.4 per cent more of all seven product classes than they expected to buy and 2.6 times as much ice cream!

There does, then, seem to be a rather clear relationship between stated preference, stated buying intention, and actual purchase of individual brands, at least within the product categories included in Banks' study. However, since many factors in addition to preference enter into the actual purchase (for example, price, salesmanship, and availability of merchandise), it is not surprising that purchase behavior does not mirror preferences exactly. One study of the effect of television on preferences and buying behavior found that "preferences changed considerably more than did purchasing behavior, although the direction of change was the same." (Howard, 1963, p. 146.) Table 5.2 gives the results of this study.

In a series of studies on car preferences (Ford versus Chevrolet, 1957 through 1962), it was found that the *direction* of change in preferences from one model year to the next was consistent with sales, but that absolute differences in preferences were not. Preference studies showed Ford below Chevrolet in 1960, but liked better than Chevrolet in 1961. Ford sales improved

Table 5.2

EFFECT OF TELEVISION ON ATTITUDE AND BEHAVIOR

	Preferences			Purchasing Behavior		
	Before TV	*After TV*	*% Points*	*Before TV*	*After TV*	*% Points*
Scotties	16%	42%	26	15%	35%	20
Kleenex	64%	40%	−24	40%	32%	−8

relative to Chevrolet in 1961, but Chevrolet sales were still higher than Ford in that year.

Further evidence comes from a proprietary research study on designs for chinaware. Women were asked to evaluate sample plates with various designs on them. They were asked to compare the sample plates with one another and with any other dinner plates they might have seen at any time, and they were allowed to handle the sample plates while judging. Instructions were to indicate the overall *preference* for each design on a 21-point rating scale. Results showed a very high correlation ($r = .90$) between rated preferences and actual sales of the plates on the market.

In studies of this kind, it is extremely important to duplicate as nearly as possible the actual decision situation. One of the authors once conducted a frustrating series of studies on automobile paint colors. A variety of techniques was used, but it proved impossible to find much relationship between paint preferences expressed by respondents and the colors of cars actually being bought. Apparently some people decide on paint while looking at actual cars, others choose from "Trim and Color Catalogs," and still others are influenced by advertisements. The paint decision is usually made jointly by husbands and wives, who sometimes "compromise" on a second choice that neither really prefers. In some cases, no paint decision is made; the buyer simply selects a car in stock without caring particularly whether it is one color or another. (In this case, it might have been more appropriate to determine the paint preferences of the dealer than those of the buyer.) Since a wide variety of paints were offered and production runs of particular paints could be stepped up or cut back easily, the problem was not too important from a marketing point of view and the research was discontinued before a "good" technique was developed.

One study used the semantic differential scaling technique to compare consumer attitudes toward two brands of the same product with actual consumer purchasing of these two brands. Each brand was rated by 199 women on 12 six-point semantic differential scales (e.g., fair tasting — excellent tasting, very healthful — not very healthful). Results showed that in the case of women who used one brand but not the other, attitude ratings of the brand used were significantly higher than those of the brand not used. However, there was a great deal of overlap in ratings of the two products, and the author concluded that the semantic differential is not a very sensitive measure of future purchasing, at least for the products studied. (Barclay, 1964.)

ATTITUDE SALIENCE

The lack of relationship between attitudes and purchasing decisions found in the Barclay study above might be explained by the concept of *attitude salience*. In the wide spectrum of all possible attitudes toward a product, brand, or pattern, there are some attitudes which predispose consumers to actual purchase and others which do not. Attitudes which are *related to actual product purchase* are said to be salient; the remaining attitudes — no matter how favorable — are nonsalient.

Salient attitudes are those which are considered *important* by the consumer *and* on which the various brands or institutions are believed to *differ*. Both criteria must be met for an attitude to be considered salient.

Nelson Foote, manager of the consumer and public relations research program for General Electric, had this to say:

In the electrical appliance business, we have been impressed over and over by the way in which certain characteristics of products come to be taken for granted by consumers, especially those concerned with basic functional performance, or with values like safety. If these values are missing in a product, the user is extremely offended. But if they are present, the maker or seller gets no special credit or preference, because quite logically every other maker and seller is assumed to be offering equivalent values.

In other words, the values that are salient in decision-making are the values that are problematic — that are important, to be sure, but also those which differentiate one offering from another. (Foote, 1965, p. 11.)

The problem is to determine which attitudes or opinions are salient in terms of the actual purchase. These can then be stressed in product design and in promotional efforts. There are two principal ways of determining attitude salience: (1) by *asking* which product characteristics or attributes are considered most important by consumers and (2) by comparing *responses* of purchasers and nonpurchasers to various product characteristics. Both approaches are widely used in current marketing research practice.

To illustrate the first approach, in one proprietary study for a savings and loan association, respondents were asked to indicate on a four-point scale how important they felt various benefits or claims were. Some of the benefits were "safety of money," "attitude of window personnel," "interest rate earned," and "years in business." In the case of the last item — years in business — the survey showed that respondents felt that there were *big differences* among the various local institutions in terms of longevity, but that this was *relatively unimportant* to them in deciding where to save. Hence, years in business was not a salient factor in this situation.

In proprietary studies asking consumers to evaluate such automobile attributes as power, comfort, economy, appearance, and safety, consumers always rank *safety* as first in importance. However, these same consumers do not see various makes of cars as differing widely with respect to safety, and safety is consequently not salient in the actual purchase decision.

A better way to determine the relative influence of various factors on the purchasing decision is to compare the attitudes of users and nonusers of a product with respect to these factors. This has the advantage of not relying on stated feelings, which may be erroneous or misleading for reasons discussed earlier.

Banks did this as another part of his study. He asked housewives to rate each of 11 brands of scouring powder on each of the following attributes: package appearance, cleansing ability, grittiness or scratchiness in use, harshness on hands, odor, and price. Similarly, 20 coffee brands were rated on package appearance, flavor, ability to make many cups per pound, and price. Using a sophisticated statistical technique which determines the relative importance of various factors, he found that only three of the rated attributes of scouring powder were related to later purchase: cleansing ability, price, and harshness on hands. For coffee, only flavor and price were important factors. Attitudes toward other product features were not found to be related to actual purchase or to overall product preference (Banks 1950).

The attitude salience of a great many possible product or brand characteristics can be determined, and those which are found most important can be used as a basis for marketing decisions of many types. Attitude salience can also be determined for the types of associations the product or brand elicits in the consumer's mind.

Changing Attitudes

By now it is apparent that attitudes are indeed related to purchasing behavior. This holds at the aggregate economic level, in the case of greater or lesser spending by consumers as a group and the direction this spending takes. It also applies at the individual consumer level, in terms of selection among products or among brands within a given product or service category.

The motivational component of attitude structure is of particular interest to the marketer of consumer goods. Basically, he wants to *motivate* the individual toward his own product category and then to his own brand within the product category. This can be done in one of two ways:

1. By determining the consumer's present motivational and attitudinal state, then *adapting* product-design and promotion accordingly.
2. By *changing* the consumer's present state to one more consonant with the vendor's product category or brand.

The second approach is the more difficult, but it may be essential as for a drastically new product (e.g., cigars for women, cosmetics for men) or new uses for old products. (Later chapters will discuss some of the major problems involved in producing changes in established social and cultural norms.)

If we want to *change* attitudes toward a particular product or brand, especially one the consumer has not yet tried, we must consider again the factors influencing the *formation* of attitudes: biological needs, information, group affiliations, personality, and experience. It is apparent that some of these cannot readily be changed — particularly the biological and personality factors (although advertising appeals can be directed to these factors). Experience can be controlled to some extent by offering free trial of an item not previously used, but this procedure has limited application in the broad spectrum of consumer products and services.

Group affiliation and information remain, then, as factors which may provide a gateway for getting consumers to change to products they have not previously used. The fact that these factors are significantly interrelated (the group often determines what information its members will receive), is discussed in Chapters 6 and 7. Since the vendor has no direct control over group membership and influence, he is left primarily with *information* as his most (only?) effective tool. The effective use of communications in the marketing context is the subject of Chapter 9, but some background on the role of information in attitude change is appropriate here.

One authority in the communications sciences, Crane, suggests that there are basically three ways to change attitudes. Before discussing them, it is necessary to define certain terms that will be used:

Attributes. These are the characteristic properties of an object or concept. Thus, a book is a solid object with specifiable dimensions, full of pages containing printed material, and covered with a binder of some particular color.

Categories. Attributes are collected into categories, based upon purpose, objective, or desire. Thus, the solid properties of a book make it useful for propping open a door or raising the height of a child at the dinner table, although these functions could be equally well performed by other objects with similar attributes (a brick and a sofa cushion, respectively). In this case, the categories are "objects for propping open a door" and "objects for raising the height of a child." The printed-page attribute of the book would fall into a different category such as "objects for entertainment" or "objects for information."

Values. These are names given to different categories to identify them (denotative) and/or evaluate them (connotative).

With this as background, Crane suggests three ways of changing attitudes through communications:

1. Give the existing categories new labels which affect both their content and evaluation.
2. Change the categories themselves by changing the attributes used in constructing them or by urging audiences to move toward larger or smaller categories.
3. Change the way in which a category is evaluated, either directly or by influencing the values of related categories.

Applying this to a consumer buying problem, suppose a cigar manufacturer wished to make cigars socially acceptable for women. (Cigarette manufacturers had the same problem at one time.) The manufacturer must first determine the category or categories of items to which cigars belong: objects for smoking, objects for relieving tension ("something to do"), objects for good oral taste or for stimulation, objects which conspicuously display business success, objects suggesting masculinity, etc.

If, for example, the latter two categories were found, Crane's first principle could be invoked by *changing category labels* — perhaps to "displaying personal success or achievement" rather than business success. Or, following the second principle, the public might be urged to *move toward larger categories* by regarding cigars as objects for enjoyment and display in a social situation. The third principle suggests that *evaluation* of the categories might be changed, perhaps by developing the idea that many objects of a masculine flavor are also quite suitable for women — slacks, suede leather goods, and electric razors are cases in point.[3]

[3] The conjecture about cigar smoking is our own, not Crane's.

Crane's book affords considerable insight into effective techniques for inducing attitude change. He summarizes by saying:

> Attitudes are not easy to change. First, because there seems to be a tendency to restore balance when it is upset and, second, because there is a tendency to avoid an upset by avoiding exposures to messages inconsistent with the existing attitude structure. Accidental exposure does occur, however. A communicator who knows existing attitude structures and the ways in which people react to their upset, can choose the method and point of attack most likely to produce, in the end, the new attitude structure most favorable to his objectives. (Crane, 1965, p. 66.)

QUESTIONS
FOR REVIEW

1. Are there situations in which attitudes would be of little or no importance in consumer buying decisions? If so, explain why not.

2. How does a manufacturer find out which consumer attitudes are most important for the product he makes?

3. What are the various avenues open to a manufacturer of cosmetic products who wishes to change the attitudes of the public toward his product?

4. What use can the large retailer make of national surveys showing overall attitudes of the public toward durable goods spending? What about the wholesaler?

5. Are attitudes generally the most important factor in consumers' choice among products or brands? What other factors might enter in? Support your position with evidence taken from other chapters of this book.

6. How are attitudes related to the consumer's perception of products or promotion efforts?

7. Should a vendor always try to *change* attitudes of the public toward his product? Under what circumstances would he be wise to try some other approach?

6

Social Groups

WE DISCUSSED EARLIER how thought processes are so rooted in social context as to affect our perception, even of inanimate objects. We also discussed how group influence may determine the standards or norms which an individual within the group adopts in making judgments in an unstructured perceptual situation. Extension of these concepts leads naturally to one of the principal mediating social forces, the *group* itself. For social groups provide most of the standards for behavior that enable an individual to live in a satisfying manner in a world filled with other people.

Groups are formed and maintained in a bewildering variety — from two men trying to push a car out of the mud to an entire army engaged in deadly combat with an enemy. Asch points out that the term *group* is quite general and may be used to refer to fundamentally different relationships between things, events, or people. He distinguishes three forms of groups:

1. A collection of *discrete objects* in the same space. These objects (or persons) do nothing to one another; each remains

169

the same whether together or alone. A group of riders on a bus is an example of this type of group.

2. A collection of units that are basically different from one another but have *something in common*. The common element might be demographic, as in the case of a group of five-year old children or a group of divorced persons, or it might be psychological, such as all individuals who exhibit compulsive behavior.

3. A collection of units which *interact* in some way, which have regular contact and communication among members, and which possess a group property. This group property characterizes the group itself, not each member singly. In this view, the group is something *more* than the sum of its individual parts; it possesses a characteristic of its own. (Asch, 1957.)

The term *aggregate* is more appropriate than the term *group* for the first two types of collections, since neither possesses the vital element of member interaction which defines a true group. Nevertheless, aggregates may be the object of study by marketers. For example, the busload of people mentioned as an instance of an accidental collection might be interviewed by the bus company in an origin-and-destination study aimed at re-routing lines and improving service. The second type of collection may be identified by particular psychological, sociological, or demographic characteristics which distinguish its members from the rest of the population. There is some amount of knowledge about the ways in which the members in the aggregate typically feel and respond, even though these members do not actually meet and exchange information. Even an aggregate as multifarious as the citizens of a country tends to possess some common characteristics: Greeks are friendly, Americans are always in a hurry, Germans tend to be brusque, and Orientals are formal and deferential. (Inkeles & Levinson, 1954.)

It is the third type of collection which interests us most for the moment — the true group, characterized by regular contact and exchange of communications. Almost by definition, the group must be small for complete social interchange to take place. When there are more than fifteen or twenty members, the number of possible interrelationships becomes so large as to be unwieldy and the group tends to break into separate subgroups. Most true groups have a dozen members or less. Groups of this kind tend to be synergistic, that is, interaction among members produces the group properties which are different from and greater than the simple sum of member properties. Thus, individuals in these groups are characterized by both a group property and a member property, and neither taken alone is sufficient to explain the behavior of members of the group.

Fortunately, social psychologists have done extensive analyses of small groups so that we have a reasonably good understanding of why these groups are formed, how they operate internally, and how they exert influence upon their individual members.

TYPES OF SMALL GROUPS

There are various ways of distinguishing among types of small groups. Two of the more common distinctions are:

Primary versus secondary. Primary groups are characterized by intimate and regular face-to-face relationships among members as in families, friendship groups, and work groups. They are considered primary because of the importance of their influence upon the individual. Secondary groups are the many other groups to which individuals belong.

Sociologists have long distinguished between primary communication, which involves face-to-face contact, and secondary communication, which is delivered through the impersonal mass media. (Cooley, 1902.) The distinction held well in the days when the two major modes of communication were speech and print, but it may have somewhat less validity in these days of radio and television. The actor delivering a television commercial is in a sense, face-to-face with the viewers and offers at least a good counterfeit of primary communication insofar as warmth, friendliness, and directness is concerned. (This is one reason for the effectiveness of television advertising.)

The concept of immediate feedback, however, suggests that the notion of primary communication still has some validity. The salesman dealing with customers on a face-to-face basis can adjust his sales messages from moment to moment as he reacts to cues supplied by the persons listening to him. Feedback from a television audience viewing a commercial is not immediate, it involves elaborate research paraphernalia, and it cannot be used to change the commercial as it is being delivered. Mutuality and immediacy distinguish a primary group relationship; unilateralism and delayed feedback distinguish a secondary group relationship.

Formal versus informal. Formal groups have an explicit structure and, usually, a clearly defined goal or objective. They are sometimes called organizations. Small formal groups may be engaged in the pursuit of economic goals (a small business or a work group within a large firm), political goals (a precinct work group), welfare goals (fathers engaged in Y.M.C.A.-sponsored youth activities), or even social goals (a committee planning a New Year's Eve party for a country club). Informal groups are usually friendship groups which exist primarily for the satisfaction of their members.

The distinction between formal and informal groups is sometimes even less clear than the distinction between primary and secondary groups. The work of Bales (1954), Homans (1950, 1961), and others has shown how informal groups develop *structure* and allocate tasks among members. Leaders emerge, for instance — and often different kinds of leaders, one concerned with *task* management (getting the group to "do" things) and another with *social* management and alleviation of intragroup or intermember tensions and frustrations. Informal groups often have "rules" governing member behavior in a relatively formal way; on the other hand, formal groups, such as the committee planning the New Year's Eve party, may sometimes behave quite informally. The distinction between formal and informal groups is nevertheless useful. The salesman who sells products to business firms for instance, is often concerned with the *formal* organization of his customers and their written purchasing procedures. Manufacturers of consumer goods, on the other hand, may be interested in the *informal* influence of friends and neighbors on purchase decisions.

Looking upon consumers as members of groups instead of as discrete individuals does not simplify the marketing task. Instead, it complicates it. There are probably more groups in the United States than there are inidviduals. Households, business firms, clubs, associations, friendship groups, political and religious institutions are all ways in which people come together in groups. It is obvious that the possible number of *combinations* of individuals is far greater than the number of separate individuals. Knowledge of the importance of group influence on buying behavior strengthens marketing but does not make it easier.

With such a range of diversity in the size, purpose, and characteristics of groups, it is easy to see why we are frequently confused by articles on consumer behavior which stress the influence of "groups" in setting clothing fashions, specifying brand to purchase, and deciding when a "luxury item" (e.g., air conditioner, automatic dishwasher) becomes a "necessity." Just which groups have this influence? Consider the plight of a typical housewife who is a member of a family, a church, the P.T.A., charitable clubs, and informal social groups. Think of the dilemma of a college student who is a member of a social fraternity and an athletic team, in addition to his family and neighborhood group connections, or a socialite who belongs to a country club, a bridge club, a charity group, and the "Metrecal-for-lunch bunch." How does one reconcile the pressures which come from such myriad sources?

One approach to clarifying *which* groups exert the greatest influence on an individual is based upon another useful distinction sociologists make among groups of various kinds:

Membership Groups versus Reference Groups. Membership groups include *all* of the smaller groups to which an individual belongs and in which he normally maintains fairly regular face-to-face contact with the other members. (However, these may also include groups such as political parties in which personal contact is absent.)

Reference groups are those with which an individual *identifies* to the point where the group becomes a standard, a norm, a point of reference for him. In effect, the individual "refers" to such groups for his standards of behavior and even for his goals and personal values. These groups influence behavior in general and buying behavior in particular. (A membership group may be a reference group, of course, and vice versa. The two kinds of groups may be thought of schematically as partially overlapping circles.) Reference groups are normally those a person meets with regularly, but they may even be aggregates, such as a social class.

Reference Groups

One writer suggests three possible definitions of a reference group: (1) a group which serves as a *comparison point* for the individual, (a) a group to which the individual *aspires,* that is, wishes to become a member of, and (3) a group whose *perspective* is assumed by the individual. He believes the third is most meaningful and establishes the following definition of a reference group: "A reference group, then, is that group whose outlook is used by the actor [individual] as the frame of reference in the organization of his perceptual field." (Shibutani, 1955, p. 565.) In this view, potential reference groups may differ greatly in size, composition, structure, and purpose. They may even be groups which do not exist, as in the case of artists or architects who are "born ahead of their times," scientists who work for "humanity," or philanthropists who give for "posterity." The important feature of reference groups is their *degree of influence* over the individual *even when he is not physically in contact with the group.*

An individual need not be a member of a group that provides reference for him. It may be a group to which he aspires; by adopting the dress, customs, and habits of that group, he hopes to be invited into membership. For example, he may wish to join a motorcycle club, so he buys a machine (called a "hog" in one such club), a black leather jacket, and a crash helmet. Or he may wish to join a golf club and, therefore, adopts the trappings necessary for such a conquest. An individual may even adopt as reference some group to which he *cannot* belong, for example, an athletic team or a group of intellectuals whose physical or mental requirements are beyond his capabilities. This need not deter him from following the group avidly and adopting those of its customs that are reasonably consonant with the realities of his own personal world. This is one reason that testimonial advertising is often quite effective — the duffer can *identify* with Jack Nicklaus by buying MacGregor golf clubs.

Goffman has described this kind of behavior in terms of drama. The individual wishing to show that he is a particular kind of person or a member of a particular reference group must use symbols as an actor does. For a motorcycle club, he must have a costume (the black leather jacket), props (the motorcycle), a setting (the clubhouse or rally), and so forth. He must even learn lines — the special language of the group — and try to surround himself with supporting characters.[1]

It is because of reference groups that the products people buy tend to "hang together" in what has been called a *life style.* (Riesman, 1950; Martineau, 1958.) A bank president knows what kind of house, furnishings, clothes, car, and so forth fit his "style." Even his amusements — golf instead of bowling, for instance — are determined by the reference group of "bankers" or "businessmen."

Another interesting feature of reference groups is that the individual may be drawn *toward* them or *away* from them. Negative reference groups are those which an individual actively *avoids* and wishes to be considered the least like. For example, a young man who would like a black leather jacket may not buy one to avoid possible identification with the motorcycle crowd; a teenage girl may avoid heavy make-up for fear of being identified with the "fast" crowd; a society matron may not serve beer at her cocktail party to avoid the connotation of lower social class.

This leads to the question: which is more important, the positive reference group (moving toward) or the negative reference

[1] Many products which are sold in the market — especially cars — function as badges of membership in particular groups. For example, Porsche clubs are legion in the United States. Before the advent of the Mustang, the Corvair Monza demonstrated among teenagers that its possessor was a swinger and a member of the youth culture; the Falcon was looked upon as a Momma-Poppa car. Station wagons are ambiguous; they tend to be owned either by rugged outdoorsmen or by solid suburban citizens.

group (moving away from)? Newcomb points out that often the two work in a complementary fashion: "In many cases (perhaps in all) the referring of social attitudes to one group negatively leads to referring them to another group positively, or vice versa, so that the attitudes are dually reinforced." (Newcomb, 1958, p. 275.) The individual tries to "be like" and also tries to avoid being like.

The knowledge that reference groups influence behavior does not answer, but merely puts off, the critical question: How does the individual select from among all present and possible groups those which he considers as reference groups for him? The answer is complex and unclear.

Often the individual selects groups whose values are similar to those of his family. This provides the hope that underlies advertising campaigns which focus the consumer's attention on his family: "If you think you can buy a better vacuum sweeper than Hoover — ask your grandmother!" In an effort to improve upon the "social image" of beer, the brewing industry undertook an advertising campaign in the late 1950's. Advertisements showed beer being consumed in a family setting, with the slogan: "Beer belongs — enjoy it." The objective, of course, was to capitalize on normal favorable feelings toward the family.

On the other hand, there is evidence that individuals do not always hold the views and values of their families. The famous Bennington College study in 1935–39 showed how college girls from familiies with a politically conservative bent often change drastically to nonconservative political inclinations while attending college in a more liberal setting. In fact, students with the highest prestige in Bennington College (as indicated by student-body nominations, in sealed ballots, for the girl "most worthy to represent the school") were those with liberal political views. Newcomb traced the manner in which girls come to grips with the problem of what reference groups to adopt — whether to adhere to the family pattern or adopt the majority view of their colleagues in the new environment. (Newcomb, 1958.)

The choice of reference groups (most individuals have more than one) is probably determined by some weighted combination of feelings toward family values or internalized personal values (if they are different), plus the powerful effects of simply being with the members of other groups. The importance of newly encountered groups must not be overlooked. For example, the student moving into a college dormitory, the man changing jobs, and the couple moving into a new neighborhood are all susceptible to the influence of others in their new environment. Whether the new groups become reference groups depends upon the individual's perception of them, but the chances are generally in favor of this happening.

To begin with, there are often selective forces at work in bringing people together. The college freshman inhabits a dormitory with others of the same sex and of similar age, intellectual capacity, and aspiration level. In private schools, the socio-economic characteristics of students' families are likely to be similar also. The couple moving into a new neighborhood probably finds itself among families of similar income level, occupational level, family structure (age of parents and presence or absence of young children), and even racial characteristics. Most of these factors are demographic, but they tend to predispose people toward similar psychological-sociological characteristics as well. Thus, new groups become, in time, positive reference groups for the individual.

REFERENCE GROUPS AND BUYING BEHAVIOR

Reference groups may have a great influence upon buying behavior, according to the available evidence. However, this influence is selective in that it does not seem to apply equally to all products or brands. Bourne cites the work done by the Bureau of Applied Social Research at Columbia University to determine the relative influence of the reference group in product and brand purchases. The results of this work, shown in Figure 6.1. indicate that there are: (1) product categories in which the reference group determines whether the product is bought at all and, if so, which brand is selected (cars, cigarettes); (2) categories in which it influences the product but not the brand (air conditioners, instant coffee); (3) categories in which it influences the brand but not the product (clothing, furniture, and other products used by nearly all people regardless of their reference groups); and (4) categories in which the reference group has no influence on either product or brand.

Figure 6.1

Reference group influence for *product* relatively:

	Weak	Strong
Strong	Clothing Furniture Magazines Refrigerator (type) Toilet soap	Cars* Cigarettes* Beer (premium vs. regular)* Drugs*
Weak	Soap Canned peaches Laundry soap Refrigerator (brand) Radios	Air conditioners* Instant coffee* TV (black and white)

Reference group influence for *brand* relatively:

(Note: The classification of all products marked with an asterisk is based on experimental evidence. Others are classified speculatively on the basis of the best experience and judgment available.) The present authors would suggest that the penetration of cars and black and white television sets in most major urban areas is now so great that group influence would be expected to be minimal in terms of product use.

Borne suggests that once it is determined whether the purchase of a product or service is influenced by reference groups, the following action should be taken:

Where neither product nor brand appears to be associated strongly with reference group influence, advertising should emphasize the product's attributes, intrinsic qualities, price, and advantages over competing products.

Where reference group influence is operative, the advertiser should stress the kinds of people who buy the product, reinforcing and broadening where possible the existing stereotypes of users. This involves learning what the stereotypes are and what specific reference groups enter into the picture, so that appeals can be tailored to each major group reached by the different media employed. (Bourne, 1956, p. 10.)

Reference group influence is probably strong when a product has *expressive value* in distinguishing one group from another. Clothing, cars, and home furnishings are all display items, and reference group influence on their purchase would consequently be expected to be strong. Reference group influence is also likely to be strong when products reflect personal taste. Books, magazines, art objects — and again clothing, furniture, and cars — fall into this category. Research further suggests that the influence of reference groups is particularly strong when the individual has little knowledge about a product. The less he feels he knows, the more he turns to a reference group for advice and evaluation (e.g., air conditioners, cars, and television in Figure 6.1).

Riesman has described the *taste exchange* process which characterizes many social gatherings. People at cocktail parties (or in bowling leagues) often discuss at length products and services they like and dislike — movies, foods, hair styles, medicinal products, drinks, and so forth. (Riesman, 1950). Once we are alerted to the taste exchange process, we cannot help but be struck by the large part that it plays in ordinary social intercourse. By exchanging and comparing tastes, people can check their tastes against those of their friends and acquaintances and use the information thus acquired to conform more closely to reference group norms.

In the case of products whose purchase is at least partly influenced by reference groups, what is the effect of such groups *relative* to the effect of the individual's *own* attitudes toward these products? Bourne describes a technique used by the Bureau of Applied Social Research which relates the actual frequency of use of a product to the individual's own attitude toward certain features of the product *and* to usage of the product by the individual's friends. For example, respondents were asked about the effects of product "X" (a food product) upon general health. Results are shown below:

Reply	Index of Product Usage*
Good effect on health. Friends use it.	.41
Bad effect on health. Friends use it.	.08
Good effect on health. Friends do not use it.	−.10
Bad effect on health. Friends do not use it.	−.51

*Higher value indicates greater usage.

The index value of .08 indicates a higher rate of product "X" usage among respondents who stated that they felt it did more harm than good *but* whose friends frequently *used* it than among respondents who felt it did more good than harm but whose friends did *not* frequently use it. Similar results emerged from questions about the fattening characteristics of the product and its cost. In this study, then, pressures from friends were apparently great enough to offset the individual's own negative feelings toward the product. The extent to which this holds for other types of products is not known, but Bourne adds:

> In a study of a beverage, it was found that, of those who drank the beverage in question, 95 per cent claimed that their friends also drank it, while of those who did *not* drink this beverage 85 per cent also claimed that their friends did *not* drink it. Some products, then, must be sold to whole social groups rather than primarily to 'individuals.' (Bourne, 1956, p. 11.)

Selective perception must be taken into account in interpreting these findings. We cannot assume that the people using the product were in fact correct when they reported that 95 per cent of their friends also used the product. The users would be sensitized to notice other users, since other users would tend to confirm their own taste. When people are asked not about their friends but about the community in general, the same kind of self-confirming behavior occurs. A question such as "What make of car do most people around here drive?" would evoke the answer "Chevrolet" from a Chevrolet owner and "Ford" from a Ford owner. In the case of automobiles, registration figures could be used to check the answers, but checking is more difficult when people say that their friends share their tastes in other products.

Also, in the taste exchanging process the user would tend to encounter other users and the nonuser to encounter other non-users. The reason for this is that people in a social gathering are more likely to agree with each other than not. When a user states publicly that he likes Brand X, people usually agree with him, if only out of politeness. The nonuser similarly finds confirmation by his friends. The fact remains that both the user and the nonuser demonstrate a need for their friends to confirm or approve their purchase decisions. The individual wants to belong — to be "with" the group — and thus tends to avoid products which are considered oddball by his reference groups.

It should be remembered that an individual normally has more than one reference group. Remember, also, that he does not have to be a member of a group in order for that group to be a reference group for him, so there may be one or more outside groups from which he adopts values or standards of behavior. It is probably reasonable to assume that an individual's total spectrum of buying behavior is governed by *several* reference groups — perhaps five, ten, or even more. This means that the identification of reference group influence is no simple task, for one group may influence the purchase of certain types of products while another group influences other types.

Thus, the marketer has two problems: (1) determining whether purchases of his product are governed to any great extent by reference groups, and (2) determining which types of reference groups are most influential. Motivation research techniques are likely to be helpful in obtaining information like this of a socially sensitive nature.

Group Structure and Operation

A great deal is known about the behavior of small groups of many types, but the discussion which follows will center on reference groups, since these are the groups which exert great influence upon *buying* behavior.

A tool which is often used by sociologists to study patterns of interaction among members of a small group is the *sociogram*. It is a graphic method of mapping the various patterns of contact, influence, and attitudes among members of a group. To construct a sociogram, one asks each member of a group to answer questions about the other members, for example, "Which members do you enjoy being with the most?" Responses from all members are depicted graphically, with arrows indicating the direction of contact, influence, or feeling. Figure 6.2 shows a sociogram from a study of doctors in a small New England community. Each doctor was asked "Could you name the three or four physicians whom you meet most frequently on social occasions?" (Menzel and Katz, 1955–56, p. 341.) In this case, there were essentially three social subclusters with relatively frequent internal interaction, a group of neutrals (Drs. 15–19), and two social isolates (Dr. 20 and Dr. 21). At a glance, then, we obtain from a sociogram information about the social pattern and structure of an aggregate.

Figure 6.2

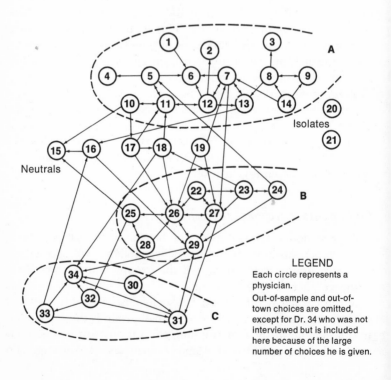

LEGEND

Each circle represents a physician.

Out-of-sample and out-of-town choices are omitted, except for Dr. 34 who was not interviewed but is included here because of the large number of choices he is given.

Some research on small group behavior has used this tool, but many other techniques have been used as well. A sociogram does give a great deal of information in simplified form. It has great potential use in consumer marketing and has already been used effectively in studies of the process of communications and influence in the adoption of a new drug among physicians (cf. Chapter 9).

From our discussion so far, the reader might be led to conclude that there is a common manner of behavior for all small groups. However, the variety of sizes, purposes, and characteristics of groups suggests that there could be no single mode of operation for all small groups, and this is indeed the case. While there are common properties, there are also many differences. Much of the research to date has been focused upon the determinants of group behavior—what *causes* one group to behave one way and another a different way; and much of it has also been concerned with *how* and *how much* the group influences the individual member.

Some of the important findings about group behavior will be summarized briefly, following the general approach of Berelson and Steiner and utilizing the information they present. (Berelson & Steiner, 1964, pp. 325–61.) We are concerned here with relatively informal social groups (neighborhood, friendships, clubs, etc.) and in the group factors which most affect buying behavior.

GROUP STRUCTURE

In most groups, some sort of order and structure tends to emerge. At the least there is some rough "ranking" of members. Each member's ranking depends upon the extent to which he realizes or represents the norms and values of the group; the more a member recognizes and acts in accordance with these norms, the higher he will rank. In groups with little or no formal objective (most informal social groups), the structure is vague and the ranking of members tends to be based upon personal characteristics and "personality." But leadership of some form emerges, and leaders *tend* to have certain characteristics: larger size, better physical appearance, self-confidence, friendliness, energy, determination, and intelligence. ("Intelligence" here may be general mental ability or specific information possessed by the individual, whichever is most suited to the needs of the group.)

The leader of a group tends to be the one who most closely reflects the standards of the group or who has the most information or skill appropriate to the goals of the group. (Note, though, that a leader has a certain freedom to depart from group standards which other group members lack.) This applies to groups of neighboring housewives, men's bowling clubs, charitable groups, hubcap thieves, or whatever.

Group Influence

The group adopts norms of behavior and/or values of some type, and members are expected to conform to them. The more important that membership in a particular group is to the individual (social approval motive), the more important it is for him to conform. What happens if he does not conform? The obvious, grosser punishments include shame, ridicule, even threat of expulsion. But more subtly, a network of communications tends to develop which rewards conformity by inclusion and greater contact and punishes nonconformity by lesser contact. The mere possibility of exclusion is often a sufficient deterrent to nonconformity. Group pressure can become very great indeed.

One study showed the extreme effects that group pressure may have on performance in a perceptual task. In this particular situation, participants were not members of the same reference group, but were a collection of male students at the same university. Experimental groups of eight students each were asked to match the length of a given line to one of three other lines of unequal length. Judgments were given *aloud in the presence of the group.* Unknown to one of the eight members, the other seven were "planted" to give wrong answers on *twelve* occasions during the testing session. The "critical" subject (who did not know the purpose of the study) was confronted with the problem of either reporting accurately what he saw or yielding to the group and reporting what he knew to be erroneous. Table 6.1 shows the frequency of erroneous reports by 50 critical subjects in 50 experimental groups. The frequency of errors of 37 control groups whose membership was not rigged are shown also.

Table 6.1

DISTRIBUTION OF ERRORS IN EXPERIMENTAL
AND CONTROL GROUPS

Number of critical errors in 12 trials	Experimental groups* (N = 50)	Control groups (N = 37)
	Frequency	Frequency
0	13	35
1	4	1
2	5	1
3	6	
4	3	
5	4	
6	1	
7	2	
8	5	
9	3	
10	3	
11	1	
12	0	
Total	50	37
Mean	3.84	0.08

*All errors by "critical" subjects in the experimental groups were in the direction of the majority "estimates."

The distribution of errors by the control groups, where no pressure was exerted, shows how easy the perceptual task really was (i.e., only two errors in 37 trials). Yet three-quarters of the critical subjects yielded to group pressure at least once, and many yielded eight or more times out of a possible twelve! And the groups here were not even *reference* groups, whose influence would likely have been even greater. (Asch, 1958, pp. 175–77.)

In a variation of this study, it has been shown that yielding occurred as much in groups of only three or four members as in groups of eight, ten, or even fifteen. Other investigators have shown conclusively that there are great individual differences in the tendency to yield and that these differences tend to be consistent regardless of the type of situation. That is, individuals who yield in one situation tend to do so in other dissimilar situations. For some people, then, the tendency to conform is great, and this tendency exists in groups of all kinds, particularly reference groups.

The tendency toward group conformity is seen clearly when people are brought together to be interviewed, for marketing research purposes, as a discussion group rather than as individuals. A phenomenon often noted in group interviews is a much greater tendency toward unanimity of perceptions and opinions than is found in private personal interviews. Group norms become established, and people hesitate to express contrary opinions even among total strangers. Groups have *sanctions* to enforce norms — withdrawal, raised eyebrows, jokes, perhaps even open hostility; and the tendency of members to follow the group norms may be overwhelming. For this reason, group interviews must be used with caution.

With such group pressure to conform, what can change the *group property* itself? Fortunately, there is room in a group for some members who maintain some independence of judgment. These individuals are, potentially, the instruments through which the group property may be changed. Also, the group has a leader of some sort, although in small, informal groups he may have less influence and be more democratic and permissive than in larger, more structured, goal-oriented groups. Does the leader of an informal, social group initiate changes? He can, but this implies an authoritarian relationship which is not characteristic of small, informal groups. One writer makes the point that the leader-follower dichotomy is an oversimplification and that the effective leader must also be an effective follower in the sense of responding to and interpreting the group's goals. The evidence tends to support this view. (Homans, 1950.)

Open versus Closed Groups. One useful perspective on the problem of group behavior is provided by the concept of *open* versus *closed* groups, that is, the degree to which a group's membership remains constant over time. In closed groups the lives of members are closely intermingled for a period of time, while in open groups members are in a greater state of flux and interpersonal relations are less stable and enduring. One writer suggests four fundamental characteristics which seem to distinguish open groups from closed groups:

A reduced time perspective. "[In open groups,] the future is indistinct; the present dominates. If the present membership is to benefit from a given group action, the action must be undertaken in the immediate future. Postponement may be tantamount to inaction for those members who may be removed or replaced."

The maintenance of equilibrium. "It has been repeatedly suggested that instability is a basic shortcoming of an open group system." This is particularly a function of the size and turnover rate of the group. The smaller the size and the higher the turnover rate, the greater the constant state of instability or disequilibrium. "Since the entire organization is more threatened by the loss of a member from a small group than a large group, the members of small groups may overreact to the threat of group distintegration and leave the group prematurely. Moreover, under these conditions, undue power is inherently accorded the mobile individual, since he possesses the power to destroy the group."

Frame of reference. Closed groups tend to develop specific and unchanging ideas, opinions, beliefs, and values. Open groups, on the other hand, have opportunity to listen to many ideologies and beliefs, and consequently their "belief systems" are more flexible. It is not hard to see why this happens. New members, even though preselected by present members to conform reasonably well with group characteristics and norms, are simply bound to infuse some new ideas based upon the different environments in which they formerly lived or operated. If change occurs with any reasonable frequency, the group tends to accept and even to expect a certain amount of fertilization from the outside. Scholars feel that societies which are characterized by a continuous flow of new members from other societies tend to be much more creative. Studies in industrial research laboratories have supported this by showing that "open" research teams are generally more creative and productive than "closed" research teams.

Changing group composition. This rather obvious characteristic has some specific implications in terms of power relationships among group members. In particular, the *newcomer* to a group immediately occupies a rather strategic position because of several factors: (1) With his extended frame of reference, he is able to make invidious comparisons among members within the new group and, also, between this group as a whole and the old group from which he came. (2) There may be competition among subgroups of the new group for his day-to-day allegiance. (3) Existing members tend to defer to the wishes of the new "guest." (4) His decision to leave shortly after joining might cause public embarrassment to the new group. "It must also be noted that in the early phase of the new relationship the newcomer is often not totally committed either financially or psychologically to the new group. Therefore, the newcomer is more mobile in a variety of ways." (Ziller, 1965.)

Is the typical consumer more likely to be a member of open or closed groups? What marketing implications are there in this distinction? To begin with, there is no such thing as a "typical consumer." Individuals and families differ widely in their participation in social activities; many people have little interaction, formal or informal, with others, while some people belong to several groups, both closed and open. Many writers overlook this and stress the social determinants of buying behavior almost to the exclusion of self-determination. "Inner-directed" individuals, in particular, are almost certainly less subject to group pressures.

The present authors would contend that a great many of the reference groups for individual consumers or family units are more accurately described as open than closed, particularly in areas of the United States which are characterized by a constant influx of immigrants from other portions of the country. Los Angeles is a notable example of an area that is in a constant state of flux. Not only are there continual newcomers from the East, but there is high internal mobility. It has been found that approximately 20 per cent of the family units in the U.S.A. change residence in the course of a single year. Such unstable conditions could be expected to produce a disproportionate number of open groups in the United States as compared with some other countries. The "other-directed" trend in our society postulated by Riesman should result in, or perhaps from, more open groups.

MOBILE CONSUMERS

Remember that in open groups *greater mobility results in greater power*, especially in the case of the newcomer and the present member most likely to leave (provided he is not a lame duck who has already publicly announced his intention to leave). This means that the factor of mobility *per se* can raise the status and influence of an otherwise average group member. It does not mean, of course, that such members necessarily become group leaders, but it does suggest that the more mobile group members may produce a relatively greater impact in open consumer groups.

What do we know about these mobile consumers? Who are they, and what effects do they have upon the market for consumer goods?

In an effort to develop a theory of *consumption leadership* (to identify individuals or families who tend to lead in the adoption of new ways of living, which often involve the early purchase of new products), the Opinion Research Corporation theorized: "The central thread of our modern society is mobility. The leadership elite is that group of people who possess this quality in greater degree than do other people." (Opinion Research Corporation, 1959, p. 51.) From this base they set forth the contention that these leaders are also leaders in the purchase of new consumer products. If these consumption leaders can be identified and their buying habits studied, it might enable manufacturers to predict the kinds of products and services that the public will eventually be buying in large quantities. The commercial advantage of information of this type is obvious.

The Opinion Research Corporation suggested eight characteristics which seem to distinguish "high mobiles" from other Americans:

1. They travel more and change residence more often.
2. They show more movement through the occupational structure.
3. They are more likely to change their economic status (upward).
4. They associate with a wider variety of people.
5. They move through more educational levels and institutions.

6. They move through more intellectual influences.
7. They are more selective and variable in their politics.
8. In these various dimensions, they have moved a greater distance from their family of birth. (Opinion Research Corporation, 1959, p. 51.)

By defining high mobiles in this objective way, it was possible for the Opinion Research Corporation to identify and locate some of these people so as to study the "value systems" which lead them to change styles and tastes and thus change purchase patterns.[2] An intensive survey of a community in New Jersey produced some very interesting results. For one thing, it revealed that there were high mobiles at every income level, so that income could not be said to be the primary factor in consumption leadership. Mobility is not synonymous with high income.

The principal finding was that high mobiles tended to lead others in the early adoption of a great many of the newer consumer products or services such as stereo equipment, power and sail boats, Irish whiskey, wild rice, travel credit cards, electric blankets, and foreign movies. In some cases, they were ahead of the medium and lower mobiles by five to ten years. High mobiles did not lead in *all* of the 75 high-growth products and services studied; approximately 15 per cent of the items were not pioneered by high mobiles. But there was clear early dominance in many items and relative dominance in some.

These findings are rather exciting, but they do pose questions:
– What about new products which were bought in large number by high mobiles but did *not* become later market successes? If these people are simply likely to buy *all* types of new offerings, promising and not, how can the manufacturer know *which* will later be widely accepted?
– How is mobility related to basic psychological factors, such as general intelligence, and to temperamental characteristics, such as aggressiveness? Are these the causal variables? What

[2] Note that these highly mobile consumption leaders constitute one of the three forms of social groups described at the beginning of this chapter — the form composed of units that are *different* from one another but that possess something in common, even though there may be no direct interaction among members.

amount of *influence* do high mobiles have upon others in their own social groups? Are these early purchasers the ones who *lead* the group into complete adoption of the new product or service?

There is some indication that the earliest adopters of a product are not always the most influential individuals in a community (cf. Chapter 9). If high mobiles did turn out to be relatively influential in their own social groups, this would be most interesting. One might expect this to be the case, since open group theory suggests that the more mobile individuals derive more power within a group, other things being equal. There is also the important factor that high mobiles often know a great deal more because of their expanded frame of reference, developed from exposure to a greater variety of experiences. This combination of factors would suggest greater influence for high mobiles, but much more evidence is needed before this phenomenon is fully understood.

The Opinion Research Corporation study is not definitive, but it does focus attention upon the importance of the mobility concept in consumer behavior. Merton and others have commented on the difference between *cosmopolitans* and *locals* in large-scale organizations. Cosmopolitan members of the organization (e.g., scientific personnel) have many outside contacts in their professional associations and possess skills which enable them to move relatively easily from one organization to another. Other members of the organization are locals in that most of their contacts are within the organization and most of their information is oriented to the organization rather than to an outside body of knowledge. An executive who has risen through an organization from salesman to marketing manager would tend to be a local.

It has been observed that much of the innovation in large organizations stems from the mobile cosmopolitan, who has had the opportunity to learn of other ways of doing things and is less committed to current organizational practice. (Merton, 1965.) The same is probably true of the mobile consumer.

In summary, the influence of small groups upon behavior in general and upon buying behavior in particular seems well established. Less is known about the way in which these groups operate and about how they can be persuaded to adopt new modes of buying behavior. We need to know if open groups tend to lead closed groups in the acceptance and adoption of new products (they probably do), what types of products are most likely to be used by open groups (e.g., expressive products?), and more about the personal characteristics and values of members of both groups, so that appropriate promotional appeals may be developed for particular products.

Group Discussion

We have discussed in some detail the important role of reference groups in setting standards and influencing buying behavior. There are other types which deserve mention, for example, face-to-face groups which are not reference groups and groups which are not even face-to-face. Evidence about other types of groups shows the many different ways in which group influence may operate.

Group Discussion versus Lecture. Lewin reported a series of studies which were designed to determine whether group discussions or lectures were more effective in producing changes in preparing and serving food products in the home. In one study, for example, six groups of women were urged to prepare and serve more often such exotic meat products as beef hearts, sweetbreads, and kidneys. Three of the groups were given a lecture on the health and economic benefits of these foods, along with suggestions for avoiding some of their undesirable characteristics (odor, texture, appearance). Recipes were distributed to make preparation of these foods easier. The other three groups were involved in separate discussions to see how "housewives like themselves" might be induced to use more of these meats. In the process, of course, there developed lively debate about the merits and problems of the products which served to inform the participants and to stimulate interest. At the end of the study, the housewives were asked who would be willing to try one or more of the meats during the following weeks.

Results showed that 32 per cent of the women in the discussion groups actually served one of the meats which they had never served before, while only three per cent of the women in the lecture groups did so. A follow-up study using different groups of women showed that group discussion was also more effective than group lectures in increasing home consumption of both fresh and evaporated milk.

A further study showed that group discussion was even more effective than *individual instruction* in inducing mothers to increase the amount of cod liver oil and orange juice they fed to their babies. Groups involved in these studies ranged from membership groups (Red Cross volunteers), who met more or less regularly on a face-to-face basis, to groups of mothers most of whom were not acquainted with each other and who were widely separated after the instruction sessions. Thus, results here were very encouraging in suggesting the power of group discussion for promoting change in groups of many types, even new and temporary groups whose members were initially strangers. (Lewin, 1958.)

Lewin's research was criticized by others on grounds of faulty methodology. Although his studies were provocative, too many different factors were involved (public commitment of decision, warning that the decision would be followed up, etc.) to permit the generalization that group discussion was the only factor to produce changes in consumer behavior. A later study by Pelz very cleverly isolated the effects of *each* of the following factors on the total process of change through group discussion:

> *Group discussion* itself, as a means of conveying information.
> *Decision* to perform a specific action.
> *Public commitment* (the degree to which the decision is indicated publicly).
> *Degree of consensus* of the group in reaching the decision.

Lectures and discussions were designed to raise students' willingness to participate in behavioral science experiments; the criterion was whether or not students actually volunteered at a later date to do this. Interestingly, it was found that neither group discussion by itself nor the amount of public commitment to the decision was influential in raising the willingness of students to participate in experiments. But there were small differences in volunteering between those who were not asked to make a decision and those who were. (Many who were asked to make a decision were not asked to make a *public commitment* of this decision.) A high degree of actual and perceived consensus among group members was also related to volunteering, that is, when a decision request yielded a high proportion of positive decisions to volunteer *and* when members of the group perceived this consensus, there was greater likelihood that group members would volunteer. (Pelz, 1958.)

Discrepancies between Lewin's and Pelz's studies may have been due to different topics for decision (food versus participating in experiments), different types of subjects (housewives versus college students), or other factors. There remains the problem of implementing group discussions in the mass consumer marketing context. How might this be done economically? Perhaps it would be worth even a high cost in the extreme case of introducing a product which runs counter to the current social and cultural norms, as in the case of "far-out" clothing styles or exotic new foods (e.g., ocean-grown fruits and vegetables).

QUESTIONS
FOR REVIEW

1. List all groups of which you are a member. Which of them are most influential in your buying decisions?

2. Are you a member of any groups which are not reference groups for you and thus do not influence your buying behavior?

3. How does an individual reconcile conflicting reference group influences in a buying situation?

4. What relationships do social groups have with the learning process? With perceptual processes? With attitudes?

5. How may a marketer of an industrial product or service take advantage of group influence in his marketing efforts? Be specific.

6. Under what circumstances are mobile consumers likely to have *less* influence than nonmobile consumers on purchase decisions?

7. What kinds of products or services might be designed for "group" purchase (in contrast to products designed for purchase by single individuals)? Are any products of this type presently available?

7

Social and Cultural Factors

EMPHASIS IN PREVIOUS chapters has been more or less on the individual himself — his perceptions, motivations, attitudes, behavior in small groups, and other processes. We will turn now to the broader dimensions of *society* and *culture* — the structure of a society, aggregate behavior patterns, ways in which a society sets norms and regulates itself, and similarities and differences among various cultures — and to their implications for the understanding of consumer buying behavior.

The Structure of Society

"Sociology is one of the social sciences. Its long-run aim is to discover the basic structure of human society, to identify the forces that hold groups together or weaken them, and to learn the conditions that transform social life." (Broom & Selznick, 1963, p. 1.) Sociology is a systematic way of looking at familiar institutions, customs, and social problems so as to understand what a society is composed of, how it is organized, and why it behaves as it does. For example, sociology is concerned with the behavior of the various *types* of social groups: family and kinship, racial and ethnic, religious, business and technological, educational and community. It is also concerned with social *structure:* social stratification, status, and role behavior. When we understand these factors, both separately and in combination, we understand the structure and operation of a given society.

What kinds of consumer marketing problems do sociologists concern themselves with? Glock and Nicosia distinguish between two types of buying behavior:

> *Consumer behavior.* This refers to the decision processes of the *individual consumer* or consuming unit (e.g., the family). Sociologists are concerned with the description and explanation of one or more acts of purchase choice and the allocation of the consumer's discretionary spending income among goods, services, leisure activities, savings, etc.

> *Consumption behavior.* This refers to the behavior of *aggregates of consumers* or consuming units, both at a given time and over a period of time. The subject matter of consumption behavior parallels at an aggregate level that of consumer behavior at the individual level.

These writers suggest that sociologists could contribute to a better understanding of *consumption behavior* by determining: (1) what major *changes* are occurring in the way populations spend their leisure time and how these changes affect the consumption of goods and services, (2) what the *social processes* are that govern the ways in which new products and services are adopted, and (3) whether there are *general patterns of innovation* and, if so, whether there is a different pattern for each of the various types of goods and services. They suggest:

> Sociologists could seriously consider the ways in which changes in the social structure and in value systems might affect consumption behavior. A large number of sociological concepts imply that these factors have an impact on consumption behavior. Such concepts as social mobility, cultural lag, social integration, life styles, and achievement orientation are directly relevant. (Glock & Nicosia, 1964, p. 53.)

Social Roles

The concept of social roles was developed by sociologists to bring order to the complex of interactions between individuals and the groups to which they belong.

Role theory holds that for every position an individual occupies in society there is a certain range of acceptable *behavior*. An individual is expected to behave in a certain way in order to carry out the requirements of a given position. Each social position has its own role requirements; for example, doctor, father, clerk, policeman, and clergyman all require certain patterns of behavior.

Roles also specify the *rights and duties* belonging to a certain social position, that is, the responsibilities to others and the demands which may be made upon others. The social context of any individual consists of a number of such roles since the same individual occupies more than one social position. For example, a male family head may occupy the positions of father, husband, truck driver, Boy Scout troop leader, bowling team member, and church trustee. Each of these positions requires a different pattern of behavior, so that the individual is constantly changing roles in the course of a typical week. His relatively subservient position as a truck driver contrasts with his position of leadership in the Boy Scouts and his prestige in the office of church trustee.

While acceptable behavior for one role (e.g., bowling team member) may be quite different from that for another role (e.g., truck driver or church trustee), the individual typically experiences little difficulty in making the transition from one role to another. Nearly every individual plays several social roles, while some individuals carry on an amazing variety.

Role behavior involves a complicated kind of feedback (called anticipatory socialization) between an individual and the group to which he belongs. The *role expectations* to which he must conform are group expectations and he must "guess" what they are. If he guesses wrong, the group then has a problem: whether to accept the person's behavior as within the allowable range of behaviors permitted by his role or whether to condemn the behavior. In effect, the person must "act out" what he conceives to be his role, while watching closely for cues as to whether or not his performance is being accepted.

This element of uncertainty in role behavior may be one of the sources of the conformity alleged to be characteristic of American life. The individual simply hesitates to display behavior which might be accepted but which he fears might not be. For example, business executives in company dining rooms usually discuss neutral matters such as work, sports events, and their golf games; they conceal any interest they may have in music, art, or philosophy. They feel vaguely that interests of the latter sort would be inconsistent with the "executive" role. People differ in their ability to perceive and carry out role expectations, and Thompson has coined the terms *bureautic* and *bureaupath* to describe, respectively, the person who fails to conform to organizational norms and the person who overconforms. (Thompson, 1961.)

In a sense, there are even *roles within roles*. The role of housewife, for example, carries requirements for other roles: mother, wife, cook, housekeeper, P.T.A. or other group participant, perhaps church member, etc. These requirements are clearly recognized and are widely understood. But within the role of housewife there are quite different perceptions that different women may have. One study of housewives in France found two distinctly different types of housewives, "traditionalists" (old-fashioned) and "modernists." Further, each of these main types was subdivided into the "devoteds," who battle with the toil and are concerned more with the quantity of work accomplished than with the results obtained, and the "blue ribbons," who interest themselves above all in the quality and the nicety of their cooking. The study related the characteristics of each of these types to the usage of dehydrated (i.e., powdered) soap. (Ferber, Blankertz, & Hollander, 1964, p. 192.)

Incongruities in Role Perceptions

One consequence of the element of uncertainty in role behavior is that marketers do not have to take role expectations as "given." A woman moving into a suburban environment for the first time, for example, wants to play the suburban-housewife role, but she is uncertain about how she should dress, how she should furnish her house, what kind of car she should drive, and so forth, so she observes her neighbors, watches Donna Reed on television, and scans the home magazines for clues as to appropriate behavior for suburban housewives. How she comes to perceive her role may be influenced, at least in part, by the advertising and other commercial messages that she accepts as valid. Marketers *shape* roles as well as reflect them.

Davidson, past president of the American Marketing Association, had this to say in his 1963 presidential address:

> There is another defect in the concept of marketing as a social process concerned with the identification and satisfaction of customer wants. The concept as commonly stated assumes that marketing is an adaptive process in our culture. In accordance with this view, it is generally assumed or stated that the firm is adjusting its product offer to market requirements which it has discovered by marketing research approaches. While this may well be true, when viewed from the standpoint of any one manufacturer, . . . the aggregate social impact of all marketing activity is, in my judgment, commonly underestimated, especially by those in the marketing field. (Davidson, 1964, p. 9.)

The aspiring suburban housewife, in seeking clues as to the artifacts and behaviors which would best express her role, cannot help but be influenced by ads stating plausibly that suburban housewives should behave in certain ways. Hair coloring, for example, encountered resistance among "respectable," upper-income women for many years until the imaginative Clairol campaign showed pictures of exactly this type of woman in a firmly middle-class setting, often playing with her children, accompanied by the provocative headline, "Does she or doesn't she?" Hair coloring was made part of the suburban scene.

An unfortunate result of the great influence that marketers have in this process is that women and other consumers are sometimes deceived. Hostess pajamas, for instance, might be advertised as "just right for a patio party" and be bought by a woman who then discovers through acute social embarrassment that the pajamas are really inappropriate for the role of gracious hostess. Many books, records, art prints, and home furnishings are sold to people who wish to appear to be cultured persons but who actually demonstrate the opposite when they display their choice of purchases, for example, overstuffed "borax" furniture.

Differences between the role expectations of others and the way people perceive their own roles may sometimes have importance for marketing decisions. For example, a research study might show that a product was looked upon by the population in general as especially suitable for young men, less suitable for young women, barely suitable for older men, and not at all suitable for older women. This would suggest that the product should be merchandised primarily to young males. Close analysis of the data, however, might show that everyone considered the product suitable for himself or herself. This could occur because of incongruities in role perceptions. Table 7.1 shows how this might happen:

Table 7.1

INCONGRUITIES IN ROLE PERCEPTION

Product Suitable For	Young Men	Young Women	Older Men	Older Women	Total
Young Men	yes	yes	yes	yes	100%
Young Women	no	yes	yes	yes	75%
Older Men	no	no	yes	yes	50%
Older Women	no	no	no	yes	25%

Exactly opposite results might be obtained in a study of some other product or service. It is commonplace, for example, that older people — parents, especially — tend to feel that young people engage in behavior inappropriate for their age. The current fad for pierced ears among junior high school girls is an instance. We suspect that older women would think of pierced ears as appropriate for themselves but as very inappropriate for their teen-age daughters and that their teen-age daughters would disagree strongly. The attitudes of older men and teen-age boys toward pierced ears for teen-age girls might fall somewhere in between.

In practical terms, the incongruities between the way people see themselves and the way others see them mean that research inquiring into role perceptions must use samples of sufficient size to provide a reasonable number of cross-breaks. In cultures with simpler role structures, the investigator examining the role of, say, the middle-aged woman can direct his inquiries to almost any representative of the culture. In the United States, however, he must talk to middle-aged women themselves.

Roles, of course, are not determined only by age and sex. Several of the factors influencing role behavior are discussed below, and they are exceedingly complex. Here it is enough to note that people tend to perceive their roles in terms of the expectations of the people with whom they interact, and that people in different age-sex groups, different social classes, or different ethnic groups can often fall into wild misunderstandings. Marketers have come to realize this, and this is one reason for the increasing sums spent on consumer research.

ROLE CONFLICT

Role conflict occurs when two or more of the social positions occupied by the same individual at the same time are antagonistic in some way. The career woman with a family may be in such a position if doing her best to meet business demands conflicts with her obligation to her family as a housewife. The university professor who engages in consulting work for business firms may have similar problems. Even within a small group such as a family, the role requirement of being a good provider suggests that the housewife give her family filling dinners and rich desserts, but this conflicts with her role as the family's chief health officer who should keep diets balanced and waistlines in trim. The more separate roles an individual has, the more potential areas for conflict there are. One would thus expect that upper-income housewives with their many group memberships would experience more role conflicts than lower-income housewives.

There are many ways of coping with role conflicts, but we are concerned here only with those which have some direct relationship to spending behavior. Common solutions such as changes in psychological processes, changes in group memberships, and elimination of one of the roles in one way or another will not be discussed.

SOCIAL ROLES AND BUYING BEHAVIOR

In his search for social identity, the individual adopts the role expectancies of either his present social position or a social position to which he aspires. They may reflect itself in both the individual's *social behavior* and his *buying behavior*.

The importance of social roles in the buying situation has been pointed out by Martineau, who says, ". . . Everything we buy helps us convey to others the kind of people we are, helps us identify ourselves to the world at large." (Martineau, 1957, p. 197.) Levy elaborates on this:

> The variety of goods available permits more ways of living than was ever the case. Because of their symbolic nature, consumer goods can be chosen with less conflict or indecision than would otherwise be the case. . . . Our choices are made easier — either more routine or more impulsive, seemingly — because one object is symbolically more harmonious to our goals, feelings, and self-definitions than is another. (Levy, 1959, p. 411.)

Staudt and Taylor take up the theme:

> Thus, our investigation becomes focused on individual reactions to specific products, and the object of the search is to determine consumers' self-image as they relate to a particular product. In this way we attempt through marketing effort to offer for sale products which will present a product-image compatible with the self-image. (Staudt & Taylor, 1965, p. 101.)

The concept of self-image is so firmly embedded in current-day marketing philosophy that it has become a shibboleth. It often forms a cornerstone of marketing policy and practice. But what *evidence* do we have that consumers "match" themselves with products or services on an image basis? Not nearly enough. The insistence of the cry leads one to believe that this matching occurs in the case of nearly every product or service purchase, but this is highly questionable for several reasons.

One key point is that not all behavior is *expressive*. Instead, many items are bought mainly for instrumental reasons. Function and price rather than image are the primary factors influencing purchase decisions of this type. Anyone who is reading this book in his own home may confirm this by glancing around at the artifacts he has acquired from time to time. Some of them will be display items such as books and pictures which clearly reflect a congruence of self-image and product image. But what about light bulbs, radios, washing machines, screwdrivers, faucet washers, common kitchen utensils, and the hundreds of other items that one finds in almost every home? A study in Los Angeles in 1963 showed that 71 per cent of all households had a jar of peanut butter on hand. Television sets are owned by more than 95 per cent of U.S. households. Items this widely distributed begin to lose their power to express a self-image.

A second consideration is that both the self-image and the product image are created by the consumer himself, often after the fact of purchase. Rationalization and attempts to resolve cognitive dissonance may enter into this process. A consumer often buys an item almost at random and then proceeds to re-work his images to bring the self and the product into congruence. Thus, a cheap wrist watch, bought because a person cannot afford an Omega, may become a symbol of rugged masculinity ("I'm hard on watches"), down-to-earth common sense ("It keeps good time"), or even democratic friendliness ("Expensive watches are a sign of snobbery"). Evans had something of this sort in mind when he advised manufacturers to try to build ambiguity into their product images:

> In promoting a brand, it would appear safest to be somewhat ambiguous with regard to both personality and objective variables. People of all kinds are customers, and creation of too strong an image in certain personality terms may narrow one's market unnecessarily. If the image is ambiguous, there is a tendency for customers to read into it what they want and to attribute what they value highly to their own brand. (Evans, 1961a, p. 26.)

Also, consumers may express a particular role in a variety of ways. A mink coat for one's wife, a $300 suit, and a Cadillac might all serve equally well to communicate that one is a successful businessman. The actual item selected by the consumer will depend on a great many factors in addition to the simple congruence of self and product image. Salesmanship, availability, sensory impressions, and other considerations may govern the actual purchase.

Just as different products may serve the same symbolic function, the same product may have different meanings in different contexts. The head of a leading Eastern market research firm, for example, buys expensive British suits and shoes, which are ordinarily used to project an image of solid financial conservatism. In the case of this gentleman, however, his suits are always unpressed and his shoes unpolished. His rationale, he claims, is to communicate that he has money and taste, but is nevertheless a "regular guy" and too busy to be bothered.

Thus, products and services *may* become a means of expressing ourselves to others, but they by no means always do so. Knowledge of the various types of consumers (cf. Chapter 3) suggests that consumers would vary widely in the matter of matching self-image and product image. The weak and even inconclusive results of trying to distinguish among brand purchasers on the basis of personality characteristic (cf. Chapter 3) indicates that we need to know a good deal more about the matching process and the conditions under which it does and does not occur.

Social Roles and Retail Shopping

In his interesting book, *The Social Context of Economic Behavior,* Tucker uses salesmen in three different classes of furniture stores — lower class, middle class, and upper class — to illustrate role behavior in the personal selling situation. He suggests that salesmen in each of these stores play quite different roles according to the position that they find themselves in and the customers with whom they are dealing.

In the lower-class store the salesman is apt to be forceful and a bit brusque. He tends to be impatient with the customer, suggesting that he, the salesman, has superior information and taste and that the customer should therefore not argue. The salesman recognizes that his own status is limited by the store in which he works, and he may have a difficult time resisting small social triumphs in his interrelationships with customers. These triumphs are likely to hurt the possibility of the sale rather than help it.

The salesman in the middle-class store is much more likely to be friendly, to treat his customers as equals, and to defer to their opinions. Unlike the lower-class store salesman, he cannot appear to be an expert in styles and fashions since he often knows little more than the customers he is serving. His primary objective is to be liked — to find some common ground with the customer. He refrains from using pressure since the role he plays gives him neither the social position nor the expertise with which to exert influence.

The salesman in the high-fashion shop generally knows furniture construction, fabrics, and current fashion much better than do his customers. His talk is not friendly and personal; he discusses only furniture and decoration. He may play any one of several roles: instructor to the intelligent but uninformed customer, fashion arbiter to the uncertain customer, or peer of the customer who is a connoisseur.

Tucker distinguishes the behavior of each of the three roles as follows:

Lower-class salesman: "Look, I'm a busy man. Make up your mind and let's get it over with."

Middle-class salesman: "Look, I'm a nice guy, and I've tried hard. Won't one of the things I've shown you do at all?"

Upper-class salesman: "This is an absolutely perfect combination. If you don't buy it, I'll know that you either can't afford to purchase in this store, or are completely lacking in taste." (Tucker, 1964, p. 76.)

The present writers would suggest that even within the same class level, the same salesman might adopt different roles depending upon the characteristics of the customer involved. For example, very dominating and egocentric customers may have to be treated with deference, while the more timid may have to be either bullied and dominated or supported in a congenial fashion, depending upon the person. Sizing up the customer's psychological make-up and adopting the proper sales approach for each personality type requires more skill than most salesmen possess.

In cases of role conflict, buying behavior becomes rather complex. Fearing censure in one role, the individual may refrain from buying something which would be quite acceptable in another. In ordinary cases, some means must be found of overcoming the resistance which one role (e.g., solid citizen) can exert on behavior desired for another role (e.g., buying a motorcycle for recreation). Such conflicts often involve a dissonance effect, and the consumer must have a means of rationalizing the two views into congruence. This should be provided by the seller.

STATUS

The term *status* is used to convey the idea that different positions in a group or in a society have different values to the group or society. Positions which have a greater value or rank are said to have higher status. Thus, each social *role* occupied by an individual has a certain *status* associated with it. One writer explains: "Status and role are thus two sides of a single coin. Status is a socially identified position; role is the pattern of behavior expected of persons who occupy a particular status. . . . Social structure is the organized system of roles and statuses that define relations among groups and individuals." (Chinoy, 1961, pp. 29–35.)

Social Class

Every society has a number of status systems — political, economic, age, etc. Social class is the most pervasive of these status systems, and it has the greatest influence on the social environment and power of the individual.

Social class is based upon the idea that a society, or even a social group, constructs some ideal or optimum which is most highly regarded by members of the society. This ideal is not absolute but relative, and each society or portion thereof establishes its own perspectives based largely upon the value systems and beliefs of constituents. Now, the more closely individuals or groups conform with the ideal, the more they are respected and admired by others and the higher their position in the hierarchy of social levels. Higher social levels or strata are said to carry more status in society than lower strata; they are of a higher *social class*.

> Every known human society, certainly every known society of any size, is stratified. . . . The hierarchical evaluation of people in different social positions is apparently inherent in human social organization. Stratification arises with the most rudimentary division of labor and appears to be socially necessary in order to get people to fill different positions and perform adequately in them. (Berelson & Steiner, 1964, p. 460.)

The problem lies in defining the criteria used to establish and to differentiate the various strata in a given society. There is no universal criterion or even group of criteria used by all societies, and changes have occurred over the centuries in some of the standards used. For example, in the more primitive societies today (and even in the most advanced societies a few centuries ago), such war-connected attributes as physical strength and success in battle are more important determiners of social status than they are in the more developed societies.

The criteria discussed below are those which seem to be most widely used in the more highly developed nations and civilizations today.

One of the most common factors distinguishing the various strata is income and/or economic position. In most societies this is not only a measure of achievement or family background, but it also provides a degree of power and a way of life which most members of the society would relish.

Occupation is another frequent criterion. An interesting study showed a very high degree of agreement among the citizens of six modern nations in the prestige value of occupations of various types; that is, occupations which tended to be regarded highly in the United States were uniformly regarded as highly in Great Britain, Germany, New Zealand, the U.S.S.R., and even Japan. The same agreement was found for lower status occupations. (Inkeles & Rossi, 1956.)

Educational level is also a widely used criterion for social stratification, but this seems to be more important in some of the European countries than in the United States (although there is some indication that this situation has been changing in recent years).

Kinship and family ancestry are important in many societies, as they are in the United States, but they tend to be of somewhat less moment to us (except at the top of the class structure) than in some other nations. Ethnic and religious factors are often considered, but they tend to vary in importance from one country to another. Other factors include political power, public service (e.g., ministry, teaching), age, and athletic prowess.

It is easy to oversimplify the problem of understanding social stratification in a given society. We Americans tend to ascribe our own stratification system (as each of us individually sees it) to other nations and cultures, and this accounts for some of the problems that United States business firms have in trying to open new markets for their products in foreign countries. Part of the problem, of course, is that there is no single set of stratification criteria observed uniformly throughout even our own country. Social class is a multidimensional construct affected by subculture values. In some cities, family heritage or background is much more important than in others; racial and even religious features are of substantial consequence in some areas of the country; and in some of the newer "think-factory" communities, educational background and intellectual achievement are more important than in most other communities.

Even when the criteria are reasonably clear and the various strata seem to be internally cohesive and uniform, one writer wonders ". . . if the social aggregates delineated by the observer are merely statistical constructs (strata) or if they have associated properties of identification (class consciousness)." (Broom, 1962, p. 432). Great care is required to establish strata which are consistent and meaningful; otherwise, there is little value in the concept of stratification.

Determining Social Class

In spite of the difficulties, sociologists have made many attempts to devise systems to categorize social stratification in the United States or various portions of it. There are three basic methods generally used for determining or mapping social strata:

Reputational. People are asked to classify other individuals with whom they are familiar. This works best in small communities where "everyone knows everyone else." When a large number of individuals or families have been classified, respondents are asked on what basis they constructed their social categories and how they decided to which category an individual or family belonged. The assumption is that in every community some form of stratification exists and the best way to find out about it is to ask members of the community.

Subjective. Each member of a community is asked to classify *himself;* that is, "In what class or category do you belong?" Answers from a large number of individuals are then combined to produce a total picture of the stratification which exists.

Objective. The various strata are determined by observations of the social system from outside. Objective criteria for distinguishing among social classes might include income, occupation, educational level, and location of residence, for example.

Unfortunately, the three methods do not always produce the same results. Some investigators feel that the subjective and reputational approaches show social stratification the way the individuals involved see it and that they are therefore a more accurate reflection of reality or, at least, what those involved believe reality is. Others argue for the consistency of the objective approach. In summary, we must remember that not only do social stratification systems actually vary from one society or subsociety to another, but the same system may appear different from one method of determination to another.

One of the pioneering efforts in this area was a series of studies done by Warner and his associates in the early 1940's. Though this was not the first attempt to define a social hierarchy, it proved to be one of the most useful and is still widely quoted. Using a *reputational* approach, they mapped the social structures of several communities in the United States and established a number of social classes which they felt applied, with minor variations, throughout the country. The most often quoted structure was set forth in the so-called Yankee City study, as shown in Table 7.2. (Warner & Lunt, 1941.)

Later, Hollingshead established five major social classes and developed an *objective* method for classification. His Index of Social Position provides a means of classifying families on the basis of a weighted combination of three factors: residence (6), occupation (9), and income (5).[1] He proposes that a family's

---

[1] Numbers in parentheses are weights used to reflect the relative importance of these factors in the Hollingshead Index.

Table 7.2

SOCIAL CLASS HIERARCHY — WARNER

Class	Definition	Percentage
Upper-upper	Aristocracy, "old family," inherited wealth	1.4
Lower-upper	Similar to upper-upper in income, occupation, and costly homes, but newer, lacking distinguished ancestry	1.6
Upper-middle	Professionals and substantial businessmen, civic leaders but not "society"	10.2
Lower-middle	Small businessmen, white collar workers, smaller homes, "good common people"	28.1
Upper-lower	Semiskilled workers, lower incomes, less desirable homes, "poor but hardworking people"	32.6
Lower-lower	Semiskilled and unskilled, worst homes, often on relief, low incomes, "level below the common man"	25.2
Unclassified		0.9
	Total	100.0

mode of living is "mirrored in its home," that occupational level reflects its skill and social power, and that formal education reflects its tastes. His strata are described in Table 7.3. (Hollingshead & Redlich, 1958, p. 387.)

These classification systems are two of the more useful and well-known attempts at describing social stratification. They are more similar than they are different. It is important to remember that these systems were developed at different times (1941 and 1958 respectively), and covered different areas. We do not know which system, if either, is suitable for reflecting the social class structure which exists today in the United States. Both investigators recognize that subclasses exist within their strata, and both know the problems in trying to classify a body as large and diverse as American society into five or six groups. It is well to heed the advice: "The American system of stratifica-

Table 7.3

Social Class Hierarchy — Hollingshead

Class	Description	Percentage
I	"Old families," top business management and professional occupations, high incomes, highly educated, expensive homes, the social elite	3.4
II	Business managers (but not policy formulators), lesser professionals, (engineers, etc.), often college graduates, socially sensitive, "on the way up"	9.0
III	Employees in various salaried administrative pursuits, small business owners, average incomes, high school graduates, modest homes in "good" areas	21.4
IV	Semiskilled and skilled manual employees, below average incomes, many are homeowners but live in multiple units, many had some high school but did not graduate, often members of minority ethnic group (Italian, Irish, etc.)	48.5
V	Unskilled and semiskilled, low incomes, no savings, live in old tenement areas, most did not finish grade school, "live today, let tomorrow take care of itself."	17.7
	Total	100.0

tion is vague and loose with much blurring and overlapping of the strata. There are no sharp lines which separate classes but rather a merging of each class with those adjacent." (Broom & Selznick, 1963, p. 199.)

At least some tested methods exist to describe the social composition and structure of the consumer market, so the marketer does not have to rely on simple observation to characterize the various social strata and their relative magnitudes. Information about social classes may guide the marketer in developing products and services and in using advertisements which appeal to social consciousness in some way.

In general, neither the upper nor the lower-lower social classes are of great interest to most marketers. The upper classes, despite their wealth, include only two or three per cent of the population and are therefore generally insignificant (although they may be highly significant to a particular marketer.) The bottom 20 per cent of the population, although sizable in number, does not have enough money to be an important market for many manufacturers. (Many of these people are the object of the current War on Poverty.) The upper-middle class of business and professional men, the lower-middle class of white collar workers, and the upper-lower class of workingmen are the three classes most important to most marketers. (There are many exceptions, of course.)

One reason for examining American class structure is that the individuals who participate in important marketing decisions (i.e., marketing management) are members of the upper or upper-middle classes. As a result, it is easy for them to make serious errors by assuming that the rest of the population is similar to them in taste, outlook, and life style. For example, contrary to what might be thought, automobile executives during the 1950's did not force chrome trim on the public. The executives themselves considered chrome vulgar, and sales-minded junior executives had to persuade them to put chrome on new models. Occasionally, an executive refused to believe that the public liked chrome and insisted on models with less glitter. Predictably, sales dropped. (Chrome is much less popular today, of course.)

SOCIAL CLASS AND BUYING BEHAVIOR

Martineau was influential in recent years in focusing the attention of marketers upon the importance of social class in determining buying behavior. He pointed out:

Income has always been the marketer's handiest index to family consumption standards. But it is a far from accurate index. For instance, the bulk of the population in a metropolitan market today will fall in the middle income ranges. This will comprise not only the traditional white collar worker but the unionized craftsman and the semiskilled worker with their tremendous income gains of the past decade. Income-wise they may be in the same category. But their buying behavior, their tastes, their spending-saving aspirations can be poles apart. Social-class position and mobility-stability dimensions will reflect in much greater depth each individual's style of life. (Martineau, 1958, p. 130.)

Not only do the various social classes differ in the types of products and services which are purchased, but the people *within* a social class vary in their spending patterns. For example, the "savers" within a social class tend to accumulate money and to spend conservatively, while the more upwardly mobile members of the same social class tend to disregard savings and to spend in the conspicuous manner postulated by Veblen. (Veblen, 1899.) In contrast to Veblen, however, Martineau finds that these conspicuous spenders exist in *all social classes* and that they often spend as a means to effect the change from a lower social class to a higher one.

Under the direction of Pierre Martineau and W. Lloyd Warner, in the middle 1950's, the Chicago *Tribune* undertook an intensive study of some 4,000 households in the metropolitan Chicago area to determine if social classes did exist and, if so, if they differed materially in various aspects of behavior of interest to the marketer. Using an Index of Status Characteristics,[2] they classified families in five social classes very similar to the Warner classes previously described. The study did indeed show social-class differences in shopping and spending behavior. For example, people in the various classes differed markedly in the stores they patronized. Not all women wanted to shop in high-status stores; many tended, instead, to prefer stores whose "social status" was perceived as congruent with their own. They felt uncomfortable in higher-status stores and expected to be "punished" by sales ladies in such stores. Customer profiles even showed that different supermarkets within the same income areas tended to attract different types of customers. A & P was stronger with the mass market, while Jewel had more strength among the middle classes. (Martineau, 1959.)

Lower-status families also differ from others in their preferences for communications. For instance, they do not comprehend or care for the subtle humor or the art in magazines such as *The New Yorker* and *Esquire*. "Most of the really big local television success stories in Chicago have been achieved by personalities who radiate to the mass that this is where they belong. These self-made businessmen who do the announcing for their own shows communicate wonderfully well with the mass audi-

[2] Occupation weighted by 5, sources of income by 4, and housing by 3.

ence . . . [they] tell the lower-status individual that here is someone just like himself, who understands him." (Martineau, 1958, p. 128.)

Differences between classes are also found in the *mode* of saving and the *purpose* of saving. Lower-status families more often choose different modes of savings (savings account, ownership of real estate) from those preferred by upper-status families (stocks, insurance). The latter also save a *larger per cent* of their income.

The working-class male, more than his middle-class counterpart, pursues outdoor "masculine" activities such as hunting, fishing, and camping. Most camping vans, for instance, are bought by lower-class men (although camping is gradually becoming important in the middle class). The upper-lower class is the prime marketing target of manufacturers of guns and other hunting and fishing equipment. (Oddly, upper-class men participate in these sports more than middle-class men.) The working-class husband is, typically, less committed to family living. He will go on hunting trips, leaving his wife at home (although she may take the opportunity to visit her mother). Among middle-class families, it is extremely rare for husbands and wives to take separate vacations. Similarly, working-class husbands often have a "night out with the boys," but the middle-class husband who suggests that he would like a weekly night out may find his wife immediately suspicious of his strange behavior.

As we noted, income is a less important determinant of class than is occupation. As a result, people in the *same* social class often have widely different incomes, and people in *different* social classes often have similar incomes. Richard P. Coleman of Social Research, Inc. describes people who have higher incomes than the average for their class as *overprivileged* and people with incomes lower than the average for their class as *underprivileged*. An upper-middle-class family (headed, perhaps, by a college professor or a young lawyer) with less than $10,000 a year income would be underprivileged in Coleman's sense. An upper-lower-class family (headed by a long-distance truck driver or a welder) with an annual income above $7,000 would be overprivileged. A lower-middle-class family (headed by a car salesman) earning more than $10,000 would also be overprivileged. (R. P. Coleman, 1961.)

These concepts clarify some kinds of buying behavior. For instance, color television sets were at one time distributed fairly evenly (though thinly) among all social classes and all income groups. Neither class nor income by itself was sufficient to describe the buyers. Social Research, Inc. found, however, that color television sets were being bought primarily by over-privileged members of each social class. The overprivileged are also the prime buyers of middle-priced cars, while compacts and foreign economy cars are bought by the underprivileged. The young lawyer, as an underprivileged member of the upper-middle class, may buy a Volkswagen as an interim car until his income rises.

This discussion of social class should not obscure the fact that there are some products which are classless in their appeal. Coleman cites air conditioning in the Southwest as an example. The person who can afford an air conditioner installs it; income alone determines whether or not a family has air conditioning.

Coleman also warns against equating high social class with highbrow tastes. Most highbrows are upper-middle-class, but relatively few upper-middle-class people are highbrows.

> At times advertisers have made the mistake of assuming that the Upper-Middle Class should be appealed to in a highly sophisticated fashion — and though this is just fine if the product itself is likely to appeal primarily to the Manhattanized type of Upper-Middle, it is not correct if it is expected to sell to the kind of doctor in Dubuque who enjoys a visit to New York every now and then but would never want to live there. (R. P. Coleman, 1961, p. 183.)

Attempts have been made to generalize differences in sensory reactions among different social classes. One suggestion is that high-income people prefer weak stimuli and that lower-income people prefer stronger stimuli. One of the authors in a study of consumers' preferences for various leather-grain vinyl upholstery materials found that the lower-income people in the sample tended to prefer coarse grains (morocco, walrus), while the upper-income people preferred the smoother grains (crushed, skiver). (Incidentally, one of the swatches tested was real leather instead of vinyl, but the people interviewed were unable to identify it.)

Aesthetic tastes are learned, of course, and this may mean only that upper-income (and upper-class) people in the course of their education learn to notice and to appreciate smaller and smaller differences among aesthetic stimuli. Their thresholds, in effect, are lowered by training. Some training in music is required, for instance, for a person to be able to distinguish the differences in technique between a fair pianist and a virtuoso.

In another study, conducted by Lippincott and Margulies, Inc., sets of designs covering 15 product fields were shown to three groups of housewives, one upper-lower-class, the second lower-middle, and the third upper-middle. The designs had been rated previously by psychologists and sociologists as "expressive," "sentimentalized," or "controlled." It was found that design preferences varied with social class. Upper-middle-class housewives preferred controlled designs; lower-middle-class, sentimentalized; and upper-lower-class, expressive. Lippincott and Margulies recommended sentimentalized designs as most appropriate for the mass market. (Helfgott, 1960.) These findings appear to be in consonance with the kinds of stories which are published in upper- and lower-class women's magazines.

The degree to which the adoption of innovations is related to social class has been investigated, and the simple "trickle-down" hypothesis apparently does not hold. That is, innovations do *not* first gain acceptance by upper classes and then trickle down to lower classes by a process of emulation. Instead, "social classes will accept innovations to the extent that the innovational features and the cultural characteristics of the classes are compatible." For example, television was much more readily accepted by lower classes than by upper; the converse was true of the card game, canasta, as shown in Table 7.4. (Graham, 1956.) Upper classes differ from lower in that they prefer "active, creative, recreational activities, such as participation in sports, visiting, get-togethers, and serious reading." (Graham, 1956, p. 177.) Also, canasta was apparently transmitted by being taught to one person by another, and the social distance separating upper and lower classes made it difficult for the game to leap across the class barrier. Television, on the other hand, could be adopted simply by purchasing a set.

Table 7.4

PER CENT ACCEPTANCE OF TELEVISION AND CANASTA

	Social Class*					
	I	II	III	IV	V	VI
Had played canasta	72	72	44	20	32	12
Owned television set	24	44	48	52	84	72

* I is highest, VI lowest

SOCIAL MOBILITY

The United States is characterized by what sociologists call an *open-class system* of social mobility, that is, movement from one social stratum or class to another is relatively free. It is not only theoretically possible for a person in our country to move from class to class, but many people in fact do so during their lifetimes. For example, one study found that approximately one-third of the sons of manual workers in America had moved up occupationally into nonmanual positions. However, the statistics on this same movement in four other industrialized countries were comparable and in Switzerland the rate was 45 per cent.[3] (Lipset & Bendix, 1959.) Thus, while we are "upward mobile," we apparently are no more so than many other highly industrialized nations.

In a caste system, such as in India, movement between social castes is not possible (although there is evidence that this is changing in recent years in some of the larger, more industrialized cities). Even though interclass movement is possible in the United States, a son is still more likely to remain at his father's occupational level than to move to some other, and most top-management men today come from families whose head was either in business management or in one of the professional or semiprofessional occupational classifications. (Warner & Abegglen, 1955.)

Consumer products marketers have shown great preoccupation with the factor of social mobility during the years since the United States changed from a production economy to a consumption economy. Promotional efforts for a product or service have often done one or more of the following:

[3] The reverse is also true; many sons of nonmanual workers move downward into manual occupations.

- Alluded to the rewards which a higher social class has to offer.
- Identified the use of the product or service with higher social levels.
- Promised to help the individual actually move to a higher level through use of the product or service.

The implication is clear. Higher-status social classes are more rewarding in many ways, and the consumer would do well to "identify" with these, either by actually moving to a higher class or by adopting the trappings of higher classes and thus acquiring more status within one's own class. This, of course, appeals to a great many people — the more mobile elements of any social class.

One group of writers points out: "We have already seen that a modern industrial society does benefit tremendously from social mobility. Without it, in fact, modern industrial societies could not function. And there are many possible benefits which may accrue to the individual from upward mobility, quite aside from material gain." (Krech, Crutchfield, & Ballachey, 1962, p. 327.)

On the other hand, the same writers indicate that upward social mobility *per se* is not an unmixed blessing. Mobility of this type often produces severe psychological and social strains upon the individual. Lipset and Bendix declare, "To assume [that high mobility is a good thing] is to ignore the abundant evidence of the social and psychic cost of a high degree of social mobility; a cost that is probably high in terms of combativeness, frustration, restlessness, and other ills that are engendered. . . . In saying this, we do *not* imply that cost is *too* high, for we lack the proper standards for comparison." (Lipset and Bendix, 1959).

A very interesting survey suggests that many people realize the strains which mobility produces, to the extent that they simply do not aspire to movement out of their own social class. This study focused primarily upon the habits and *life style* of wives of blue-collar workers. At the time of the study, such workers were estimated to constitute nearly two-thirds of the nonfarm population of the United States. The study sample consisted of 420 working class housewives in four cities: Chicago, Louisville, Tacoma, and Trenton. In addition, 120 middle-class women, who were similarly occupied as mothers and wives, were interviewed to provide comparative data. This study provided so many insights into the patterns of behavior of blue-collar wives and the mental processes which underlie this behavior that it deserves considerable emphasis here. After all, we are talking about a large market segment for some types of products, and the importance of understanding how people in this segment think and live cannot be overestimated.

Extracting selectively throughout the book, we find that the workingman's wife:

- Feels that every day is pretty much the same — dullness; drudgery; restricted to home, children, husband. (In contrast, middle-class wives find more variety in their everyday lives.)
- Exhibits continual anxiety about being deprived of fundamentals — income, husband — and about fights in the neighborhood.
- Sees the world beyond her home as rather chaotic. If this world is to come to her, it must be on simple terms.
- Is not drawn to social groups, but wants to be with "people" — her family, relatives, close friends. She has a great fear of loneliness.
- Dislikes thinking. She prefers things she can believe in with certainty.
- Feels the lack of power to control or even relate effectively with the outside world. She becomes very passive and dependent upon husband, close family. (Middle-class wives are out and about more, have more confidence in their ability to meet people, join more social groups.)
- Has no involvement in her husband's work, but controls household finances.
- Has a phobic concern for her children. She feels that a happy, contented life for them is more important than mobility and accomplishment and indulges them lavishly within her means. (Middle-class wives tend to think in terms of "investing" in children, with college educations, wider experiences of all kinds.)

- Is not a clubwoman. Only 25 per cent belong to a club of any kind.
- Reads magazines such as *True Story* for escape. She finds magazines of this general type realistic, filled with warm human experiences. By focusing on others' problems, she tends to forget her own.
- Feels that her home is her castle, spends upon heavy appliances to save work (instrumental motive) but also to "anchor-down" her surroundings (security).
- Looks to authorities for advice in raising children, but not for advice on foods and cooking. She prefers plain foods, does not try new recipes.

The authors summarize the *five basic goals* which, in their view, activate the purchasing behavior of the workingman's wife:

- To achieve social, economic, and physical security.
- To reach the "common man" level of respectability and recognition.
- To gain the support and affection of people important to her (family, relatives).
- To escape from household burdens and chores.
- To decorate or "pretty-up" her world (with decorations for her home).

The picture which emerges is one of a wife who is not too interested in being fashionable, who is "plain and simple, modern, up-to-date (as *she* knows it)." She will spend money for a home in a nicer neighborhood, but this is primarily to avoid the potential violence and other undesirable features of her present neighborhood and to give her children a nicer place to grow up in. She has no great interest in spending large amounts of money for recreation or other matters of personal interest, no great interest in gourmet foods or high-fashion clothes. She is happiest when buying "brand name" merchandise, for this gives her a feeling of security. (Rainwater, Coleman, & Handel, 1959.) There are many additional findings which relate to her preferences in advertising and to the types of appeals which motivate her the most. And these will be discussed later.

The message is rather clear. Many blue-collar wives do not want to "move up." They have their own patterns of spending behavior which make them feel secure and acceptable to others who have the same value systems as they. Urging these people to change even some portion of their buying behavior amounts to asking for a drastic change in their way of life, their role in the world. Many are simply not interested. The marketer who wishes to reach such women will have to become more familiar with their life style, their habits, their preferences, so that he can appeal to them *on their own terms*. Failure to do this will meet with selective perception on the part of the consumer and the message will not even be noticed.

Culture

Chinoy defines *society* as: "that group within which men can live a total common life, rather than an organization limited to some specific purpose or purposes. From this point of view a society consists not only of individuals related to one another, but also of interconnected and overlapping groups." (Chinoy, 1961, p. 28.) American society thus consists of over 190,000,000 individuals linked together by a complex of 60,000,000 families, many city and farm communities, religious denominations, political parties, racial and ethnic groups, social and economic classes, and so on. Any society, then, may be considered in terms of its constituent groups and the relationships of one to another.

Chinoy defines *culture* as the aggregate of *patterns* or *norms* which regulate or prescribe behavior in a given society. Included in this definition are the following:[4]

Institutions. As it is now used by sociologists, this term refers not only to formal organizations (e.g., church, city government), but also to patterns of approved or sanctioned behavior. For example, marriage, higher education, the family, and child care are institutions in our society. Institutions encompass mores, laws, folkways, and customs.

[4] Patterned after Chapter 2 of Chinoy's book, *Society*.

Mores. These are institutions or standards of behavior which have strong moral sanction, for example, love of father and mother, patriotism, and refraining from killing or stealing. Many aspects of sexual behavior are governed by social mores.

Laws. Many mores are so important as to be codified in legal form. Laws are enacted by those who exercise political power and are enforced by some formal agency of government. They may or may not have the sanction of tradition behind them.

Folkways. These are more or less conventional practices which are accepted as appropriate, but are not insisted upon. Examples are wearing neckties on dress occasions, women wearing hats in church, and writing thank-you notes. Slacks and, later, bikini bathing suits for women represented, at the time of their adoption, changes in the folkways of American women. The cigar commercial, "Should a gentleman offer a lady a Tiparillo?" is a teaser aimed at one of our folkways.

Customs. These are standards of behavior which have gradually become accepted as appropriate modes of conduct. In our society, for example, the normal workday is from nine to five, while many other societies observe a two- or three-hour break for lunch and work later into the evening. Such customs as the observance of religious holidays and the etiquette of social behavior are in the nature of traditions in a given society. They are preserved by the pressures of group opinion. Turkey-farm owners, for instance, are hopeful that the traditional American Thanksgiving continues to be observed.

Admittedly, the lines of demarcation between some of these constructs are not clear and distinct, but the various terms do serve a useful function in distinguishing the *origins* of various regulatory norms and in pointing up the *methods by which they are enforced.* Some norms or institutions can be changed rather easily, while others require extensive effort. Difficulties experienced by business firms in trying to change buying behavior — and the amount of promotional effort required to do this — are a function of the type of social norm most closely associated with control over the buying behavior which is to be changed.

For example, a product designed for the good of all members of society but of no particular value to any one member (e.g., a smog-control device for automobiles) must be ushered in and maintained by law. Trying to get people to change their custom and eat fish instead of turkey on Thanksgiving Day would be almost equally difficult, but would not require legislation. (Stan Freberg gave an amusing twist to this particular custom in a radio commercial in which he urged people to serve Chun King chow mein for Thanksgiving. The commercial was delivered "straight" and at its conclusion another voice asked announcer Freberg, "Are you some kind of a nut?") On the other hand, institutions sometimes change. For example, the custom of many generations' standing that the bride buy and own her wedding gown is currently being challenged by small retail stores which offer such gowns on a rental basis. Folkways and customs are easier to change than mores and laws, but even the former require time and extensive promotional effort.

ETHNIC SUBCULTURES

The term *subculture* is often applied to the values and behavior patterns characteristic of subgroups in a society. The youth culture of teenagers is an instance. Properly, the term subculture should be applied only to the patterns of *subsocieties* which include both sexes, all ages, and institutions paralleling those of the overall society. *Group culture* is perhaps a suitable term for the cultural patterns of less inclusive groups which are not actually subsocieties. (Gordon, 1964.)

Four major factors play a part in defining subsocieties: region, rural or urban residence, ethnic group, and social class (although subculture membership may, in turn, define social class). Thus, for example, it is not sufficient to speak of "the Negro subculture." Instead, one must recognize that there are a variety of Negro subcultures depending upon region (North or South), rural-urban residence, and social class. A Northern, urban, college-educated Negro professional leads a far different life than the Southern rural Negro. Thus, the idea of a single Negro market is largely a fiction. (An ethnic group, incidentally, is any group of people distinguished by a sense of "peoplehood" and "common fate," whether because of race, religion, or national origin.)

It has been argued that the United States is characterized by *cultural assimilation* and *structural pluralism.* Cultural assimilation means that the major ethnic groups in our society tend to share a common culture, but structural pluralism means that each of these groups retains a sense of identity, that there is little intermarriage between ethnic groups, and that friendships and other social relationships tend to be intra-ethnic. For example, approximately 90 per cent of all marriages are between people of the same religious faith; people asked to name their best friends rarely name someone of a different faith; there are Catholic schools and Protestant, Jewish fraternities and Christian, Italian neighborhoods and Polish, and so forth.

Structurally, Gordon speaks of the "three melting pots," Protestant, Catholic, and Jewish. Sephardic, German, and Eastern European Jews are all part of the overall Jewish community and intermarry and interact socially. Similarly, Polish and Italian Catholics have a "sense of identity," and Protestants of whatever national background see little difference among themselves. Religion, rather than national origin, has become the most important source of *ethnic enclosure* (although some groups — Puerto Ricans and Mexican-Americans, for instance — are still "separate").

In spite of this structural separation, however, cultural assimilation of the behavior patterns of the Anglo-Saxon core group has tended to erase differences among the various ethnic groups in our society. Gordon has commented on the American Jewish community:

> With regard to the acculturation process, it is clear to any close observer of the American scene that in extrinsic culture traits, native-born Jews at various class levels are very similar to native-born non-Jews of the same social class. . . . Communal life and ethnic self-identification flourish within the borders of a group defined as one of the 'three major faiths' of America, while at the same time its members and, to a considerable extent, its institutions become increasingly indistinguishable, culturally, from the per-

sonnel and institutions of the American core society. (Gordon, 1964, p. 190.)

In the same way, while second-generation working-class Italian-Americans are ethnically enclosed, they are overwhelmingly acculturated to an American working-class way of life. Gordon concludes:

> . . . It is a matter of commonplace observation that the descendants of the Irish and other Northern European Catholic immigrants of the nineteenth century are indistinguishable in appearance and manner from the core group members of the same class, and the descendants of later arrivals from Southern and Eastern Europe are rapidly approaching this acculturation stage. (Gordon, 1964, p. 216.)

Nevertheless, there are some ethnic cultural differences that are worthy of notice. Glazer and Moynihan have examined the major ethnic groups in New York City. Jews, for example, for various historical reasons tend to be businessmen or free professionals rather than working-class or organization men. (Less than one-half of one per cent of executive personnel in leading corporations are Jews, although Jews constitute eight per cent of the college-educated population.) Jews are important consumers of "cultural" items. Glazer and Moynihan comment:

> Once again, statistics are not available; but it is clear that neither tourists, the working-class masses, nor the small Protestant elite could have filled or could fill today the audiences for chamber and contemporary music, modern dancing, and poetry reading, or the subscription lists for avant-garde magazines. As they have become wealthier, Jews have also become patrons and collectors. Many descendants of the older German-Jewish immigration have played important roles in New York's cultural life as patrons, collectors, and organizers.

> Their independence of the American tradition makes Jews a market for the new. They do not as often fill their homes with early American, but they are receptive to new painting, new household design, and new houses. In New York there are relatively few contemporary houses, but outside New York Jews have been

among the most important patrons of advanced architecture. (Glazer & Moynihan, 1963, pp. 173–74.)

Some empirical support for this observation was obtained in a study of innovators and early adopters of new products in metropolitan Detroit. Innovators were defined as people who bought a product before it reached a ten per cent level of saturation, and early adopters were defined as those who bought a product before it reached a 50 per cent level. Ownership of products with different levels of market saturation was studied. The products included in the study (and their levels of market saturation) were color television (0.6 per cent), stereo (9.3), dishwashers (5.2), air conditioning (6.1), hi-fi equipment (22.7), and clothes dryers (43.0). It was found that Jews and people of French descent were significantly more likely to be innovators and early adopters and to own at least one of the low-saturation products than people of British, German, or Italian descent. (Bell, 1963).

On the other hand, Jews have been slow to accept some new convenience food items. In a study of the New York market, as shown in Table 7.5, Jews ranked below Negroes, Italians, and Puerto Ricans in their usage of frozen red meat, cake mixes, and dehydrated soup. They ranked above Negroes but below Italians and Puerto Ricans in their usage of frozen dinners and frozen fruit pies. Instant coffee was the only one of six new products tested in which usage by Jews exceeded usage by the other ethnic groups. (Alexander, 1959.)

The Puerto Ricans in this study were the only group showing much enthusiasm for convenience foods. The other ethnic groups probably rejected the foods for different reasons. The

Table 7.5
RANK ORDER OF CONSUMPTION

	Negroes	Jews	Italians	Puerto Ricans
Frozen dinners	4	3	2	1
Frozen red meat	2	4	3	1
Frozen fruit pies	4	3	2	1
Instant coffee	4	1	3	2
Cake mixes	3	4	2	1
Dehydrated soups	3	4	2	1

low income of many Negroes, for instance, would tend to bar them from purchasing the foods, while the much higher income of Jews would permit them to buy fresh meat and baked goods. Italian-Americans tend to be traditional and conservative — Glazer and Moynihan call them "urban villagers" — and this may have caused their rejection of the foods.

The study, unfortunately, is not reported in sufficient detail for close analysis. It points up, however, two crucial elements of ethnic groups that are important to marketers. First, food habits tend to persist among immigrant groups long after other habits have been adapted to American core group patterns. "One of the chief reasons given by Italian men in New Haven for marrying within the ethnic group was the fact that Italian girls knew how to prepare Italian meals." (Woods, 1956, p. 219.) Second, differences among ethnic groups are far more important to retailers than they are to manufacturers. A retailer selling food products in an Italian neighborhood would have to be thoroughly familiar with Italian food preferences, but Italian food preferences would disappear in the statistical food preference profiles prepared by a national manufacturer.

It is obviously impossible to describe within the scope of this book the cultural patterns eixsting among the many ethnic groups in America. For what it is worth, on the basis of the study by Glazer and Moynihan, Italian-Americans appear to be strongly attached to neighborhoods and their families. Affluent Italians do not move to the suburbs; instead, they rebuild or renovate their homes in the old districts. (Italians tend to be home-owners, incidentally.) The family is seen as all-important, and success is prized because it makes the whole family stronger and more secure. Italian mothers, like Jewish mothers, overfeed and overprotect their children, and it has been suggested that this is one reason for the low incidence of alcoholism in both groups.

Irish-Americans, in contrast to Jews and Italians, have extremely high rates of alcoholism. The rates of admission to hospitals for alcohol psychoses per 100,000 people in 1947 in New York State were: Irish, 25.6, Italian, 4.8, Jewish, 0.5. Glazer and Moynihan suggest that this may be one reason that the Irish have tended to remain working-class.

Puerto Ricans, on the other hand, seem extremely business-minded and have opened many small businesses in the relatively short time they have been in New York. They are far less church-minded than the Irish, partly because of the scarcity of priests in Puerto Rico (one priest per 7,000 Catholics, compared with one per 750 in New York). They have large families, and possibly because of frequent trips back to the island, seem to be successfully maintaining a distinctive culture. They read books, magazines, and newspapers printed in Spanish and go to Latin American movies. There is a tradition of dignity and respect for the man of the house. (Somewhat the same is true of Mexican-Americans.)

The Negro Subculture. Social class is as central a concept in understanding the Negro American as it is in the case of the white American. The Negro upper class is a small group composed primarily of college-educated professionals and some businessmen. It is not a wealthy group (although it includes a few extremely wealthy individuals), and its life style is similar to that of the white upper-middle class. Much of the social life of the class is centered around traditional churches (Episcopal, Congregational) and college alumni groups. Many of the members of this class are active in the civil-rights movement.

The Negro middle class corresponds to the white lower-middle and upper-lower classes. It is composed of white-collar workers, small businessmen, and skilled and semiskilled workers. "Respectability" is the key value of the class. Its members are likely to be Baptists or Methodists and to belong to clubs and lodges.

The Negro lower class is one of the major elements in the lower-lower class of our general society. The recent headline-making so-called Moynihan Report,[5] "The Negro Family: The Case for National Action," prepared by the Office of Policy Planning and Research of the Department of Labor (1965), summarizes graphically the social structure and culture of this disadvantaged group. The Moynihan Report stresses the disastrous consequences of the Negro's low position as a result of

[5] Moynihan, co-author (with Glazer) of the previously cited *Beyond the Melting Pot*, was largely responsible for the preparation of this report.

discriminatory pressures over many years. "Keeping the Negro 'in his place' may be translated as keeping the Negro male in his place; the female was not a threat to anyone." Thus, the woman tends to be the principal wage-earner in poor Negro families and the father a drifting, unrespected, somewhat shadowy figure. Twenty-five per cent of Negro families — almost all lower-class — are headed by women, compared with eight per cent of white families. The absence of a male model, such as the dignified Puerto Rican father, contributes to delinquency on the part of male children and to the persistence of what most middle-class whites would describe as socially undesirable cultural patterns.

Gordon says, "The subculture of the Negro lower class testifies eloquently to the power of prejudice and discrimination to retard the acculturation process both in external behavior and internal values." (Gordon, 1964, p. 173.) Gordon cites, however, a study by Davis and Havighurst of child-rearing practices in white and Negro families. The investigators concluded, "There are considerable social class differences in child-rearing practices, and these differences are greater than the difference between Negroes and whites of the same social class." (Davis & Havighurst, 1946, p. 707.)

The Negro market has been studied intensively by market research firms specializing in Negro motivations (e.g., the Center for Research in Marketing in Peekskill, New York), by Negro media (e.g., radio station KGFJ, which calls itself "The Voice of the Negro in Southern California"), by social workers and others interested in Negro problems, by academicians; and so on. (A great deal of proprietary information on Negro attitudes is still locked up in corporate files.)

There are some surprising data about the Negro market in general. The average Negro man, for example, annually buys 2.3 pairs of shoes, compared with a figure of 1.3 for whites, and spends some 33 per cent more per pair than the white shoe buyer. Negro per capita consumption of Scotch whisky is approximately *three times* that of whites, and Negroes account for about 25 per cent of all the Scotch sold in the United States.

These data suggest, first, that since the Negro is prohibited by segregation practices from spending money on housing, expensive restaurants, resorts, and the like, he spends relatively more on consumption items such as shoes and Scotch; second, middle-class Negroes tend to be "strivers," a term coined by Bauer, Cunningham, and Wortzel, and are anxious to buy the "right" things or, more precisely, to avoid buying the "wrong" things. Negroes tend to be highly brand-conscious with respect to products with symbolic values and "the regular Negro drinker of Scotch, in contrast with his white 'opposite number' is more anxious about the possibility of making a mistake and serving an inferior brand." (Bauer, Cunningham, & Wortzel, 1965.)

Bullock has described the "self-rejection side of the Negro split self-image" and how this leads relatively well-off Negroes to overconform to what they see as "white" community norms:

> Furthermore, many upper- and middle-class Negroes have developed 'country-club ways' without a country club. They like to appear 'out of type' before their guests or when visitors come to town. Consequently, they attempt to surround themselves with visible symbols of whiteness. Those who feel they can afford the luxury try to maintain a country club at home. The play room has become a fad, and domestic bars for dispensing drinks have achieved the status of standard equipment. Lawns are fenced and hedged to accommodate outdoor snacks and entertainment, and almost every householder of these classes aspires to give his place a festive air. Thousands of Southern urban Negro consumers go into the furniture, appliance, food, and liquor markets in search of products capable of feeding their country-club aspirations. (Bullock, 1961, p. 96.)

This point is recognized by many marketers selling to the Negro community. Advertisements in *Jet, Ebony,* and other Negro magazines often show products in home entertainment settings involving hosts and guests.

The Negro market, incidentally, is relatively easily reached by mass media, contrary to what might be expected. About 60 per cent of Negro households listen to Negro-oriented radio stations, 85 per cent read some Negro newspapers, and the magazines published by the Johnson Publishing Company — the Negro equivalent of the Luce enterprises — have far greater penetration in the Negro community than similar magazines among whites. There are striking figures showing that advertisement of automobiles, gasoline, beer, cigarettes, canned milk, soft drinks, and refrigerators in Negro media pays off handsomely (the Gestalt "context" effect enters in here — cf. Chapter 1)

White retailers are only belatedly recognizing that Negroes, like other people, are sensitive to humiliation and react by taking their business elsewhere. "Salutations like 'Honey,' 'Child,' 'Mary,' or 'Sam,' have driven many potential Negro customers from fully stocked department store counters." (Bullock, 1961, p. 113.) Retailers would do well to remember that Negroes like to deal with salesmen with whom they have dealt before and who can be trusted to treat them with ordinary respect. It would be to further advantage to have floorwalkers and supervisors conspicuously present, ready to enforce store policies against racial discrimination.

There are some unpleasant peculiarities in the marketing system serving the lower-class Negro (and other lower-lowers) which should be mentioned. One is the "customer peddler," selling door to door, calling on his customers weekly to collect payments due and often making additional sales at the same time. (Caplovitz, 1964,) Many of the customers are aware that they are paying exorbitant prices for shoddy merchandise, but the alternative is the strange, impersonal, and possibly humiliating bureaucratic structure of the large downtown department store. Lower-class Negroes often have narrow shopping horizons.

Bait advertising, selling used merchandise as new, apparently easy credit at disguised high rates of interest, and other deviant marketing practices prevail in low-income Negro neighborhoods. Few low-income Negroes are familiar with institutions such as the Legal Aid Society, Small Claims Court, or Better Business Bureau. Stopping payment on faulty merchandise leads to garnishments and often to the loss of employment. Some low-income customers, when they learn that a purchase contract has been sold at a discount to a finance company, come to the mistaken conclusion that the merchant has gone out of business and that no more payments need be made. Some salesmen misrepresent themselves as government or housing-authority officials and insist that sink cabinets and other items have to be bought or the low-income tenant will be evicted or possibly brought to court.

Legitimate merchants have tended to steer clear of the high financial risks involved in dealing with low-income Negroes. Hopefully, as the position of the Negro in our society improves, more conventional marketing practices will replace those described.

FOREIGN CULTURES

Anthropology is the study of human beings as creatures in society. It fastens its attention upon those physical characteristics, industrial techniques, those conventions and values, which distinguish one community from all others that belong to a different tradition. The distinguishing mark of anthropology is that it includes for serious study other societies than our own . . . [The anthropologist] is interested in human behavior, not as it is shaped by one tradition, our own, but as it has been shaped by any tradition whatsoever. He is interested in the great gamut of custom that is found in various cultures, and his object is to understand the way in which these customs change and differentiate, the different forms through which they express themselves, and the manner in which the customs of any peoples function in the lives of the individuals who compose them. (Benedict, 1934, p. 17.)

Inkeles and Levinson[6] define *national character* as "relatively enduring personality characteristics and patterns that are modal among the adult members of the society." (Inkeles & Levinson, 1954, p. 983.) They cite over 200 studies of the cultures of various societies and describe the major approaches used. Freudian theory has been especially important in the development of the many analytic issues which have been investigated (e.g., relationships to authority, conceptions of self, handling of aggression, internal security systems).

For example, a common practice among some Russian cultures is the swaddling of children, apparently to keep them from damaging themselves. The adult traits of impassivity and controlled rage, noted among these cultural groups, have been attributed to

---

[6] Much of the material in this section is drawn from an overview of the literature by Inkeles and Levinson (1954).

this practice. Russians also seem to introject guilt and shame and accept group standards more readily than most Americans, which may explain the confessions and recantations in Russian political life that many of us find hard to understand. Another Freudian-oriented study found Germans to be preoccupied with order, status, and authority because of the stern male parental authority typical of the German family. The extended Chinese family has been alleged to produce adults with weak superegos and an absence of competitiveness (except outside the family).

In the United States,

> culture is, naturally, a major influence in economic decisions, since it not only forms the broad base of the value system, but also provides a misleading account of human nature. When someone makes an economic decision, he often bases it on his concept of human nature. And he often makes the mistake of thinking, 'this is what people are like,' rather than 'this is what people are like *now* in *this culture*.' (Tucker, 1964, p. 23.)

Tucker goes on to point out the effects of this in terms of the past tendency of large corporations to resist developing major innovations such as the automobile, frozen foods, and the motion picture because they "knew" it was against human nature to want these things.

Some of the contributions of anthropologists to understanding consumer buying behavior are cited by Winick:

> A manufacturer of central heating equipment was planning to introduce central heating to an area which previously had used other heating. Since people generally grow up to accept a certain approach to heating which they take for granted, introduction of the new central heating posed marketing problems in coping with deeply imbedded consumer resistance to what would be a major innovation. An anthropologist was able to draw on his knowledge of the folklore and symbolism of heat and fire in order to suggest methods of presenting the new system so as to make it as consonant as possible with the connotations of heat, even though the nature of the heating method had changed radically. There was considerable consumer resistance to the central heating, but it decreased substantially after the first year.

In addition to a marketing problem, the introduction of central heating also posed problems of public policy which the manufacturer had to overcome before he could obtain approval for the introduction of the heating equipment. The area was one which suffered from a declining birth rate, and officials were concerned about the extent to which central heating might cause the birth rate to decline further, because of their belief that heated bedrooms would cause a decline in sexual activity and ultimately in births.

The anthropologist was able to point to some cultures in which the birth rate had declined and some in which it had not done so after the introduction of central heating. The anthropologist's data made it possible for the manufacturer of the central-heating equipment to discuss its probable effects realistically with the appropriate officials. (Winick, 1961, p. 56)

Buying patterns and motives often differ among nations for reasons which do not depend upon differences in social institutions. For example, one familiar food product tends to be used primarily by *lower-income* families in the United States; since it is *unaffordable* by the lower-income families in one Latin American country, it is used there primarily by middle- and upper-income families; in another Latin American country it is used almost equally by people of all income levels. Even within the United States there are great regional differences in usage of this product, based partly on income and partly on historical factors.

One west coast distributor of frozen seafoods discovered to his surprise that his products were selling extremely well in Mexico without much in the way of promotional effort. By his own admission, his products were not noticeably superior to those of his competitors. After considerable thought, he could only conclude that the major factor was his package colors. red, white, and green, which are the colors of the Mexican flag. Along the same line, it is interesting to note how often the best-selling brand in a particular product category in the United States tends to have red and white colors in its label or package.

Color is one of the areas in which a manufacturer marketing to a foreign culture may make significant errors. Among Chinese, for example, red means good luck and pale blue is a funeral color. Blue is also a mourning color in Iran. "Green is the nationalist color of Egypt and Syria and is frowned on for use in packages. White is the color of mourning in Japan, and therefore, not likely to be popular on a product. Brown and gray are disapproved in most Latin American markets because of [their] association with death." (Winick, 1961, p. 59.)

Hall has described differences among United States and foreign cultures in terms of differences in attitudes toward time, space, things, friendships, and agreements.

Time. Ethiopians think that the importance of a decision is proportionate to the time required to make it. Americans in a hurry thus lower other people's opinion of their importance. Middle Easterners resent deadlines. Lateness for an appointment is interpreted as an insult by Americans but not by Mexicans.

Space. In the United States, business is discussed at a distance of five to eight feet. Latin Americans conduct conversations at much shorter distances, so short, in fact, that Americans edge away uncomfortably, embarrassing the person with whom they are dealing.

Things. Americans use offices and possessions as status symbols to impress customers and other businessmen. No Middle East businessmen would expect things of this sort to induce a banker to lend more money than he should.

Friendships. Friendly acts in the United States carry some implication of reciprocity. In India, they are presumed to be for the good of the soul and reciprocal acts of friendship will not necessarily be forthcoming.

Agreements. Americans emphasize contracts. Greeks tend to look upon the signing of a contract as the beginning of serious negotiations. (Hall, 1959.)

The president of a large United States market research firm, engaged in setting up a network of European research firms, once arranged to visit the president of a Spanish firm to discuss possible working relationships. He set aside a week for the discussions. Upon his arrival in Spain, he was met at the airport by his potential colleague and whisked away to a series of parties, dinners, and entertainments. His week in Spain was magnificent, and he enjoyed it thoroughly, but it was necessary for him to return again a month or so later to discuss business. "Getting acquainted" was the only purpose served by the first trip. Later, he commented that he was glad that he was head of his firm, for he would never have believed a junior executive who reported spending an extremely pleasurable week in Spain on an expense account without ever getting around to business!

Dichter has compiled masses of data on cultural differences that the businessman dealing with foreign cultures should take into account. He notes, for example:

- Only one Frenchman out of three brushes his teeth.
- Four out of five Germans change their shirts only once a week.
- French women are more interested in durability of clothing than in fashion.
- Many countries prefer nonlocal products, for example, Venezuelans like American cigarettes, and the French distrust French gasolines.
- Excessive care of the body (scented soaps and lotions) is looked upon as immoral in Catholic and Latin countries, and about 80 per cent of French women use laundry soap instead of toilet soap for personal care.

Dichter distinguishes six kinds of world consumer markets, including:

- The "classless, contented" countries, such as the Scandinavian, which are primarily interested in functional, reliable products.
- The "affluent" countries, such as Switzerland and West Germany, which are becoming increasingly similar to the United States.
- Countries in transition, such as Italy and South Africa, which are beginning to be industrialized but with low-income working classes.

The other three groups are the revolutionary or potentially revolutionary countries (e.g., Venezuela), the primitive countries (e.g., some of the new African nations), and the "new class" societies of Russia and her satellites. (Dichter, 1962, p. 122.)

This discussion of American ethnic subcultures, including the Negro subcultures, and foreign cultures was intended mainly to suggest the richness of the materials which are available. It should not be looked upon as a compendium of things known, but as an attempt to indicate the range of things not known. The marketer dealing with different or "strange" cultures should seek the advice of cultural anthropologists, knowledgeable local inhabitants, and any other well-informed persons he can find. He should not assume that if his marketing strategy works in Peoria, it will also work in Harlem or in Stockholm.

QUESTIONS
FOR REVIEW

1. Culturally unacceptable products sometimes can be made acceptable. Cigarette smoking among women, men's deodorants, and hair coloring for women are cases in point. What promotional strategies would you use to overcome cultural resistance to such products as cigars for women, motorbikes for middle-class adults, and wrinkle-remover cream for men?

2. Explain the relationship between social roles and social groups. Which is the more important concept to a consumer products manufacturer? Why?

3. To what extent might social roles influence the development of a marketing strategy for stationery items such as ball point pens, Magic Marker felt pens, desk sets, and so forth?

4. It has been alleged that successful salesmen can shift easily from one role to another in dealing with customers. Would this be true for all kinds of salesmen: retail, industrial, and door-to-door, for example?

5. What kinds of products and brands do you think are especially expressive of social class? How would an upwardly mobile consumer learn about these products and brands?

6. What mistakes might an upper-class marketing manager make in marketing products to lower-class consumers? To upper-class consumers?

7. Social roles are determined by a variety of factors. What are these factors, how do they interrelate, and how can a manufacturer determine which is most important for his purposes?

8

The Family

THE FAMILY IS ONE of those phenomena which are so familiar to us that they are difficult to discuss without seeming to belabor the obvious. Most of us are brought up in families and eventually head families of our own. We *live* in families. Yet there are certain features of American family structure which have important consequences for marketing and which are not at all obvious.

The most striking feature of our family structure is that the typical American is a member of *two families*, the family in which he is born and reared and the family which he later heads himself. (Parsons et al., 1955.) This kind of family structure is not found universally. In purely patrilineal-patrilocal societies, for example, the wife leaves her original family to join that of her husband, who remains a member of his original family instead of leaving home to start a new one. In matrilineal-matrilocal societies, it is the husband who joins the wife's family. In the United States, however, the husband and wife *both* typically leave their original families behind to form a separate conjugal nuclear family. Let us examine what this two-family structure means in terms of buying behavior.

First, the old folks are left alone. As a result they constitute a separate and identifiable market. Houses are built for senior citizens, and medical insurance plans are tailored to their needs. Older people without children constitute a kind of "detached" family in that they no longer perform such family functions as supporting and rearing children and participating in PTA and other community functions. Del Webb, with his Sun Cities, has faced this "detachment" frankly, and many older people have responded by moving into housing developments designed expressly for them. (Why, incidentally, does the Cartwright family in the television show, *Bonanza*, not seem strange to Americans? The program originally showed three grown-up sons, at least two of whom were in their thirties, still at home and still subject to the authority of their father. According to some observers, the show appeals nostalgically to those who miss the parental authority and support they put behind them when they married and left home.)

Second, marriage in our culture normally establishes a new household. The wife does not simply move in and the family make room for her. Instead, new housing is required, new furniture, new appliances, and so forth. An extended family living in one household can absorb new members without immediate major additions to its physical plant, but our two-family structure requires massive expenditures for new "artifacts" whenever a marriage occurs. Consequently, household formation rates are closely watched by marketers; they are a key to the growth of the economy. Considerable data, including much of the information compiled by the United States Bureau of the Census, are reported in terms of "households."

Third, the two-family structure means that household size is severely limited. The typical family consists of a husband and wife and two or three children. Modern dinette sets seat four to six people, and many other products are similarly geared to a small conjugal family. Over 90 per cent of American cars seat between four and six persons; refrigerators are about eleven cubic feet in size; home washers handle about nine pounds of laundry; and milk is sold in quarts and half-gallon containers. Anyone launching a new product should certainly take family size into account. A question which is asked fairly frequently is why Ford Motor Company dropped the original two-passenger Thunderbird, a car which is still greatly admired. The reason is that its limited passenger capacity made it impractical for most families and kept its sales from rising above 20,000 units a year. The four-passenger Thunderbird which replaced it sells over 100,000 units a year.

Fourth, as new families are formed, the authority of the elders is rejected — and rejected is not too strong a word. When a young man marries, he is "on his own" and feels that it would be a violation of his new-found status for him to seek advice from those to whom he was formerly subject. Many older people, reacting to this, are hesitant to offer advice and counsel (although others react the opposite and offer far too much!)

In the case of women, this situation is reflected in some recent evidence that a rather large percentage of young housewives use different styles and brands than their mothers used. A Gallup survey stated that a young woman undergoes a major transition when she becomes eighteen years old and reaches adult status. "When these women were asked, for example, in what style or period they would furnish their living room, 61 per cent indicated a choice different from that of their mother." (Los Angeles *Times*, 1964.)

Independent young couples must rely less on their elders and more on their own resources, their friends, and the mass media than would be the case in a different kind of society. Other structures and institutions must take the place of grandparents and other relatives. As a result, husbands and wives consult *each other* about major purchases instead of soliciting opinions from their parents. (This is especially true of mobile middle-class families.) The typical husband does not behave as an independent horsetrader when he buys a car, but talks to his wife about the purchase. Similarly, the wife does not look upon the purchase of a new washer as a purely feminine prerogative, but instead consults her husband. This consultation process extends to home furnishing, clothing, and entertainment. The isolation of the nuclear family from relatives means, also, that young couples must use opinion leaders — people in the neighborhood — as sources of information about new products and projected purchases. (The opinion-leader phenomenon will be discussed in detail in Chapter 9.)

Fifth, the new family lacks an established status. Because of American mobility, it cannot be pegged immediately as a branch of the Tarletons, the Taliaferros, or some other larger and older family of recognized status. Each new family must establish its own status among strangers. The situation is somewhat analogous to that of the American frontier in that kinship and "connections" have only limited relevance to the status system. This is one reason for the emphasis in American life upon status symbols to impress acquaintances and accidental neighbors. In our society, each family stands alone, and people have to deploy material objects — houses, cars, clothing, and so forth — to demonstrate their values, roles, status, and personality. (To return to *Bonanza*, suppose that Hoss married an heiress and moved to Chicago; what steps could he take to establish the fact that he was a person of worth, a Cartwright of the Ponderosa? His principal recourse would be conspicuous consumption and the display of status symbols.)

Sixth, the change in status when a youth marries and becomes a household head is much greater than the change which occurs in other types of family structure when a son simply brings a new wife home to his established family. Developmentally, it has more meaning. The period of transition from childhood (in the original family) to adulthood (in the marital family) has consequently been recognized institutionally. It has been given a name, the youth culture or youth society, and we take for granted that young people necessarily undergo a time of breaking away in which they are neither children nor adults. The youth market is discussed more fully below. It is enough to note here that this market exists because of the two-family structure of our society.

This discussion has been intended mainly to show that we tend to overlook the importance of family structure as an influence in the way we behave as people and as consumers.

Role Differentiation Within the Family

All human groups, the family not excluded, have needs and values which may be classified as instrumental and expressive. *Expressive values* are those valuable in themselves, for example, love, personal dignity, religion, and art. *Instrumental values* are mainly economic; they are means rather than ends. Expressive values may be "higher" in the sense that they are further along the means-end chain, but instrumental values take priority since they are a necessary precondition of the attainment of expressive values. Both sets of needs have to be attended to; they are equally important in that a group could not survive if either were neglected.

Bales and others have observed that small groups in laboratory settings tend to produce leaders who specialize in either instrumental or expressive functions — *task leaders* and *social leaders*, respectively. The task leader directs himself to the "real" problems confronting the group and the social leader to the maintenance of intragroup cohesion. The task leader gives and asks for advice and information; the social leader reduces tensions and gives emotional support to group members. (Bales, 1954.) In families, the instrumental role is usually played by the father and the expressive role by the mother. (The mother often plays both roles in lower-class Negro families.)

This difference in family roles is reflected in buying behavior. The father tends to take the lead in buying decisions when the product is primarily instrumental, and the mother when the product has important expressive values. This distinction tends to hold even when the major user of the product will be the other person. For example, sport shirts, ties, and cuff links are expressive items which are often bought *by* women *for* men. In many families, in fact, the wife buys almost all her husband's clothing. By the same token, most wives seek their husband's advice before buying a new washer or other major household appliance. The husband is not expected to comment on the appearance of the item, since that is a feminine prerogative; his contribution is with respect to such functional matters as soundness of constructon, thickness of steel, size of motor, noise, and service requirements.

Furniture salesmen know that the purchase of an important piece of furniture is a *family* decision and that each spouse has a part to play in the process. A man or a woman walking into a furniture store alone is not nearly as good a prospect as a husband and wife together, and the aggressive salesmen will pass up a single person to latch onto a husband-wife team. The expressive-instrumental differentiation of roles is apparent in this situation, also. The wife will look at the upholstery and finish of a chair, while her husband turns it over to look at its springs and joints.

Families, as well as other organizations and groups, must develop *decision rules* to avoid conflict over goals. The expressive-instrumental dichotomy is an implicit rule which gives the husband or wife a way to resolve conflict in situations in which they happen to disagree. In expressive matters, the husband will defer to the wife; in instrumental matters, she will defer to him. Each knows the items that may be bought without consultation and those which require consultation. Conflict is thus minimized and, when it does occur, is resolved by reference to a simple rule.

Families have other decision rules which work in the same way. In the purchase of a new car, for example, the decision on the make to be bought is usually made jointly without conflict. Often the family simply buys another car of the make previously owned. If the husband and wife disagree, however, a kind of "decision tree" comes into play, as illustrated in Figure 8.1. If the husband and wife want to buy different makes, the ultimate purchase decision may depend on whether the two makes fall into the same or different price classes. In the first case, with both makes approximately the same price, the husband usually makes the decision on instrumental grounds. In the second case, the spouse favoring the *lowest priced make* tends to win in the family decision process. (Brown, 1961.) In either case, once the decision is made, the husband then decides on such matters as engine and transmission options while the wife decides on color, trim, and upholstery.

In this connection, one proprietary research study indicated that women's preferences with respect to cars are swayed more than men's by interior appointments and color. A factorial experimental design was used in which men and women were asked

Figure 8.1

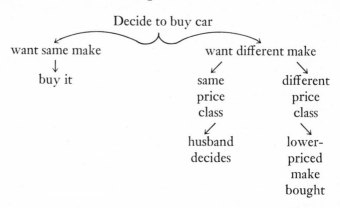

to evaluate a pair of different cars with different trims. The trims were then interchanged and preferences recorded again. As diagrammed in Figure 8.2, the preferences of the men remained stable with respect to the cars tested, regardless of trim; but the preferences of the women showed a tendency to follow the change in trims.

Figure 8.2

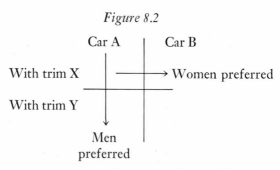

Family role differentiation is also seen in the tendency of husbands in our society to be concerned primarily with matters *external* to the family and wives with matters *internal*. This distinction tends to hold less and less as time goes by and women become increasingly active in the world outside their families. Many wives work nowadays, for instance, and many participate more than their husbands in community and civic affairs. There are also class differences, as pointed out earlier. But the distinction still holds generally. It is the man who typically leaves the family to go to work in the morning, while the wife stays at home. It is the man who generally takes the lead in dealing with the major external institutions of the society. (Parsons et. al., 1955.)

The external-internal division of roles is an overlay on the instrumental-expressive split, as depicted in Figure 8.3.

Figure 8.3

	External	Internal
Expressive	?	Wife
Instrumental	Husband	?

Internal-instrumental matters and external-expressive matters, since they are areas in which husband-wife roles overlap, are likely to be handled jointly. For example, husbands and wives share an interest in home repairs (an instrumental-internal matter) and make joint decisions about amusements outside the home (expressive-external).

In fact, there are not many purchase decisions which are made solely by a husband or by a wife or in which one or the other is clearly the deciding party. The concept of colleague spouses, with each spouse having a definitely marked area of authority, does not adequately describe the actual situation. Husbands and wives tend to *share* tasks rather than to *divide* them. Husbands, as noted, have more influence in deciding on the make of car to be bought, and they have more influence in life-insurance purchases. Wives, on the other hand, have more influence in how much money to spend for food, and they play a bigger role in the purchase of household durables and furnishings. (Sharp & Mott, 1956; Wolgast, 1958.) Nevertheless, in most families, most major purchase decisions are made jointly by the husband and wife.

Moreover, there seems to be a steady trend toward *more*

joint decision making. Kenkel has noted that there seems to be a general movement in husband-wife relationships toward more sharing of authority, less division of labor, and more companionship. (Kenkel, 1961.) Younger middle-class couples, especially, seem to show a high rate of joint involvement. (Kemarovsky, 1961.)

This suggests that a tension in family structure, noted by Parsons in 1949, may be on its way toward becoming resolved. Parsons contrasted the subservient traditional domestic wife, devoted to her home and children, with the career wife, who works outside the home and whose role is not clearly differentiated from her husband's. He suggested two other possible roles, a glamour-girl pattern in which courtship behavior is carried over into marriage and a companion role in which the wife participates in community affairs, manages her home, and takes an active and equal part in family decision-making. (Parsons, 1949.) The companion role seems to be winning out, and marketers seem to be aiming their appeals more at this type of wife than to the domestic, career, or glamour-girl type. Family situation comedies and family drama shows on television, for example, typically show the wife as a companion in Parsons' sense.

The role of *children* in purchasing decisions varies widely among families, from the one extreme where children have almost no say, to the intermediate position where they influence food, clothing, and entertainment purchases (which they participate directly in using), to the other extreme where purchases of such major durable goods as automobiles, color television sets, and even homes are influenced to at least some degree by the insistent demands of children in highly permissive families. (Children, sometimes facetiously described as "small household pets that turn economic goods into junk," are often the marketer's best friend.)

In many cases, manufacturers have long exploited the influence of youngsters (breakfast cereals, soft drinks and confectionery, toys and other recreational items). In other cases, where a connection between children and the purchase decision seems remote, almost no promotional efforts are made to appeal to these small "influencers." Yet there are many purchasing situations where alternative products are so similar in quality, features, and use characteristics that the choice among them is based upon the flimsiest of preferences. In such cases, children may exert a powerful influence.

For example, the selection of an airline for a trip between any two major cities in the United States cannot be based to any great extent upon time schedules, safety records, or other "rational" factors. Competing lines are similar in these aspects. In the case of family recreational trips, then, it would matter little to parents which line were selected, and children's voices would tend to be heeded to at least some extent. Their influence upon such purchases as color television (*when* as well as *what* to buy), vacation trips (destination and accomodations), and even some household furnishings might also be considerable. The influence of children on purchasing decisions has not been adequately examined to date.

THE FAMILY LIFE CYCLE

The term *life cycle* refers to the series of changes in the family status of the individual as he grows older. The marriage of a single man causes him to become a husband; the birth of his first child makes him a father; when the children grow up and leave home, his status changes again.

These changes in status are related to age, but there are many kinds of consumer behavior for which *stage* in the family life cycle is a better predictor than age. For example, of two young men of the same age, one married and one single, the single man is much more likely to be interested in hot rods and high-performance automobiles. One proprietary study of attitudes toward a dressed-up engine with chromed valve covers showed a marked difference in the "likelihood of buying" of men under and over 25 years of age. Men 26 to 30, however, were much like men 31 to 40, 41 to 50, and even older. The break at the age of 25 and the subsequent leveling off were attributable to the fact that most of the single men in the sample were in the under-25 age group. Single men *over* 25 were as interested in the engine as younger single men, and married men under 25 were as disinterested as their elders. The fact of marriage, in effect, had forced the married men in the sample to put such glittering things as chromed valve covers behind them.

The Survey Research Center at the University of Michigan has studied intensively the influence of life cycle upon buying behavior. The Center classifies the life cycle into seven stages: young single, young married with no children, young married with children under six, young married with children over six, older married with children, older married without children, and older single. (About ten per cent of the spending units in the country do not fit this classification scheme, e.g., divorced people with children.)

The conjugal family of parents and their children is firmly engrained in our minds as the typical mode of living for human beings, at least for human beings in our society. Life cycle analysis shows, however, that *over half the adults* in this country are not couples with children. About 52 per cent of the spending units in the United States are single adults, married couples without children, or other *"nonfamily" households*, as shown in Table 8.1 (Lansing and Kish, 1957.)

Table 8.1

STAGES IN THE LIFE CYCLE

Per Cent of Spending Units in U.S.

	Family Households	Non-family Households	
Young single		10%	
Young married, no children		7	
Young married, children under six	23		
Young married, children over six	9		
Older married, with children	10		
Older married, no children		18	
Older single		13	
Others		4	
Not ascertained	6		
All stages	48%	52%	100%

The nonfamily spending unit is especially interesting to firms in the transportation business. Mass transit systems, for example, do better than average business on lines operating in areas in which there is a relatively small number of children. Airlines have found that the nonfamily household accounts for a proportionately greater share of nonbusiness travel. The implications for the housing market are also important.

As we have noted, many consumer durable goods are designed for the needs of the "typical family." But it is possible that products and advertising appeals aimed at the nonfamily household would pay off handsomely. The Volkswagen, for example, has some obvious deficiencies as a family car, and, in fact, the main reason that people trade in their Volkswagens is that they need a bigger car, usually because of children. However, the Volkswagen admirably fits the needs of the nonfamily household, and this is probably one of the reasons for its success. (The advertising of the Volkswagen bus is, of course, aimed directly at the family with children.)

The percentage of households with working wives is much more closely related to stage in the life cycle than to age. The wife works in 57 per cent of the spending units composed of young couples without children, but is only 21 per cent of the spending units with children under six. The percentage of working wives then rises to 40 per cent in spending units with children over six. The low number of working wives in households with preschool children is obscured if age alone is used as the independent variable, ignoring the life cycle concept, the percentage of working wives is about the same — 25 per cent — in spending units in which the head of the household is 25 to 34, 35 to 44, or 45 to 54 years of age. (Lansing and Kish, 1957.)

Young couples with young children are thus under a double financial burden. The wife stops bringing in an income exactly at the same time that they face increased expenditures because of children. Their debts rise steeply, and they defer such major expenditures as the purchase of a new car. Their entire structure of purchase objectives tends to shift toward the more rational, economic, instrumental, security-oriented motivations.

The twin concepts of *stage of the life cycle* and *social class,* both from the sociologist's inventory, offer improved methods of survey analysis that are being overlooked by most market researchers today. Present practice calls for cross-breaking survey results by such demographic variables as age, income, and family size *separately*. In contrast, the stage and class concepts call for the *combination* of subsets of these variables to produce more meaningful behavioral concepts that have been found to explain certain types of purchasing much better than single variables. The necessary information has often already been gathered in many surveys and could be used rather easily.

For example, an index of social class could be constructed on the basis of income, education, and occupation (cf. Chapter 7). A stage of the life cycle index could be constructed in terms of age, marital status, number and ages of children, and similar variables. At the very least, future surveys should gather the necessary information from respondents so that meaningful indices of this type can be constructed and used for analysis of survey results. They could even be used as a basis for interviewer quotas, in samples of this type.

This is only one example to show that marketers do not always make the fullest use of meaningful behavioral concepts.

THE YOUTH CULTURE

The youth culture has been defined as the period of transition between the family in which a person is born and the family which he establishes when he marries and has children of his own. The transition, in effect, is from childhood to full adulthood. Three stages have been distinguished in this developmental process:

1. *The clique.* Boys socialize with boys and girls with girls, with little intermingling of the sexes.
2. *The crowd.* Boys and girls make up a bisexual group, but there is little pairing off of couples.
3. *Competitive dating.* Boys and girls pair off and break away from the crowd.

It is difficult to assign definite ages to these stages, but the clique tends to phase into the crowd at about the age of fourteen and the crowd to break up at about sixteen. (Smith, 1962.)

The marketer trying to reach youth should consider carefully to which of these three stages he should direct his appeals. For example, the "lively ones" advertising campaign sponsored by Ford Motor Company in the early 1960's showed groups of teenagers at beach parties, building bonfires, playing volleyball, and engaging almost exclusively in crowd activities. The campaign was notably ineffective among young people who had put the crowd behind them and moved into the dating stage. A survey of university students showed that graduate students, while they disliked the campaign personally, thought that it might appeal to college seniors; seniors thought it might appeal to freshmen; and freshmen thought it might appeal to high school students. Overall, however, the campaign was looked upon as juvenile and actually evoked negative attitudes toward Ford. Ford, learning from this experience, has used only couples — *not* crowds — in its Mustang advertising.

Youth is a period of movement toward greater independence and autonomy, and age is therefore an important source of status in the youth culture. Older young people look down upon those younger than themselves, and younger age groups look forward to acquiring age and status. The "greasy kid stuff" campaign by Vitalis took cognizance of this drive toward maturation by urging young males of dating age to use products appropriate to their age status and by attempting to attach the opprobrium of childishness to competing products. Many marketers, however, make the mistake of urging youth to use their products as a sign that they are still young. The "Pepsi generation" campaign is an example, although the appeal here may be to adults who want to "think young." Young people respond better to products (e.g., cigarettes) which they may use as a sign that they are growing up. (The recent use of people in their twenties in cigarette advertising to discourage smoking among teenagers may backfire and be effective in *encouraging* teenage smoking.)

The drive of young people toward independence and autonomy necessarily involves some conflict with parental authority. Teenagers, experimenting with their new-found freedom, tend to engage in forms of behavior which they suspect their parents would find reprehensible. This gives rise to what Smith has called the *teenage conspiracy*, the solid front that teenagers present to adults. Young people display a compulsive conformity to teenage fads and customs to demonstrate that they are full-fledged members of the youth conspiracy and not "spies" from the adult culture. This is one reason for the importance of fads in the teenage market. They are badges of membership.

Another reason for the rapid spread of fads among youth is that young people have a high rate of social interaction. Grade school students socialize more than high school students, high school students more than college students, and all members of the youth culture — including school drop-outs — a great deal more than adults. The increasing demands of study, work, and family responsibilities account for this decline. Youth, because of this interaction, are "wired in" with their contemporaries and fads can spread more easily among youth than among adults isolated in their families.

Rural youth are less integrated in the youth culture than urban youth, and their attitudes are more similar to those of their parents. They ride the bus to school in the morning and back home at night and lack the opportunity to hang around the candy store or drive-in snack shop. They participate less in the ongoing youth interaction process. (Bealer and Willits, 1961.)

Sex typing (teaching boys masculine behavior and girls feminine behavior) begins early in our society and, not surprisingly, there are many differences of marketing significance between teenage boys and girls. Popular music, for example, means a great deal more to adolescent girls than boys. Free record offers used as a sales promotion device are apt to elicit a lackadaisical response from boys and thus should not be used by marketers of male products (e.g., hair oil or shaving cream). Cars have about the same importance for teenage boys as records do for young girls. (J. S. Coleman, 1961.)

Girls tend to have a romantic attitude toward sex and boys a more exploitive attitude. This difference is reflected in the names of two hair creams marketed mainly to young males, Score and Command. "Score" is actually a slang expression among adults for making a sexual conquest. However, the communications problem enters in here. Adults use the term "make out" for a sexual conquest, but this term means something quite different to teenagers. Teenagers use it to mean "succeed" or "get by." Making-out almost means simple survival. The marketer must be sure that he understands the *current* teenage lingo (which changes rapidly), or he will surely fail to communicate with this important market segment.

Peer groups have probably been overemphasized in the analysis of the youth culture. Young people tend to absorb their values and attitudes less from their age-group peers than from slightly older age groups. Smith has commented on the influence of college students on the attitudes of younger middle-class youth. (Smith, 1962.) The age-status system of the youth culture and the emulation of older youth by younger is fairly well documented.

This would account, of course, for the similarity in peer group attitudes toward saving and consumption reported by Cateora. Instead of developing a closed-loop, other-directed, peer-group oriented society, each succeeding wave of youth strives to duplicate the behavior and attitudes of older age-groups. (Cateora, 1963.) This is part of growing-up. The implication for marketers is that their primary efforts should be directed toward young people who are at the peak of the youth culture, that is, those who have achieved autonomy and independence but have not yet relinquished (by getting married) their high status among youth for a low status among adults.

Typifying the importance of age-grading and sex-typing among youth is a description of the rationale purportedly followed by American International Pictures in producing the "beach party" movies starring Frankie Avalon and Annette Funicello:

- A younger child will watch anything an older one will watch.
- An older child will not watch anything a younger child will watch.
- A girl will watch anything a boy will watch.
- A boy will not watch anything a girl will watch.
- In order to catch your greatest audience, you zero in on a 19-year-old male. (Levy, 1965.)

Playboy magazine is similarly aimed at the top of the youth culture.

The importance of age-grading as a source of status in the youth culture means that adult sources of status have less significance and may actually be looked upon as phony. J. D. Salinger's novel, *Catcher in the Rye*, depicts the contempt of youth for adult status concerns, and Salinger's position is supported by sociological evidence. One writer notes that display of adult status symbols (e.g., fancy cars) or attempts to exploit family status (e.g., "my father, the doctor") are condemned as ostentatious by most teenagers. (Smith, 1962.) Another investigator has presented convincing empirical data indicating that the attitudes of youth are less influenced by social class than by other youth. (Cateora, 1963.) (The class system closes in, of course, when the young person joins the adult community and his high school athletic prowess or guitar playing becomes irrelevant to his standing.)

Attempts to use status drives to motivate youth are thus fraught with peril. The marketer must be sure that his status appeals have meaning within the youth culture and are not looked upon as an attempt to impose adult values.

The college years, in particular, constitute an important transitional period for young men and women. Many are almost completely freed, for the first time, from the confines of the family home and from parental authority. The making of an adult begins. The student has considerably more autonomy in the selection of the brands, styles, and even products which he purchases. Surveys show that the brands and styles adopted in college tend to persist rather well through at least the early years of marriage. For this reason, manufacturers are giving more and more thought to direct means of reaching the college market. *Time* magazine, for example, publishes special "college demographic" issues with special advertisements for student subscribers.

Another reason that college students are important to marketers is that they tend to be *style leaders*, even for their elders, in the case of some products. They are often the first to try new products and to innovate trends for the country. As experimental consumers, collegians were among the first to use filter cigarettes, beer in cans, and electric shavers (now owned by 63 per cent of college males). Conversely, their rejection of the extreme continental style in men's suits was a foreboding of the dismal future for this style among adults. It has been suggested, also, that college students are important vectors in the *transmission* of fads; they carry the new things they learn on campus back to their home communities. (Smith, 1962.)

It may be that the youth market receives more attention from marketers than it ought to. Teenagers have little disposable income ($11 billion out of over $500 billion total disposable income in the United States in 1965). Moreover, brand preferences formed before approximately 18 years of age are notoriously unstable. (Gilbert, 1963.) The attention given to the youth market may reflect the general American preoccupation with youth. Appeals ostensibly directed at the youth market may be looked upon as appeals to the adult market based upon this preoccupation.

On the other hand, the purchasing power of teenagers is magnified by their influence on purchases made for the entire family, where the final decision is often made by adults. Table 8.2 shows the results of a survey in Sacramento, California, covering 300 teenagers. (Samli, 1965)

Table 8.2

EXTENT TO WHICH TEENAGERS MAKE BUYING DECISIONS
FOR DIFFERENT ITEMS

Item	Do Not Have or Use	Teens Have All the Say	Teens Have Most of Say	Teens Have Some of Say	Others Have All the Say	Don't Know
Entertainment	1.8	23.4	30.1	38.5	1.6	4.6
Sports Equipment	16.6	31.4	19.3	19.3	3.0	10.8
Radio	2.9	29.0	24.6	32.2	6.0	5.3
Records	8.1	53.8	18.5	14.2	2.4	3.0
Fountain Pens	4.2	65.8	11.5	9.5	1.0	8.1
Watches	8.7	30.6	20.6	25.2	7.5	7.3
Vacations	4.8	10.3	12.0	49.6	18.0	5.3
Toothpaste	2.6	8.2	12.5	30.1	32.0	14.6
Jewelry	10.0	49.4	17.2	11.6	5.0	6.8
Shoes	.6	68.7	22.1	7.2	1.0	.4
Coats	.6	58.8	28.8	10.0	1.0	.8
Suits	4.2	51.6	26.8	11.1	3.6	2.6
Furniture for the Home	4.7	1.8	2.9	46.8	35.8	7.9
A New Family Automobile	4.4	1.8	4.0	48.4	34.0	7.4

The only justifiable conclusion is that the full extent of teen-ager influence on purchasing decisions has yet to be determined.

Older People

Both youth and age are relatively new phenomena. Primitive societies lack the equivalent of American youth since they ordinarily have no long transitional period between childhood and adulthood. Old people are scarce in primitive societies because the absence of modern medicine makes it difficult to achieve old age. The fact that old people are scarce may be one reason that they tend to have a higher status in primitive societies than in our own society. At any rate, gerontology (the study of aging) and geriatrics (the medical treatment of old people) did not evolve much before the 1920's. (Barron, 1961.)

The older couple is an especially recent phenomenon. Not too long ago, at about the turn of the century, it was rare for both spouses to live until their last child was married. Either the husband or wife was likely to have died by the time the conjugal family was broken up by the dispersal of the children. (Because many women died in childbirth, husbands were as likely to outlive their wives as vice versa; nowadays, of course, widows far outnumber widowers.) Few people spent much time in the life cycle category of "older couple, no children." In contrast, most married couples today may look forward to *fourteen years* as a couple after the children have left home and before the marriage is terminated by the death of a spouse. (Glick, 1955.)

The stereotype of the aging person alone in a rented room is thus not an accurate picture from a marketing point of view. Instead, it might be more profitable for the marketer to envision a vigorous group of people in their fifties and sixties, freed of parental responsibilities, with major household expenditures behind them, more mobile than at any other time in their lives. Modern retirement communities tend to aim their appeals at this market. They require only that prospective buyers be childless and at least fifty years old, and not necessarily retired.

It has been suggested that older couples of this type, properly directed (by marketers as well as by other institutions of the society), might well prove to be the leisure innovators of tomorrow. (Friedmann, 1960.) Certainly, no marketer in the recreation and leisure field can afford to overlook this important market.

It has been observed, however, that people in the course of their lives learn to perform better in their central roles of spouse/parent/worker/homemaker than in their peripheral roles of friend/citizen/leisure-user. (Havighurst, 1953.) Older people thus have difficulty in responding to the leisure created by the departure of their children and the declining demands of the world of work. In addition, many older people were brought up in a more strict, more disciplined, less permissive manner than young people today and consequently suffer guilt when they try to enjoy themselves without work. (Streib and Thompson, 1960.)

Gerontologists define their field to include people from about 45 on, but many studies of older Americans — partly because of retirement practices — focus on the group over 65. These people make up about one-tenth of the population, but since about 40 per cent of the population is under 21, people over 65 are actually *one-sixth* of the adult population. Moreover, because of the higher incidence of single-person households among older people, about one-fifth of American households are headed by a person over 65. Older people generally have lower incomes, but at least in numbers, they constitute a sizable portion of the total market.

The leisure problem becomes especially critical with retirement. One writer has suggested that retired people are interested in formal associations more than in ordinary sociability, in games more than in "creative" pursuits, and in immobility more than in exploration. The reason seems to be that retired people seek structured uses of their leisure time to overcome the anxieties stemming from the unstructured nature of retirement. (Kaplan, 1960.) This implies that there is a market among retired people for physically undemanding but elaborately organized "games" involving many people. For example, arts and crafts facilities in retirement communities are not as popular as one might expect them to be. This is probably because they are individual pursuits.

Retirement, by the way, except for the problem of money, may not be as traumatic as has been supposed. One recent study indicates that men who are actually retired are better adjusted in many ways than men who are close to retirement. The latter may feel frustrated as they watch their life chances narrow down. Retired men, on the other hand, apparently lower their aspiration levels and feel more accepting of what they are, what they have been, and what they have done. (Reichard, Livson, & Petersen, 1962.)

Older people are nevertheless ambivalent in their attitudes toward age. This makes them a difficult marketing target to reach. Much like young people, they tend to resent products (e.g., puréed foods) and advertising appeals which single them out as "different" and possibly inferior. At the same time, like youth, they feel that more attention and consideration should be given to people in their age bracket. An advertising rule-of-thumb might be established on the basis of the apparent difference between the retired and the preretired. The preretired might respond very well to a slogan such as, "Now that you don't have to look after the children . . . ," while they might resent (or at least not notice because of selective perception) a slogan calling attention to their age. People in their seventies, on the other hand, seem more accepting and less resentful of an approach based upon age.

Finally, cross-cultural studies indicate that older people the world over seem to have five basic needs or goals:

- To live as long as possible.
- To get more rest.
- To keep what they have, rather than to achieve more.
- To remain active, with something to do but nothing which has to be done.
- To die comfortably in the hope of a happy life after death. (Simmons, 1960.)

This list sums up fairly well the more important differences in the motivations of the old as compared with younger people.

A caution is in order. It has been argued that although retired people over 65 have low incomes, they spend the limited amount of money that they have in about the same ways as younger people. (Reinecke, 1964.) However, the over-65 group, at least at the present time, is *not* as important a market as the foregoing discussion might suggest. Still, Medicare and the current War on Poverty may improve the financial position of older people and, indeed, more and more marketing appeals are being aimed directly at their needs. The picture is consequently subject to change.

RITES OF PASSAGE

Anthropologists use the term *rites of passage* to refer to rites used by primitive and other societies to mark or observe a significant change in social status or life situation. The Jewish bar mitzvah, marking the transition from childhood to manhood, is an example.

Given the pervasiveness of the family, most of the changes in status deserving of a rite of passage have to do with changes in family status. Weddings, for example, are a recognition that a boy and girl have moved from the status of unmarried people to full participation in the adult married community. The boy and girl have formed a "family."

Strictly speaking, of course, the term *rite of passage* is no more applicable to changes in family status than it is to fraternity initiations, commencement exercises, showers for expectant mothers, oaths of office or of allegiance, ordinations, retirement dinners, or any of the other multifarious ceremonies that mark the changes in status that we undergo in our lives. Van Gennep, the classic writer on rites of passage and originator of the term, described how the equivalent of christenings are used in some cultures to admit newborn infants to the society of the living and how funerals are used to detach the dead. (Van Gennep, 1908.)

As the individual moves from one status to another, he necessarily moves from one *status group* to another. The boy must be treated as a man, and the girl as a wife. The former companions of the boy and girl must, after the appropriate rites, treat them differently. Rites of passage consequently tend to exhibit three phases (although one or more may be omitted): (1) *separation* from the previous status group, (2) *transition*, and (3) *incorporation* into the new status group.

Rites of separation are ordinarily symbolic "castings away" such as disrobing (a preliminary to baptism in some fundamentalist religious sects), cutting the hair, or throwing away the bridal bouquet. Examples of transitional states are the novitiate period before a girl becomes a nun and the engagement period before a girl becomes a bride. Of particular interest to marketers are the rites of incorporation in the new status group. It is at this point that the "initiate" *accepts*, instead of "casting away," a variety of artifacts (or products) symbolic of the new status.

Think for a moment of gift-giving occasions in American culture. We give presents to people when they graduate from school, marry, become parents, move into a new home, retire, or otherwise change their status. Moreover, the presents are *appropriate*. New parents get baby clothing and products; house-warming presents are usually decorative household objects; the graduate receives a watch or a car. The giving of gifts which are symbolic of the new status is one of the primary characteristics of rites of incorporation.

Some marketers are acutely conscious of the importance of significant "passages." Graduation ceremonies (and gown rentals) have been pushed down to kindergarten. Diamonds are linked with engagement. Department stores have wedding advisors. (But why the gold watch on retirement, when clock-watching is suddenly no longer necessary? Recently, sets of golf clubs and power tools seem to be replacing the watch as more appropriate retirement gifts.)

The point of a rite of passage is that it is not a wholly personal thing, marking a personal event. It is a *social* occasion. For example, in primitive societies, initiations into manhood are not necessarily connected with the personal biological event of puberty, but may occur before or long after puberty. The rites change the status of the youth in the eyes of the group.

Similarly, marriage in our society and in many others is a concern not only of the central couple, but of their parents, their relatives, their age-set mates, and the community at large. After the wedding, all of these groups must begin to treat the young man and woman as different in the behaviors expected of them and due to them. Wedding gifts symbolize this difference. Who, for example, would give an unmarried person towels or bed linen as a present?

Deliberate efforts have been made by some marketers to attach the importance of a rite of passage to particular changes in status. Chevrolet aims advertising messages at young people who have just acquired their driving licenses. A shoe manufacturer has exploited "learning to tie shoelaces" as a sign of growing up in an attempt to reach the preschool shoe market. (Winick, 1961.) Manufacturers of women's foundation garments and sanitary products are stressing the transition through puberty. Other marketers might follow the lead of these innovators.

Sherlock Holmes once asked Dr. Watson the number of stairs leading up to their flat at 221 Baker Street, and when Watson confessed ignorance, Holmes said smugly, "You see, but do not observe."

It is hard to look at the phenomenon of the family closely — to think of young people struggling from one family to another, married couples discussing and *deciding*, people moving from one family status to another, older people with role opportunities narrowing down, and the ceremonies marking these changes. The family is part of our lives. Thus, we often see, but do not observe.

Astute marketers, however, *do* observe. (And many, of course, intuitively adjust themselves perfectly to American family structure without taking thought at all.) But remember: The classical economic *man* is really the economic *household*. Most purchase decisions are made by families, and family considerations color even purchase decisions made by individuals.

QUESTIONS
FOR REVIEW

1. Are family influences more or less important in marketing today than previously? What major changes do you think might take place in family structure and influence in the next twenty years?

2. What similarities do you see between the youth market and the senior-citizen market? What do these similarities suggest with respect to the development of marketing strategies?

3. Several "decision rules" for resolving family differences with respect to major purchases were cited in this chapter. What

other decision rules do you think might be important? How might a retail salesman handle a sales situation in which a husband and wife have different opinions?

4. List products with respect to which life cycle influence would be particularly important. Unimportant.

5. What are some of the differences in family structure in different social classes and different ethnic groups which have marketing implications?

9

Communication
in Marketing

ALL OF THE BEHAVIORAL topics previously discussed converge on at least one aspect of marketing —the matter of communications. If communications is not *the* critical element in competitive consumer marketing today, it is very nearly so. For, almost everything the marketer *does*, as well as what he *says*, communicates something to the consumer about the product or the company behind the product. Communications, in this sense, involves far more than the substantive content of the written or spoken word. It involves all of these elements about the product, package, price, channel of distribution, and other factors which shape the consumer's awareness and buying behavior. The realization of this simple fact has been one of the more important developments in consumer marketing in recent years.

263

But the problem of external communications does not end with the consumer. Indeed, nearly every marketer finds he has several audiences outside of his firm to whom he must direct messages. Some of these audiences may be even more important than the ultimate consumer, for example, a distributor for whom the manufacturer produces private-brand merchandise. Consider the various audiences for the typical consumer products manufacturer:

Consumers. They are male and female; old, and young, and in between; socially mobile; conservative; and so on ad infinitum.

Distributors and dealers. They determine whether or not the product will reach "the shelves," the point of ultimate sale. Both distributors and dealers exercise considerable power in this regard (McVey, 1960), and the less well known a product or company is, the more important the dealers and distributors become. The corporate image study discussed in Chapter 1 was done by a large manufacturer of household cleaning products to determine its image *among distributors*, not consumers.

Financial institutions. Nearly all companies of any size must obtain long-term or short-term financing from a variety of sources. Communications in this area may take the form of advertisements in financial journals or general business publications, of stockholder reports, or of the results of special analyses of the firms by an outside consultant. Even defense-oriented electronics and aerospace companies advertise in consumer magazines. A spokesman for one such company was asked why this sort of thing is done, since the general consumer public does not buy defense products. His answer was brief: "They buy stock." (Advertisements of this type are also used to recruit professional and semiprofessional personnel, of course.)

Government and community. Business must have a favorable climate in which to grow and prosper. Communications must continually be directed to governmental officials and to the general public to stress that the company or industry is a "good citizen." This is particularly important in industries with some degree of public regulation (finance, transportation, communications) and in industries on the fringe of social respectability (distilleries and, in more recent years, tobacco and pharmaceutical companies). Many communications of this type are not disseminated in the mass media but instead take the form of participation in community activities and lobbying.

Suppliers. Strangely enough, suppliers must be kept informed to some extent about the condition of the manufacturer's company and industry. Price increases by the manufacturer are often signals for suppliers to consider price rises of their own, unless something is done to counteract this.

There are still other external audiences in the form of trade associations, educational institutions, families of employees, and labor unions. The wise businessman does not neglect any of these.

The rest of this chapter will focus upon mass communications which are directed *to the ultimate consumer products user*. Emphasis will be upon the written and spoken word, transmitted both face-to-face and through mass media. Techniques of effective personal selling will not be discussed separately, because many (if not most) of the principles of effective mass communications also apply in the individual sales process. Many aspects of product and package design which we have discussed do communicate meaningfully to the consumer, but more by association and implication than by the process conventionally known as *communications*.

Factors Determining the Effectiveness of Communications

There is a considerable body of knowledge about factors which affect communications and which determine how effectively a given message is transmitted. Much is also known about the way in which information is disseminated among consumers. Before reviewing this, we should look at the entire communications process, from sender to receiver.

Generally speaking, there are four principal elements in a written or spoken communication:

Sender. Whom the message comes from and the manner in which it is spoken or written.

Message. The substantive content of the message, the choice of words, and the organization of material.

Transmission medium. The method of carrying the message, whether by a mass medium or face-to-face contact.

Receiver. Those characteristics of the recipient which determine what will actually be received (as opposed to what is sent) and what type of message and medium should be used.

Each of these is a factor in *every* communication, and it is not possible to understand the communications process fully without considering all four factors. For example, a truthful, accurate message from a convicted criminal is often rejected, while a successful speech in a political campaign may be characterized by little substance but smooth delivery by a respected incumbent.

In our discussion, a number of principles which have been developed for each element of the communications process will be stated briefly, some supporting evidence will be reviewed, and inferences for effective marketing communications will be drawn. Only principles which have particular relevance to the problems of marketing communications have been selected from the vast body of knowledge which exists on this subject. Before reviewing the evidence, however, we should note the comments of one writer:

> One note of warning is in order. The conditions faced by a particular advertiser may be quite different from the conditions on which research findings are based. For example, the subjects used in some of the experimental studies which will be reported were college students who are not entirely representative of the audience to which most advertisers address their appeals.

> It would therefore be unwise to accept the findings of any one research study at face value without first determining whether the conditions on which the research is based do apply to the advertiser's particular situation.

> It would be equally unwise to reject the research findings unless one is quite confident that the conditions on which the findings are

based are quite irrelevant and that if the advertiser's unique conditions *were* substituted, the findings would be different. It is all too easy to reject, out of hand, information which does not agree with our own preconceptions. (Cox, 1961, p. 161.)

THE AUDIENCE

It might seem more logical to begin our discussion with the sender — the communicat*or* — since that is where the message originates. However, a good case can be made for starting at the opposite end of the transmission chain, since the recipient really determines *what* the message will be, *who* will send it, and *how* it will be sent. *We cannot know too much about our audience if we are to communicate effectively.*

Principle A-1

People tend to see and hear communications that are favorable or congenial to their predispositions. They are more likely to see and hear congenial communications than neutral or hostile ones. And the more interested they are in the subject, the more likely is such selective attention." (Berelson & Steiner, 1964, p. 529.)

This principle has been confirmed by a wide variety of controlled laboratory studies and field studies on political campaigns, radio listening, and television viewing. Its similarity to Bruner's concept of selective perception (cf. Chapter 4) is obvious, and it further suggests the pervasiveness of the human predilection for screening out things that are not interesting or are not harmonious with existing beliefs. But note that this does not rule out the possibility that some individuals will listen to information which is contrary to a predisposition of theirs. There are always those who are open-minded, who will consider changing their opinion. Although they tend to be a minority, particularly on issues of any personal significance, they do constitute the element of potential for change. Even many of the hard core can be changed, given enough time and the repeated availability of information contrary to their initial view.

One writer points out that this tendency for people to see and hear what they want to accounts for the fact that users of a product are more likely to notice an advertisement for that product than are nonusers. This same tendency probably accounts for the fact that readership is typically greater for advertising about high-interest products than about low-interest products. (Maloney, 1963.) Two authorities go so far as to state:

> Considering the state of our present knowledge, the reasonable conclusion to reach in any given instance (in the absence of specific information to the contrary) is that any correlation between communications behavior and the personal characteristics of the people involved is a result of *selective exposure*, rather than evidence for the effects of communications. (Bauer & Bauer, 1960, p. 29.)

Another authority puts it this way: "The people you may want most in your audience are often least likely to be there." (Abelson, 1949, p. 54.) This was demonstrated by a study undertaken to evaluate the effectiveness of an intensive campaign to inform the people of Cincinnati about the United Nations. The investigators reported:

> At the end of the first survey, we made the recommendation that the campaign be addressed in particular to women, the relatively uneducated, the elderly, and the poor — the classes which showed themselves to be most in need of enlightenment. But who, in the end, were the people reached by the campaign? They were the better educated, the younger, and the men — precisely the people most likely to be interested and, being interested, also to be informed. (Star & Hughes, 1950, p. 397).

The vendor trying to reach a new market segment has this problem. He may well need massive promotional expenditures to break through the selective screening which is usually exercised by those who do not initially consider themselves a part of his market (e.g., women smoking cigars, adults owning motorbikes).

In the classic study of selective exposure in political communications, *The People's Choice*, Lazarsfeld and his co-authors report that Democrats tend to expose themselves to Democratic campaign messages and Republicans to Republican messages. In retrospect, this is not too surprising. Few loyal party members would trouble themselves to attend a rally sponsored by the opposing party. Somewhat more surprisingly, independent voters do not seem to expose themselves to the campaign messages of either party. They listen neither to Democrats nor to Republicans. (Lazarsfeld, Berelson, & Gaudet, 1944.)

In marketing terms, this means that a manufacturer should not expect much success in "converting" people who are strongly attracted to competing brands. Such people simply will not expose themselves to his messages. Similarly, like independent voters, people who are not in the market for the product he sells will notice neither his advertising nor that of his competitors.

This does not mean that the manufacturer is helpless or that advertising is useless because it reaches only people who are already convinced. Lazarsfeld notes two effects of political campaigns other than "conversion." One effect is to *reinforce* the attitudes of loyal adherents, for even they are likely to drift into inaction — and possibly even fail to VOTE — without some kind of reinforcement. Manufacturers may lose customers in this same way.

The other effect of campaigns is to activate *latent supporters,* that is, people who share the social and economic characteristics of the members of one party or another but who are not politically active. People who are rural, high-income, and Protestant (to take three demographic characteristics) tend to be Republican, but they may not be active supporters of the party. They can be stimulated to become active, however, since they will tend, at least to some extent, to expose themselves to Republican messages more than to Democratic. The converse is true of urban, low-income Catholics. (Lazarsfeld et al., 1948.) The implication is that a marketer should direct his messages primarily to present customers and to people *like* his present customers; these are the audiences most likely to notice his advertising efforts.

Principle A-2

Communications that are thought to represent some particular interest or characteristic of the audience are more influential on opinion than general, undifferentiated sources. Thus, communications directed to particular audiences are more effective than those directed to 'the public at large.' (Berelson & Steiner, 1964, p. 540.)

Commercial starting with "Mr. Homeowner, I'm talking to you!", "We mothers know that . . . ," and "This message is only for people who want . . ." illustrate the attempts which are frequently made to differentiate the public at large and to form a bridge of identification which brings speaker and audience closer together. This is based on sound communications principles.

Obviously messages of this kind will be less noticed and less effective among people to whom it is not directly addressed. Fathers will screen out messages directed specifically to mothers, and apartment dwellers will screen out messages directed to homeowners. Manufacturers must consequently be careful in limiting their appeals in this way, for they may be ruling many potential customers out of their audience. Principle A-1 suggests, however, that people who are not potential customers will rule themselves out of the audience anyway, so if a marketer can identify his primary market with reasonable accuracy, appeals aimed directly at it are likely to be effective and economical.

Industrial marketers often can use this principle effectively. Many industrial markets are "thin" or "vertical," composed of relatively few customers. Thus, specialized trade media may be used to reach, for example, petroleum engineers or gray-iron foundrymen. Many advertisements for industrial goods are, in fact, highly specific in seeking the attention of particular audiences.

In consumer goods, advertisements for nonprescription medicines and prosthetic devices are perhaps those which can be directed most specifically. It has been speculated, for instance, that advertisements promising relief from medical conditions may be small and in the back of the magazine, since they are ignored by noncustomers and are invariably noted and read by potential customers. Thus, people with arthritis and bursitis tend to notice ads about palliatives for these conditions.

The problem is to get the same kind of direct personal appeal into messages directed at the general market. A large company, with a massive advertising budget, can make a variety of appeals to a series of small markets. Advertisements for the Mustang, for example, can be aimed variously at young people, older people, men, women, and so forth, with some confidence that people will notice only the particular advertisements directed at them. Advertisers with smaller budgets cannot aim their limited number of messages at as many different targets and must consequently use more of a shotgun approach. Somehow, they must try to make their shotgun look like a rifle, so that each audience will consider itself as the primary target.

Principle A-3

Persons with high intelligence will tend — mainly because of their ability to draw valid inferences — to be *more* influenced than those with low intellectual ability when exposed to persuasive communications which rely primarily on impressive logical arguments, . . . and [they] will tend — mainly because of their superior critical ability — to be *less* influenced than those with low intelligence when exposed to persuasive communications which rely primarily on unsupported generalities or false, illogical, irrelevant argumentation. (Hovland, Janis & Kelley, 1953, p. 183.)

Data relating opinion change to intelligence (as measured by standard mental tests) indicated that sometimes highly intelligent people were more persuasible and sometimes less. However, this apparent contradiction tended to resolve itself when the content of messages was examined closely. In one study, high school students were exposed to communications containing crudely propagandistic statements concerning each of several ethnic groups they had rated (e.g., "When we hate Jews we hate Jesus."). Results showed that the most intelligent students were *least* influenced by this kind of propaganda. However, a troop indoctrination film, *Why We Fight*, was more effective in changing opinion in the *more* intelligent soldiers, probably because of the sensible approach attempted by the film. (Hovland, Janis & Kelley, 1953)

The implications of this are obvious. The study demonstrates clearly that a knowledge of the audience is essential to proper communications. We might expect advertisements in selective, "higher-type" magazines such as *The New Yorker, Holiday, Saturday Review*, and *Harper's*, to differ somewhat from ads in "mass-distribution" magazines, and indeed they often do. But usually this is because different *products* are advertised in these magazines, rather than because different *ad formats* are used for products which are also advertised in the mass-distribution magazines. Normally we find the same advertisement for the same product running concurrently in both types of magazines. Research evidence suggests that more thought might be given to developing several alternative ad formats which would run concurrently in different types of magazines reaching different audiences for the same product.

So many of today's ads appeal to social considerations that we wonder if more would not be gained in some cases from the greater use of logical argument, particularly in selective-distribution magazines. For example, there is good reason for suggesting that some of the newer appliances, in addition to their other advantages, produce a real dollar savings for users. For example, automatic dishwashers, which get dishes cleaner than is possible by hand washing, may help to prevent the spread of colds and other virus infections among family members in the wintertime. A home air conditioner may well increase the efficiency of the wage earner who is on a variable income (e.g., a salesman) more than enough to offset the cost of the unit, when one considers the importance of a good night's sleep during hot summer months. Yet little of this sort of thing is done and, when it is, it is likely to appear in mass-distribution rather than selective-distribution magazines.

One advertising firm, which handles the account of a prominent foreign manufacturer of motorbikes, has not talked at any length about many of the several advantages which accrue to the owner of such a vehicle; the main message is that you meet the "nicest people" on this motorbike. While this is aimed at changing the image of products of this type, there are undoubtedly important segments of the market (e.g., college students, who do form a major market segment for motorbikes *and* who are normally of higher intelligence) who are not very concerned with image but are searching for some "sensible reason" to buy. One reason for the great success of Volkswagen advertisements is undoubtedly their appeal to reason; the practical features of these automobiles are stressed repeatedly.

Principle A-4

> The individual's personality traits affect his susceptibility to persuasion. (Abelson, 1949, p. 65.)

One investigator exposed a group of people to a variety of attempts to change their opinions, with the idea that there might be people who would be more likely to change their opinions no matter what the situation and others who would consistently resist change. He found that people who were influenced in one situation did not tend to be the same as those influenced in another different situation. On the basis of this study, there does not seem to be any *general* susceptibility to persuasion which characterizes some individuals but not others. (Linton, 1955.)

However, relationships have been found between certain personality characteristics of the audience and the type of appeals which are likely to have the greatest effect. In one experiment, four groups of subjects were exposed to communications of various types about Negroes; in another, college students were tested before and after receiving communications about movies, punishment of criminals, and tariffs. Both studies showed that individuals with *authoritarian personalities* (i.e., people who tend to act in a dominating manner and to hold unquestioning respect for those in leadership positions, such as teachers, and policemen) were more likely to be swayed by communications from business and military leaders. Those with low authoritarianism were more susceptible to anonymous informational literature. (Rohrer & Sherif, 1951; Berkowitz & Lundy, 1957.) The latter study showed also, that students who were low on *self-confidence* were more readily influenced by college student peers than by authoritarian figures.

Other personality correlates of persuasiveness found by various investigators include:

Aggressiveness. There seems to be an inverse relationship between aggressiveness and susceptibility to social influence. The more hostility, irritability, and overt aggression a person displays, the less likely is he to be persuaded by communications which stress the majority opinion.

Social withdrawal. "Persons who display social withdrawal tendencies are less likely than others to be influenced by persuasive communications from sources in the community." (Hovland, Janis & Kelley, 1953, p. 195.)

Acute psychoneurotic symptoms. Overt symptoms of this type are often associated with defense mechanisms, emotional blocks, and similar problems which might be expected to interfere with persuasiveness. And, indeed, the available evidence suggests that individuals with psychoneurotic tendencies tend to exhibit greater resistance to opinion change than other people.

One writer observes:

It may occur to the reader that of all the aspects of persuasion that could be studied, the least useful to the practicing persuader are those that have to do with individual personality traits. All shades of all of these traits are present in a mass audience. Because this kind of objection is brought up occasionally, we should like to indicate some reasons for the importance of these studies. (1) In many cases you try to reach audiences that are highly selected and who may exhibit a preponderance of similar characteristics. . . . (2) As more becomes known about the influence of the small group on its members, communicators will devote more thought to how they can capitalize on similarities of personality and circumstance which bring people together in the same neighborhood, work group, social club, and other centers of influence. (3) A continuing awareness of the existence and force of individual characteristics will help any propagandist to avoid the trap of seeing his audience as a lump of humanity instead of as separate, distinct individuals. (Abelson, 1949, p. 70.)

To this the present authors would add the observation that individual personality traits of the *seller* as well as of the *buyer* are more pertinent in formal, face-to-face, personal selling than in mass communications. Recent work has focused upon the "matching" of buyer and seller personality traits and upon the clues which tell a salesman what type of individual he is talking to and what type of appeal would probably be most effective. Media advertising could at least try to capitalize on basic sex differences in personality and develop copy along a more aggressive line for males. Personality factors have been taken into account in ads by Metrecal which utilize the fact that persons with weight problems may have psychological complications, such as self-doubts, that contribute to the problem.

Principle A-5

> Persons who are most strongly motivated to retain their membership in a group will be most resistant to communications contrary to the standards of that group. (Hovland, Janis & Reilly, 1953, p. 277.)

Group membership has a definite influence upon the effect of communications to group members. In one study, boy scouts who highly valued their troop membership were more resistant than boy scouts who did not value their membership to suggestions from an adult that they would be better off to participate in community activities than to waste time on woodcraft activities. (Kelley & Volkart, 1952.) In another experiment, Catholic college students were exposed to opinions contrary to Church doctrine which allegedly came from other Catholic students (but which in fact were fabricated by the experimenters). These communications had a much greater influence on those who placed little value on their group membership than on those who valued their membership highly. (Kelley, 1955.)

This would be expected from the evidence on the influence of groups upon individual perception and behavior (cf. Chapter 6). Note, however, that individuals differ widely in their choice of groups and in their degree of identification with the groups they choose. Despite the normal human gregarious tendencies, there are social isolates as well as many others who "belong" in a half-hearted way. Only those persons with a strong sense of commitment to a group are highly resistant to appeals counter to the group's standards. Many others with a lesser sense of identification are willing to listen to contrary views. Note, also, that in many if not most cases the marketer of a consumer product is not selling something so contrary to group norms as to be resisted. Many products are "group-neutral" as far as the consumer's choice of brand is concerned and even as to whether he

uses the product at all. Most groups do not specify makes of refrigerators, air conditioners, soaps, or television sets; there is great
variety among members of all types of groups.

In summary, group membership may, but does not always,
determine the effects of a given communication upon a mass
audience. The extent to which group membership is influential
depends upon the importance of this membership to a given individual as well as upon the type of product involved. We would
expect, however, that advertisements appealing directly to members of some group, be it formal or informal, would succeed only
to the extent that they really mirrored the values of that group
(e.g., "*Business Week* is read by business executives," "Take
your family on United Air Lines.")

THE MESSAGE

Once everything possible has been learned about the intended
audience (within time and cost limitations), the problem of designing the message itself must be considered. (In the case of
visual media such as television and magazines, artwork and
layout are part of the problem, but since these factors were discussed at some length in Chapter 1, they will not be covered
again here.) We are interested in the presentation of verbal
material, both written and spoken, to develop maximum impact.

So much has been written on the development of effective
messages as to make it seem impossible to provide even a cursory
review of the knowledge in this area. However, a great deal of
this material has been presented by writers and advertising men
and reflects their own personal experience in designing effective
communications for particular objectives. At the opposite extreme is the strictly theoretical material, which examines the
communications process from a conceptual point of view. We
prefer to concentrate here upon the *principles underlying effective message design which have emerged from research studies by
behavioral scientists*. While the field is broad and its bounds are
not yet in sight, there are a reasonably limited number of
principles which have particular relevance to consumer marketing. A discussion of some of these principles follows.

Principle S-1

> When the audience is generally friendly, or when your position is the only one that will be presented, or when you want immediate though temporary opinion change, present one side of the argument. When the audience starts out disagreeing with you or when it is probable that the audience will hear the other side from someone else, present both sides of the argument. (Abelson, 1949, p. 2.)

The evidence for this comes primarily from studies conducted in the 1940's. In one study, three groups of American soldiers were asked how long they thought the war with Japan would last. Two of the groups were then exposed to arguments about the probable length of the war. One group was told the war would be long. The other was told the same but was also given some information about Japan's weaknesses. The control group heard no arguments at all. The effects of communication were measured by asking each man, *after* he had heard the arguments, how long he thought the war would last. There was *no difference* in opinion change *in the aggregate* between the one-sided argument group (Japan was strong and the war would be long) and the two-sided argument group. However, there were individual differences in the effects of the two arguments, *depending upon how the person felt initially*. Men who had indicated before the communications that they *expected* a long-war were more influenced by the *one-sided* argument in favor of a long war. But men who had initially expected a *short* war were swayed more toward expecting a long war by the communication which presented *both sides* of the issues. (Hovland, Lumsdaine, & Sheffield, 1949.)

In an experiment to determine how audiences might best be inoculated against counterargument, two groups were given arguments about how long it would take Russia to get the A-bomb. One group heard a one-sided presentation to the effect that it would be five years or more before Russia got the bomb. The other group heard the same argument but, along with it, observations about some of Russia's strengths and resources. A week later, the same subjects heard a counterargument, suggesting that Russia had probably already developed the A-bomb and would be producing large quantities within two years. Results showed clearly that the subjects who initially received the two-sided presentation were more resistant to the counterargument than those who received the one-sided presentation. The latter subjects were much more likely to swing to the new view. (Lumsdaine & Janis, 1953.)

Of all the principles of effective communications, this is perhaps the least obvious and most widely overlooked among consumer products marketers today. Madison Avenue executives have a long tradition of the hard sell, which deplores any mention of product weakness or limitation. Yet the evidence clearly indicates that there is another side to this. During the depths of the depression, when real estate was scarcely moving, one home-owner placed an ad in a local newspaper to this effect:

HOUSE FOR SALE

Rather old, roof leaks in heavy rain, needs painting, but this place has served well, has made a good home for us for 15 years until we outgrew it. Our family will miss it.

This advertisement reportedly drew two hundred responses. Would such an approach work again? No one seems to have tried. The temptation to "accentuate the positive" is apparently overwhelming, despite the fact that the potential audience for a given advertisement may be generally disinterested or even hostile to the product or service in question. However, in very recent years two-sided arguments have begun to make an appearance in commercial advertising. Perhaps the most noteworthy attempt has been by Avis Rent-a-Car: "Avis is only No. 2 in rent-a-cars, so why go with us"? was widely circulated. Avis' response to this question was, "We try harder!" What was the reaction to this campaign? In a short period of time Avis rentals jumped 28 per cent and revenues reached a high of $31.2 million. (*Time*, 1964.) As a result, the company has continued to feature ads with a similarly two-sided approach. One such ad viewed with alarm a burned-out directional signal on one of its cars in

Poughkeepsie, New York, where Avis is Number One in sales. This ad warned the local manager: "A few more complaints and we may have to put in someone a little less complacent [as manager]. So watch it, Jack."

Another company using a similar approach was *Woman's Day* magazine, which advertised: "Since everyone else is 'first,' we'll be second. Okay?" And the Williams Furniture Company advertised: "What happens when you drop Casual Oak [furniture] from a third story window? It smashes to bits!" Volkswagen hints at, but does not come to grips with, imperfection in advertisements headlined "Lemon," and "Nobody's perfect" above a VW with a flat tire.

All of this tends not to set well with the advertising veteran. An editorial in *Advertising Age*, a widely circulated, highly respected advertising trade publication, comments: "This bitter kind of honesty we frankly find hard to take. Advertising was easier to take back in the old days when every advertiser believed his product was the best damned product made and anything competition made was pure junk."

Apparently the majority of the advertising world holds this position, for we see very little two-sided advertising even among the smaller companies who might use it to advantage. Yet the available evidence suggests that a case can be made for advertising copy which is completely honest, rather than selectively honest, as in the case of most advertising today. The late President John F. Kennedy grasped the full significance of two-sided appeals and frequently argued in his 1960 campaign: "If you are content with the way things are going in this country today, you should vote for my opponent; but if you want to get America moving. . . ." In the present authors' opinion, the potential effectiveness of two-sided arguments and appeals has yet to be recognized in consumer products marketing.

In fairness to the advertising man, we should note that the two-sided approach is more effective than the one-sided, primarily when the audience disagrees with you or will surely hear the other side of the argument from someone else. This means that it is valuable when a product has obvious and unmistakable disadvantages which the public is sure to notice, but with a friendly audience, and little likelihood of rebuttal, the one-sided approach is probably more appropriate. The two-sided approach points out one's own weaknesses and competitors' strengths. There is no reason, of course, for a firm with a solid consumer franchise to do this. Why draw attention to its own weaknesses? President Johnson, for instance, was probably strategically as correct in refusing to debate with Goldwater in 1964 as Kennedy was correct in 1960 in wanting to debate with Nixon. The two-sided approach is more appropriate for small, struggling, or second-place firms than for large well-established firms; it is a good strategy for Avis, but not necessarily for Hertz.

One happy fallout of the two-sided approach is that a small firm may sometimes goad a larger competitor into retaliatory advertising. Hertz, for example, replied directly to Avis in a series of somewhat petulant ads which could only have had the effect of calling the Avis ads to the attention of the public. Similarly, American Motors in the late 1950's ran a two-sided campaign comparing the strengths and weaknesses of the Rambler and larger "gas guzzlers." Ford Motor Company responded by sponsoring an "Economy Run" to prove that a Ford was just as economical as a Rambler. The rebuttal probably strengthened the plausibility of Rambler's claims.

Principle S-2

Strong appeals to fear, by arousing too much tension in the audience, are less effective in persuasion than minimal appeals. (Berelson & Steiner, 1964, p. 532.)

The primary evidence for this comes from a study of the effects of different intensities of "fear" or "threat" in a communication on dental hygiene. Three levels of threat intensity were studied: strong (71 references to unfavorable consequences), moderate (49 references), and minimal (18 references). For example, one strong statement said, "If you ever develop an infection of this kind from improper care of your teeth, it . . . can spread to your eyes, or your heart, or your joints and cause secondary infections which may lead to diseases such as arthritis, paralysis, kidney damage, or total blindness."

Each of the three communications, strong, moderate, and minimal, was given to a separate, randomly chosen group of high school students as a part of their standard instruction on hygiene. Questionnaire results showed that the group exposed to the strong threat became more *worried* about the condition of their teeth than did the other two groups. However, when it came to *doing* something about the problem, such as brushing teeth more often, it was found that the group exposed to the *minimal* threat increased their conformity with the recommendation in the message, while those exposed to the strong threat did virtually nothing constructive about the matter. The minimal-appeal group also proved more resistant to later propaganda which contradicted the main theme of the original message. (Janis & Feshbach, 1953.)[1]

The investigators were careful to point out that their findings apply to situations involving voluntary acquiescence, but that strong threats may be effective in situations involving severe physical punishment. (Hovland, Janis, & Kelley, 1953.) They also suggest that a threatening message *can* be handled more effectively by reassuring the listener immediately after the threat, for example, by presenting a suitable means of avoiding the undesirable effects. They postulate an "habitual chain of response" to reflect the process that occurs when a strong threat is countered by reassurances within the same message:

$$C \longrightarrow E \longrightarrow R$$

where:

C = content cues, i.e., the fear-arousing portions of the message,

E = emotional reaction, i.e., the high state of tension which results if the message is sufficiently threatening,

R = reassuring recommendations, which make assertions about ways of averting the threat.

When the reassuring recommendation is successful in reducing the emotional tension, this reduction in tension itself operates (according to learning principles) as a *reinforcement* of the recommendations, so that this same response or assurance will

[1] Proponents of the cognitive dissonance phenomenon would argue that this study supports their case. The group receiving the greater threat would have greater dissonance between the cognition (knowledge of the threat) and their own previously inadequate dental hygiene efforts. To reduce this dissonance, they would deny *either* the threat *or* their own inadequacies. The former is easier and personally more acceptable.

tend to occur automatically the next time the individual hears the same or similar threats. However, these investigators suggest that even the most carefully planned reassurance may not be successful in reducing tension, and thus the complete habit chain is not built up. When this is the case, the fear-arousing appeal may elicit only a defensive-avoidance reaction, in which the individual rationalizes, represses, or otherwise minimizes the importance of the threat. The investigators suggest that this is what occurred in the "dental threat" experiment in spite of the investigators' careful efforts to reassure subjects after the threat.

The life insurance industry, in particular, was a long time in learning how to handle threat appeals. Early advertising used the "back the hearse up to the door" theme, implying great problems for the family purchasing no insurance. The most noteworthy break in this approach came in the early 1950's, when the Equitable Life Assurance Society began stressing "living insurance," to emphasize the fact that approximately two dollars of every three paid out by life insurance companies are paid to living policyholders (in the form of annuity payments, endowment maturities, annual dividends, etc.).

A recent illustration of how threat may backfire is furnished by the safety campaign of the Ford Motor Company during the 1956 car year. So much stress was placed on safety features (e.g., padded dashboards, recessed steering column, safety belts) that follow-up interviews showed that people were growing shy — of all things — of the safety of Ford automobiles! It was found that consumers evaluated safety in an automobile more in terms of accident prevention features (e.g., solid frame, good brakes, steering, road-holding ability) than in terms of such features as the padded dash which would reduce the number and severity of injuries in the event of an accident. Emphasis on injury reduction caused people to doubt the safety of the car with respect to accident prevention. The advertised safety features reminded prospective car buyers of the threat of accident and did not really reassure them that the threat could be averted. In fact, the features suggested that accidents were inevitable, since otherwise there would be no reason for them.

Chevrolet's slogan in 1956, incidentally, was "Sweet, hot, and sassy," and Chevrolet beat Ford decisively in sales that year. An explanation may lie within the "threat" principle of communications: Consumers begin by shutting out information they do not wish to hear. In this sense, the threat principle demonstrates the selective nature of our perception and supports Freud's concept of repression (cf. Chapter 3).

Consumer reaction to the report of the Surgeon General of the United States on the relationship of smoking to lung cancer provides further evidence of the effects of excessive threat. Table 9.1 shows sales of cigarettes for the first four months which followed release of the report on January 11, 1964; sales for the same four months of 1963 are shown for comparison. Note that sales for February, one month after the report, were drastically reduced, but that they were almost entirely recovered by the following month, then climbed to an all-time high in April, 1964.

How do we account for this strange behavior? Several explanations are possible. Returning to smoking might be based in part upon some sort of physiological addiction syndrome. Or perhaps smoking habit pattern, established over many years involving thousands of reinforcements, is compelling. There is also the possibility that the psychological effects of excessive threat had something to do with the matter. Smokers may have reacted to this message in much the same way that students reacted to the threatening dental message discussed earlier.

Table 9.1

SALES OF CIGARETTES IN THE UNITED STATES*

(*In billions*)

	1964	1963
January	41.0	43.0
February	29.2	37.9
March	37.8	39.5
April	44.0	42.0

* From *Advertising Age*, June 22, 1964.

It has been suggested, only half-facetiously, that the threat of cancer may actually make cigarettes *more* attractive to heavy smokers. The personality of the heavy smoker has been investigated intensively and apparently involves a sizable element of self-directed aggression or self-destructiveness. (Pflaum, 1965.) Heavy smokers know, whether they admit it or not, that cigarettes damage their health in many ways, and this may be one of the important reasons that they do smoke. This is not a far-fetched hypothesis. Many common sports and activities (e.g., skiing, surfing, and auto racing) are thrilling and attractive because they involve some physical danger. To the extent that this is true of smoking, the possibility of cancer may be simply an added attraction. (It is significant that heavy smokers also tend to be drinkers and gamblers.)

The evidence does not, of course, indicate that fear-arousing appeals should never be used, but it does point up the critical importance of providing *sufficient reassurance of a specific nature* so that the defensive-avoidance reaction is overcome by the $C \rightarrow E \rightarrow R$ habitual chain of response and the net effect is positive and favorable toward one's product or service. Presumably the stronger the implied or specified threat, the greater must be the reassurance to reduce the resulting emotional tension. This may well explain why some threat advertisements are less effective, that is, the fear aroused may be so great that it cannot be reduced by the amount of assurance that is possible in printed media.

Principle S-3

> In persuasive communications which present a complicated series of arguments on impersonal topics, it is generally more effective to state the conclusion explicitly than to allow the audience to draw its own conclusions. (Hovland, Janis & Kelley, 1953, p. 105.)

A communication on the topic "Devaluation of Currency" was presented to two groups of college students. Both groups heard all the arguments for and against devaluating United States currency. From the arguments and a statement of conditions prevailing in the United States, the logical conclusion was that the currency should be devaluated. One group was left to draw this conclusion for itself, while the other was given the conclusion as well as the arguments. Opinion change was measured by asking the same questions before and after the message. The net per cent changing opinion (i.e., the per cent changing in the direction of the message minus the per cent changing in the opposite direction) was 19.3 per cent for the "no-conclusions" group and 47.9 per cent for the "conclusions" group. (Hovland, Janis, & Kelley, 1953, pp. 100–102.)

It was later reasoned that perhaps the conclusions group had changed more because they had *understood* the message better. To check this, another study was done in which arguments for and against our entry into the Korean War were presented to recruits in the armed forces. One version of the message was well organized and the other poorly organized, to produce differences in understanding. Both versions were given to four separate groups, as follows:

1. Poorly organized presentation and conclusion drawn.
2. Poorly organized presentation and no conclusion drawn.
3. Well-organized presentation and conclusion drawn.
4. Well-organized presentation and no conclusion drawn.

As expected, the well-organized presentation was better understood than the poorly organized, and each of the groups showed some opinion change in the anticipated direction. However, both groups that heard the conclusions drawn tended to understand the arguments better than the no-conclusion groups. On the whole, spelling out the conclusions seemed to be more effective. It was also found that in the case of the more intelligent men, who could draw the conclusions for themselves, it made no difference whether the conclusion was stated or not. Thus, stating the conclusion was more important among less intelligent subjects. (Thistlethwaite, deHaan & Kamenetsky, 1955.)

Since so many consumer marketing communications are personal rather than impersonal in nature, it cannot safely be generalized from the studies presented here that conclusions should always be drawn in advertisements. But it is probably wise to assume so, since many ads, while attempting to talk to the consumer about *his needs,* are perceived by the consumer as impersonal, at least upon initial impact. It was pointed out in Chapter 1 that attention may be produced by ads using the Gestalt principle of closure but that individuals differ widely in their ability to effect closure. For this reason, the majority of advertisements today carefully include the explicit conclusions which the vendor wishes the consumer to draw, rather than leaving this open to the interpretation of the viewer or reader. Advertisements that end, "And so, get a. . . ." or "For these reasons, you should. . . ." are utilizing the conclusion principle to good effect on the mass audience. On the other hand, ad copy directed to more sophisticated audiences may effectively substitute inference and innuendo for direct statements, as is done in many cases.

Principle S-4

No final conclusion can be drawn about whether the opening or the closing parts of the communication should contain the more important material. (Abelson, 1949, p. 8.)

Learning theory (cf. Chapter 2) suggests that retention is highest for the items at the beginning and at the end of serially-presented material. It does not, however, suggest *which* of these is best remembered. Experiments by Ebbinghaus and others tend to show a *slight* superiority in retention of nonsense syllables learned first over those learned last. However, any slight advantage of the beginning over the end might easily be overcome by differences in content of the beginning or end items in a *meaningful* communication.

In the communications context, one investigator read a series of narrative biographical statements to subjects and tested how well each statement was retained. To control the "memory value" of each statement, the order of presentation was varied systematically. Results showed that statements read at the beginning were remembered better than those at the end. Subjects remembered 64.3 per cent of the first three statements as against 50.9 per cent of the last three. (Jersild, 1929.) Another investigator conducted a study which essentially replicated this one yet yielded the opposite results. Subjects were told they would be tested for memory and were read a series of statements. They were able to recognize items at the end of the list better than those at the beginning. (Ehrensberger, 1945.) Other studies, dealing with statements about the desirability of wartime marriages and the desirability of federal medical aid, also show better retention of end-items than beginning-items.

As of now, the evidence is not clear, and we are reduced to speculation. One writer hypothesizes: "If the audience is not very interested in the communication, the major arguments should be presented first. Where interest is high, save the punch for last." (Abelson, 1949, p. 9.) He reasons that saying the most important things first to an interested group will lead them to expect even more important points later on, which will make for disappointment. On the other hand, a relatively disinterested group is not likely to develop interest from hearing weak messages, so the punch is needed at the beginning.

A great deal of work has yet to be done in the commercial context to determine the proper organization of arguments or claims presented in a serial fashion. One group of authorities states: "In view of the contradictory conclusions it is unlikely that one or the other order will turn out to be universally superior. Our interest is, then, in an analysis of the factors which will make either the climax or the anticlimax order more effective under a particular set of conditions." (Hovland, Janis, & Kelley, 1953, p. 114.)

The sensible conclusion is that *both* the beginning and the end of a message are especially well remembered and that a copywriter should therefore be careful not to bury important points in the middle of his copy. There is no reason that an advertisement should not begin with a "grabber" and end with a "shocker." The copywriter does not have to weigh the relative importance of primacy and recency; he may — and should — use both to good effect. Copy which does not initially capture the attention of the reader and copy which trails off into inconsequentialities are equally bad.

Principle S-5

. . . Studies tend to show moderately high retention of *opinion change* over a period of time even in the case of rather brief communications. But in some studies little effect appears to be retained, while in several investigations there is an apparent *increase* in the extent of the change with the passage of time.[2] (Hovland, Janis, & Kelley, 1953, p. 244.)

[2] Our italics.

The increase of opinion change over time is called the *sleeper effect*. Evidence for the sleeper effect comes from a study during World War II involving a film, *The Battle of Britain*, shown to United States soldiers to increase their confidence in our British ally. All soldiers in the study were given an opinion questionnaire before the film, then one group was given a second identical questionnaire *five days* after the film and another group *nine weeks* after. The retention of *factual material* declined over time, in line with expectations based upon learning theory. However, for some items there turned out to be an increase in *opinion change* over time. The investigators coined the term *sleeper effect* for these changes. They hypothesized that the items toward which opinions were changed were more consonant with the views of the socioeconomic and educational groups to which the individuals belonged and, thus, that repeated exposure to these views could be expected over a period of time. (Hovland, Lumadaine, & Sheffield, 1949.)

In a similar study identical communications on four topics ("The Future of Movie Theaters," "Atomic Submarines," "The Steel Shortage," and "Antihistamine Drugs") were presented to two groups of subjects. For the first group the material was attributed to a trustworthy source and for the second to an untrustworthy source. As expected, the material from the trustworthy source produced a much greater opinion change than the same material from the untrustworthy source. However, a retest after an interval of four weeks showed that the net opinion change for both groups had converged and *was now the same*, that is, opinion change in the "trustworthy" group had decreased and that for the "untrustworthy" group had increased. The latter group's change exemplifies the sleeper effect. The investigators conjectured that this had occurred because the initial reaction to the untrustworthy source was negative, and since the source tends to be forgotten faster than the message, opinion was gradually swayed in the direction suggested by the communication.

Does the sleeper effect apply to commercial advertising? One observer thinks not. He writes:

A factor which distinguishes [the studies] cited from the situation found in advertising is that advertisers are concerned with the effect of repetition of their advertising messages, whereas [these studies] dealt with the effect of a single exposure to a communication. The 'sleeper effect' is not a 'coming around' to a point of view as a result of frequent exposures to a communication. . . . It may well be that the frequent repetition common in advertising is likely to create conditions the very opposite of those requisite for a 'sleeper effect.' Repetition of an advertising message which is initially rejected because of the environment in which it is presented is likely to *increase* spontaneous association of the message with the unacceptable environment. If the consumer is frequently reminded of the unacceptable environment he is less likely to disassociate the advertising message from that environment. In short, the conditions necessary for the 'sleeper effect' are less likely to occur with each repetition. (Weinberger, 1961, p. 66.)

A phenomenon which may be confused with the sleeper effect is the delay that often occurs between attitude change and the behavior resulting from the attitude change. In experiments on the sales effectiveness of advertising, for example, in which one area is saturated with advertising and another is not, it has been found that the saturated area sometimes continues to produce sales long after the experiment has been terminated and the differential in advertising expenditures removed. While a true sleeper effect may be involved, it is more plausible that attitudes changed by advertising simply take a certain amount of time to be translated into buying behavior. A housewife buys a "26-ounce round of salt" only about once in six months and, if she has a full box of Brand A salt on hand, will not rush out to buy a box of Brand B even if an advertising campaign convinces her of its superiority. It will take six months for her change in attitude to be reflected in her buying behavior. It is not necessary or even reasonable to assume that her attitude toward Brand B becomes steadily more favorable in the intervening period because of the sleeper effect.

It might be helpful to think of the sleeper effect, if it does occur, as another instance of cognitive dissonance. The recipient of a believable message from an untrustworthy source (or an unbelievable message from a trustworthy source) is thrown into a state of confusion, which he can resolve only by changing his opinion of either the *source* or the *message*. Either change might cause the message to become more believable over time.

That is, the recipient might repress the untrustworthiness of the source of the believable message or come to believe the unbelievable message because of the trustworthiness of the source.

According to one theory, however, it is more likely that both the source and the message will "lose ground." For example, if a trusted doctor advocates some medical course of action not in accord with a person's previous beliefs, the doctor may tend to become *less* credible as a source and the message to become *more* credible. (Osgood, Suci, & Tannenbaum, 1957.) In this view, the sleeper effect would almost always follow a dissonant source and message.

THE COMMUNICATOR

Another factor of extreme importance in communications is the sender or the communica*tor* — the source from which the message comes. In face-to-face transmission, the source is obvious, but in commercial advertising there may be several "sources" behind a particular message and the consumer may attach a differential importance to each of them. For example, an advertisement for Clairol in *Good Housekeeping* magazine contains at least two sources: the company and the magazine itself. While the latter may be technically the *medium of transmission* and thus not one of the communicators, we must remember that products advertised in this particular magazine carry the "Good Housekeeping Seal of Approval," which speaks loudly for the quality of the product. Women who respect and trust *Good Housekeeping* tend to impute favorable characteristics to the products advertised therein. Thus, the magazine "speaks" for the product. Along the same line, we occasionally see point-of-purchase displays proclaiming that a particular product was "Advertised in *Life*" magazine.

Suppose Clairol decided to employ testimonial advertising, involving perhaps a prominent movie personality. There would then be *three* sources: the company, the magazine, and the movie star. In such cases (and there are many examples in consumer advertising), the various sources may amplify one another to produce a greater impression than any one source alone or even than the sum of the separate effects of each of the three sources. Conversely, if one of the two or three sources carried unfavorable connotations, the net effect might be confusing or even unfavorable. The important point is that the medium may but will not always be a source in the consumer's mind, as will an individual or group quoted directly in the advertisements. With this in mind, let us proceed to the factors which affect the communications process.

Principle C-1

> The more trustworthy, credible, or prestigious the communicator is perceived to be, the less manipulative his intent is considered to be and the greater the immediate tendency to accept his conclusions. (Berelson & Steiner, 1964, p.537.)

Since this principle is rather obvious, we will not provide extensive evidence in its support. The Clairol example in the preceding section illustrates the important initial effect of a communication when different sources present the same message. Remember, however, that in some cases the effects of the *source* may fade over time more quickly than the effects of the *message*, so that the long-run net influence upon opinion may be the same for both high- and low-credibility sources. A number of studies support this hypothesis (e.g., Kelman & Hovland, 1953; Hovland & Weiss, 1951.) It is for this reason that Berelson and Steiner have included the words "immediate tendency" in their statement above.

Testimonial advertising is perhaps the most forceful example of utilizing a high-credibility source. Advertisements of this type range from endorsements by individuals ("Play the woods Jack Nicklaus plays — MacGregor") to endorsements by professional associations (Crest toothpaste, by the American Dental Association). The use of a high-prestige medium may also support a message, as pointed out earlier. And, finally, the corporate image of a company itself may have a great effect upon opinion change when the company name is shown in the advertisement. For example, the months following the conviction of General Electric, Westinghouse, and other electrical products manufacturers involved in price-fixing would have been precisely the wrong time for these companies themselves to initiate campaigns designed to change consumer attitudes or opinions toward some product line. The initial impact would probably have been low, and the total effect of a campaign at that time would have been minimal.

What constitutes a *credible source* for a particular communication? This would obviously vary with the type of product and the audience itself. Credible sources range from teenage rock 'n roll idols to influential businessmen and statesmen. Usually a source which the audience would consider credible is not hard to select, although occasionally mistakes are made.

In general, "majority opinion" is more effective than "expert opinion" in changing opinions (Berelson & Steiner, 1964, p. 538), but it is difficult to determine for a particular situation whether the source should be an individual (e.g., testimonial) or a group (e.g., reference). If an individual, what characteristics should this individual possess? We discussed in Chapter 3 the problem one household baking-products manufacturer had in trying to decide what kind of image to build for the housewife-type woman whose name was used as part of their trade mark and brand name. One motivation research firm recommended a next-door-neighbor approach; another felt that the authority image (Mother knows best") would be most effective. Problems of this kind have no easy solution.

What happens when the audience does not know anything about the source?

> When the audience has little or no prior knowledge of the communicator's trustworthiness, it tends to decide a question on the basis of the content itself — i.e., the conformity of the content to predispositions, [but when] the audience does expect or attribute manipulative intent — except perhaps where that is taken as 'normal,' as in advertising — it develops resistance to acceptance of the message. (Berelson & Steiner, 1964, p. 537.)

A certain amount of manipulative intent is imputed by consumers to all advertising, but this is undoubtedly overcome in most cases by message content which follows reasonable lines.

People do not necessarily distrust manipulative messages. Jim Moran, an enormously successful Chicago automobile dealer, has established himself as a credible source to many people in the Chicago area. He acts as master of ceremonies on his own television show and delivers his own commercials. His commercials are consequently not received as if they came from a paid announcer. Instead, they have the double impact of the warm rapport built up during the show and the prestige of being delivered by the owner of the business himself. The president of American Motors, George Romney (who later became governor of Michigan), did something similar by featuring himself in Rambler ads and actually signing many of them himself.

It is well known that television commercials are much more effective when delivered by the star of a show. In part, this is because the star can "slide" into the message without losing the audience, while the appearance on the screen of a regular announcer is a signal that a commercial is beginning. But the credibility of the star as a communicator is also a factor. People really do build up affection and respect for their favorite television performers. One of the most effective commercials ever evaluated by Gallup and Robinson, Inc., was a five and a half minute commercial for Chevrolet featuring the entire cast of *Bonanza*. A commercial of this length risks losing its audience, but viewers apparently watched it with interest from beginning to end.

Principle C-2

A communicator's effectiveness is increased if he expresses some views that are also held by his audience. (Abelson, 1949, p. 78.)

Politicians often employ this principle by promising support to, or expressing views known to be held by, that segment of the electorate to which they are speaking. This normally makes the audience more receptive to other statements the speaker wishes to make which may not be so palatable (e.g., the need to raise taxes). In one study, students known to be mildly in favor of fluoridation of public water were exposed to arguments against fluoridation. One group first received a communication in support of academic freedom (which they unanimously favored), then the fluoridation communication. Another group received only the fluoridation message. Results showed that the group receiving the preliminary favorable communication regarding academic freedom reversed their opinions of fluoridation more than the group receiving no preliminary agreeable communication. (Weiss, 1957.)

In another study, two groups of subjects having a favorable opinion of Henry Ford were exposed to the same unfavorable communication about him. For one group, the communicator claimed his purpose was to make people feel *more* favorable toward Ford and for the other group, to make them feel *less* favorable. There was more opinion change in the direction suggested by the message (against Ford) in the group that had been told the communicator was *favorable* toward their views than in the other group. (Ewing, 1942.) It is interesting how the communicator's opening comments produced a Gestalt effect which influenced everything following.

The Mutual Life Insurance Company of New York used this principle effectively in its ads to farmers and ranchers which began, "I'll take livestock over life insurance any day!" (attributed to a sheep rancher with a 19,000-acre spread in Montana). Preliminary remarks of this kind put the audience "in tune" with the advertisement and induce them to read further and learn why this rancher changed his mind in favor of life insurance.

One curious feature of this principle is that it seems almost to contradict the third message principle (M-3), stating that conclusions should be drawn explicitly. As noted, the message that claimed to be favorable to Henry Ford but was actually unfavorable (message "a") was more effective in inducing negative opinion change toward Ford than the message explicitly stating that it was meant to induce unfavorable attitudes (message "b"). Message "b," in effect, stated the conclusion to be drawn; message "a" actually stated that an opposite conclusion should be drawn. These "conclusions" were presented, however, at the beginning of the messages rather than at the end. This suggests that, in efforts to induce opinion change, a successful message structure might be initial agreement with the position of the audience, then more or less logical arguments in favor of a contrary position, and finally an explicit conclusion that the opposite position should be accepted. Mark Anthony followed this pattern in the famous speech in Shakespeare's *Julius Caesar* in which he first claimed to support the "honorable" men who had assassinated

Caesar, then presented evidence that they were ungrateful murderers, and finally concluded that they were in fact ungrateful murderers. This message structure is a rhetorical sequence well known since at least medieval times, and traces of it can be found, for instance, in the writing of St. Thomas Aquinas.

Principle C-3

What the audience thinks of a persuader may be directly influenced by what they think of his message. (Abelson, 1949, p. 81.)

In one study, persons who originally favored legalized gambling, read a story which indicated that labor leaders also favored it. The subjects showed a more favorable attitude toward labor leaders as a result of this communication. (Tannenbaum, 1956.) Another study found that students exposed to a 15-minute Drew Pearson rebroadcast changed more toward a *favorable view of Pearson* than did a matched group which did not hear the broadcast. (The group hearing the broadcast also learned more about the factual issues.) (Freeman et. al., 1955.)

This principle suggests that the long, laborious road to a good corporate image *can* be travelled by a newer firm through continuous attention to the *quality of its messages* as well as to the *merits of its product*. Credibility of a source may be developed over time with the proper kind of messages.

THE MEDIUM

A great deal of interest over the past thirty years has centered around comparison of the effectiveness of the different media. Hovland is careful to point out the methodological problems involved in making these comparisons:

For one thing, the uses of two media are often so distinctive that direct comparison is not meaningful (for example, in subjects requiring visual presentations).

A second problem is the differential selection of audiences by different media. . . . Thus, comparisons involving captive audiences which have been given one or the other medium may not sustain generalization to real life situations where a high degree of self-selection obtains.

The third difficulty is to obtain a sufficiently large sample of different communications using the same medium to permit valid generalization about a population of cases involving some particular medium. The bulk of the literature involves a comparison of, say, one radio presentation and one directly given speech. The obtained results may be attributable to unique characteristics of the particular comparison made. (Hovland, 1954.)

Another problem is that much of the work done to date has compared mass media with nonmass media such as personal delivery and printed messages administered under laboratory conditions. It is no great help for the consumer marketer to know that *personal* delivery of a talk is more effective in changing attitudes, since he often has little chance to deliver his message personally or even in printed editorial copy. What he wants to know, basically, is whether he gets more impact per dollar of advertising budget from television, radio, magazine, or other forms of advertising.[3]

Keeping Hovland's warnings in mind, we shall review the limited evidence on the comparative effectiveness of different media. An early study by Hollingsworth in 1935 involved the presentation of information in three different ways: spoken, shown visually, and both shown and spoken. Effectiveness of the various presentations was measured by recall immediately after the presentation and again three days later. Table 9.2 shows the results in terms of the per cent of total content recalled. (From Baker, 1961.)

Table 9.2

PER CENT OF TOTAL CONTENT RECALLED

	Immediately	After 3 Days
Spoken only	71	10
Shown only	72	20
Shown and spoken	86	65

From these brief results, we might infer the superiority of television over other commercial media, but this is far from certain.

---

[3] Of course, local newspapers, billboards, direct mail, and other potential media greatly complicate the problem for many marketers.

In the absence of objective evidence about the relative importance of sight and sound in television, it is interesting to note the rebate policy of the major networks. If the picture is lost but not the sound, the rebate is 75 per cent, while in the reverse situation where the sound is lost but not the picture, the rebate is only 25 per cent.

Principle D-1

Since audience attention is self-selective, exposure to communications in different media tends to be supplementary, not complementary; that is, those who read about a topic also tend to listen, and those who pay attention at one time also tend to pay attention at another. (Berelson & Steiner, 1964, p. 532.)

Table 9.3, taken from a study by Larzarsfeld, Berelson, and Gaudet in 1948 on overlap among the various media, shows that approximately two-thirds of respondents were either frequent users or nonusers of both radio and newspapers, while only one-third were frequent users of one and not the other. Similar results hold for radio and magazine overlap.

Table 9.3

PERCENTAGE OF PERSONS EXPOSED TO
DIFFERENT COMBINATIONS OF MEDIA

Exposure to newspapers	*Exposure to radio*		*Exposure to magazines*	*Exposure to radio*	
	High	*Low*		*High*	*Low*
High	66	31	*High*	66	27
Low	34	69	*Low*	34	73
Total	100	100	Total	100	100

These findings may be either comforting or disturbing, depending upon one's point of view. On the one hand, the overlap provides some amount of "reinforcement" in that the same advertising theme run concurrently in different media is likely to produce multiple exposure for the individual who uses many media. On the other hand, the duplication reduces the total number of potential buyers who may be reached by a given advertising budget, unless great care is taken to select media which are not similar in content and which reach different audiences.

Principle D-2

There is no one medium (or type of medium) best for everything —all media have their place, dependent upon circumstances. (Lucas & Britt, 1963, p. 285.)

Even if, for example, television with its combination of audio and video were found to produce a greater impact per dollar than other media, this would always be *with respect to a given message, product, and audience target.* In some cases, television advertising is not at all feasible (e.g., in defense marketing), and even in consumer marketing there are many types of goods which appeal primarily to higher-income groups, which are less frequent users of television than lower-income groups.

The solution for a given firm can only be determined by careful research of the type that is now being done by the Du Pont, Ford Motor, and Scott Paper companies. These firms have expended large sums of money and time in recent years to learn which media are best for which purposes and under which circumstances. Results from one of these proprietary studies suggests that the medium selected is relatively unimportant, at least for the product offered by this firm. The same amount of money spent in different media combinations tended to produce about the same sales results. This may or may not be true for other consumer products companies.

Advertising Believability

It has long been held by some observers of the advertising scene that there are three principal factors which determine how effective a commercial is. These factors are:

Exposure. Was an individual *exposed* to the commercial?

Credibility. Was the advertisement *believed* by the individual?

Influence. What *motivating force* did the advertisement have?

These three factors are linked by the following propositions:

(1) An advertisement cannot be believed nor can it influence someone until it is seen or heard. (2) An advertisement cannot influence anyone unless it is believed. In a sequential flow diagram,

Exposure —)   Credibility —)   Influence

where the symbol —) means "may but does not necessarily lead to." It seems reasonable that an advertisement not seen or heard has no chance of influencing anyone, and that an ad which is not believed cannot have any positive effect. The trouble with this sensible conception is that recent evidence suggests that neither one of these propositions may be so.

But how is it possible for unseen and unheard advertising to affect a consumer purchase decision? The answer to this will be clear from a study of the next section of this chapter, "The Flow of Information and Influence," which points out the power of transmitting information through certain key friends and neighbors known as opinion leaders. These leaders are generally more receptive to the commercial media and, upon being exposed to a particular ad, they often pass along its content orally to others in their social group or groups. The effects of this are often great.

Can commercial advertising which is not *believed* have any influence upon buying behavior? One authority believes it can. He says:

> . . . It is now apparent that *no advertisement is likely to be completely 'believable' when its purpose is to change people's minds. Moreover, an advertisement need not be believed completely to be effective.* These views are based on three years of background research conducted by the Leo Burnett Company and [on] a survey of hundreds of books and articles concerning all phases of persuasive communications. (Maloney, 1963, p. 1.)

Maloney's view is that believability is not a property of the advertisement itself but depends upon the *interaction* of each advertisement with the consumer's accumulated attitudes and memories. Thus, an ad that is believable to one person may not be to another. By definition, a *persuasive* message (designed to change one's mind about a product or brand) is sure to run into conflict with the pre-existing beliefs it seeks to change. In such a case, it is almost impossible for a single advertisement to completely change a particular belief; rather, each successive exposure may put the consumer into an increasing state of tension about his present beliefs until, eventually, he makes a "quantum jump" to adoption of the new or different brand or product.

But an appeal for change will tend either not to get through at all (selective perception) or to be forgotten (leveling) simply because it is an appeal for change, so the net total impact will tend to be low. The first thing that must be done, according to Maloney, is somehow to relate the advertisement to previous beliefs or attitudes to establish some basis for a common ground with the consumer. This task falls primarily to the creative advertising staff. If they do their work well, the consumer receives the impression that the ad is in some way germane to his own view of the product, and the ad will at least pass initially through his "mental filter". After this is accomplished, interest must continue to be maintained in some striking way, or the preliminary advantage is lost. Maloney suggests one very effective way of doing this which draws upon still another principle of effective communication:

> The more extreme the opinion change the communicator asks for, the more actual change he is likely to get. (Abelson, 1949, p. 84.)

This principle suggests that the best way to produce opinion change is to claim *enough* to get people *interested* in the product so that they may develop a *tentative belief* in its advantages. Maloney says, ". . . The advertiser need not be too concerned about advertising messages which 'sound too good to be true' *if* the consumer has a real opportunity to find out that they *are* true." He finds that many consumers who say about an advertisement, "I don't believe it," are not reflecting an *actual disbelief* of the product but rather a *curious disbelief* — "It sounds too good to be true." He states, "The author's research has shown that the latter sort of response, although it may seem negative in a superficial sense, is actually conducive to 'nudging' the consumer along the path of the product adoption process." (Maloney, 1963, p. 7.)

If this curious disbelief is supported — by actual use of the

product, by comments from friends or neighbors, or by a formal
sales presentation — the consumer is well along the road to a
more complete belief in the product's merits. The more complete the belief, the less the probability of the consumer's
switching to a competitive product at some later date. Particularly in the case of inexpensive products and those which involve
little risk of failure (that is, if the product is no good, the consumer simply buys another brand the next time), it is relatively
easy for the consumer to *try* the new product, thus passing the
biggest obstacle to brand-switching. If the new product has the
advantages it is claimed to have, if a habit chain is established
despite the fact that the new product is little or no better than
the old, the desired switching action is accomplished.

What types of appeals are most likely to produce the desired
curious disbelief? They are probably not the claims we see so
often — "new," "faster-acting," "greatest," "easy," and similar
expressions which characterize advertising copy in the United
States. (The study by Whyte reported in Chapter 4 suggests
that such copy is often relatively ineffective.) Appeals which
effect curious disbelief are likely to be of the following type:

- "You will never need another set of tires for your car (if
  you buy brand X)."
- "With this mix, your eight-year-old daughter can make a
  delicious cake."
- "Our preparation has eliminated the need for surgery in
  many cases."

At first glance, the foregoing discussion may seem to be primarily
manipulative; if you tell the customer *this*, he will do *this*. But
remember that Maloney suggests that startling claims should be
no cause for worry "*if* the consumer has a real opportunity to
find out that they *are* true." This puts the responsibility directly
where it belongs — with the product planning and development
function. Unless this function can devise a product or service
that is measurably better than its competitors' or a new product
that offers advantages not available in present products, the long-
run consumer response to the total market efforts of a firm will
be less than maximal for a given amount of time and resources.
*The most important job of marketing management today is to
see that products that are really new or meaningful in some way*

are continually brought to the market, to give the communications function something to talk about.

The Flow of Information and Influence

Most large firms today consider media advertising almost exclusively when mapping promotional strategy for a new consumer product. A great deal of effort is spent on ad message and copy and on the proper choice of media to reach the segment of the market which seems to have the greatest sales potential. While this conventional approach has been *effective* in the past, there is some doubt that it has been an *efficient* method of communicating to consumers. The reasons for this are many.

The fact that advertising is, by definition, impersonal makes it generally less persuasive than personal communications. And even a moment's reflection suggests that advertising is a "shotgun" approach to communications in the sense that: (1) many potential purchasers do not read or watch the particular media selected by the advertiser for the job at hand; (2) many readers or viewers of the selected media do not constitute potential purchasers of the product or service; (3) even regional advertising does not always hit "pockets" where the product is available on the shelf and, conversely, advertising often covers markets where the product is not available. A list of all shortcomings would be lengthy.

A schematic outline of the communications link implicit in most American advertising today is given in Figure 9.1 on page 303. Here we see manufacturer M directing messages to individuals A through I, who constitute the market for his product. Through an appropriate choice of media, theme, and copy, M hits market segment D, E, F harder than segment A, B, C and gives little attention to segment G, H, I. In this way, the manufacturer is clearly utilizing a strategy of *market segmentation*, communicating more intensively with some portions of the market than with others.

This structure might be referred to as a *one-step flow of communications*. The manufacturer directs his appeal to *each consumer* in hopes that the consumer will: (1) notice the advertisement, (2) be informed, persuaded, or reminded by it, and (3)

Figure 9.1

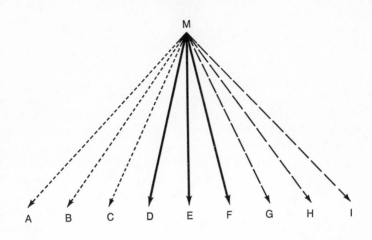

purchase the product or service. Most of the mountainous volume of advertising research to date has been undertaken to evaluate the effectiveness of the one-step communication structure in terms of these three objectives.

The Two-Step Flow of Communications

Recent research findings suggest that the one-step scheme is an oversimplification or even a gross distortion of the actual channels through which information flows. As a result, the *two-step flow* hypothesis was developed to explain more adequately the flow of communications to and among the general public. Katz has written an excellent discussion of the two-step flow and the supporting research evidence. (Katz, 1957.)

Briefly, the two-step hypothesis proposes a communications structure as diagrammed in Figure 9.2.

Information is directed from manufacturer to each consumer, but B, D, F, and I do not respond directly. However, C, E, and H not only notice the message but pass it along orally to B, D, F, and G. C, E, and H are known as *influencers* or *opinion leaders*, to whom B, D, F, and G look for information and evaluation. These opinion leaders not only reach potential consumers who may not have seen or heard the original advertising message, but

Figure 9.2

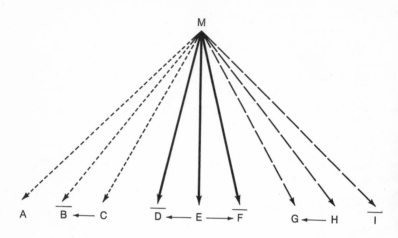

they also *reinforce the message impact* among those who have (e.g., individual G), thereby adding a personal motivation dimension to the communications process. In effect, the opinion leaders are acting, without pay, as salesmen and saleswomen for the manufacturer. Their importance should not be underestimated.

An interesting study by Whyte illustrates this phenomenon rather well. Observing the presence of home air-conditioning units among row-type houses in a Philadelphia suburb, he found that adoption proceeded in *clusters of adjacent homes* on one side of a street or alley, while identical clusters of homes across an alley or across a street would have no air conditioners at all. Whyte felt this phenomenon was due to the "web of word of mouth" among neighbors, whereby an early purchaser — perhaps an opinion leader — would exert a direct influence upon his neighbors and thus initiate a chain reaction of influence in his immediate area. The findings of this study convinced the investigator that the importance of local communications networks is very great. (Whyte, 1954.)

Further evidence comes from the consumer spending-intention research conducted over the past fifteen years by the Survey Research Center at the University of Michigan.

In studying information-seeking on the part of buyers of large household appliances (TV sets, refrigerators, washing machines, kitchen ranges), Eva Mueller found that more than half of the buyers turned for advice to acquaintances and in most instances also looked at the appliances used by them. A third of the buyers bought a brand or model that they had seen in someone's home, often the home of relatives. Information-seeking through shopping around in stores appeared to be of lesser importance than information-seeking from relatives, friends, and neighbors. (Katona, 1960, p. 157.)

This two-step flow implies a more involved communications process than the one-step, yet it may still be an oversimplification of reality. At least one study has shown that opinion leaders in the medical profession do not necessarily formulate their own views in isolation, but may be influenced by the very individuals whom they later influence. (Menzel & Katz, 1955–56.) If this is the case, we have something like the proverbial chicken-and-egg dilemma, and the entire communications process is far more complicated than it has been assumed to be. It is certainly more involved than the one-step flow structure would indicate.

Opinion Leaders and Social Class

At this point, it is important to distinguish between two meanings of the term *opinion leader*. This expression has often been used to refer to individuals of high social, political, or industrial status, that is, those who make decisions of major consequence in a society or community. The eminent sociologist C. Wright Mills refers to such individuals as *the power elite*, those who "occupy the strategic command posts of the social structure." (Mills, 1956, p. 3.) Advertisers often secure product endorsements from such individuals to motivate consumers, but such communication still takes place within the *one-step* flow structure.

In contrast, opinion leaders in the two-step flow seem to be found *in approximately equal proportions at all strata of society* (at least for marketing types of information). (Katz, 1957.) In this context, the emphasis is upon communicating with neighbors and friends *horizontally*, that is, within the same social level, and every neighborhood or social group would be expected to have its share of opinion leaders. In their own way, these leaders constitute one of the basic regulating mechanisms of society. They are instrumental in deciding when a luxury item becomes a "necessity" and whether a fashion style adopted by a higher social level is suitable for their own stratum.

The fact that opinion leaders seem to be *found* at all social levels does not necessarily imply, however, that they are equally *effective* or important at all levels. On the contrary, it appears that social communications networks may be more prevalent at the upper-income and social levels than at lower levels and that they are more important and influential at the upper levels. Support for this view is found in Warner's classic Yankee City studies indicating that "joining" is more of a middle- and upper-class phenomenon (Warner & Lunt, 1941) and in the "Workingman's Wife study mentioned earlier. The latter study, in contrasting the workingman's wife with the middle-class wife, concluded: Overall, it appears that the lives of working-class wives are more constricted to the triangle of home, children and husband than is the case with middle-class families. . . . Three out of four [working-class wives] are not taking any active part in a club, [while] more than three out of four of the middle-class wives . . . are actively engaged in club work. (Rainwater, Coleman, & Handel, 1959, p. 40, 114–15.)

These clear differences in social behavior suggest that somewhat different communications patterns may exist in lower and upper social classes. For if the working-class wife gets around less than her middle-class counterpart, it seems likely that she receives less information by word of mouth from other and relies upon impersonal media or spur-of-the-moment decisions in making purchases. Two recent studies provide support for this view. (Myers, 1964.)

Locating and Utilizing Opinion Leaders

At the present time, there appears to be sufficient evidence that: (1) the informal communications networks hypothesized by the two-step flow do exist, (2) these networks can be extremely important in informing and influencing potential buyers of consumer products, and (3) these networks are more prevalent and more influential at upper than lower income levels. How can one capitalize on this knowledge in developing a competitive edge in marketing communications? The key lies in locating, at a reasonable cost, opinion leaders for a given product or service. Once this is done, special communications may easily be directed to these individuals on a "rifle" basis to supplement the current "shotgun" media advertising approach.

However, the evidence available suggests that it is by no means a simple task to identify opinion leaders, for a leader for one type of information (e.g., older family women for homemaking) is not necessarily a leader for another type (e.g., younger, sometimes single, women for fashions). This seems to be true even within a fairly narrow product category (e.g., groceries). And, as pointed out in Chapter 6, some product categories appear to be unaffected by personal influence (e.g., laundry soap, refrigerators). Whether or not a person becomes an opinion leader seems to depend upon at least three major factors: *who* one is (prestige), *what* one knows (instrumentality), and *where* one is located (accessibility). In effect, opinon leaders are *selected* by their followers, rather than vice versa, and they may actually be *lower* in status!

For these reasons, it would be futile to expect that the informal group leader (of a family or reference group) would be the opinion leader for products of all types. Group leaders are influenced by many others in the group, so that it is *possible* for each member of a reference group to be an opinion leader for one or more types of products. Further, there almost certainly are intellectual or personality correlates of opinion leadership. Some individuals possess a psychological "need structure" which compels them to "sell" other individuals a product they themselves have bought, as a means of self-justification for their own actions. There are undoubtedly other complexities.

The direct approach to locating names and addresses of opinion leaders for a given product would call for a complete sociometric mapping or sociogram (cf. Chapter 6) of all geographical areas in which the product is offered for sale. In the case of a consumer household product, the utter impossibility of this approach is obvious. But a bit of thought reveals that communication links which *directly* connect manufacturer and consumer are possible and, indeed, have been available in one form or another for some time.

For example, manufacturers often obtain names of product users or potential users by sponsoring consumer contests which call for the mailing addresses of entrants. Free gifts or premiums are offered to those sending in coupons from printed media (opinion leaders seem to have greater exposure to mass media). Warranty cards might be used, when available. A brief mail survey of selected upper-income homes might be conducted on one pretext or another, and space could be provided on the return postcard or letter for the name and address of the respondent. While the number of returns would be low, respondents might well include a high proportion of opinion leaders.

A firm might also ask questions designed to identify these leaders as part of large nationwide consumer surveys planned for other purposes. Listings from direct-mail organizations might be of help. Lazarsfeld suggests that members of certain types of community organizations (e.g., women's clubs, men's service groups) might be more likely to be opinion leaders. (Lazarsfeld, Berelson, & Gaudet, 1948.) Also, since opinion leaders are far greater users of the mass communications media than nonleaders, a comparison of subscription mailing lists of appropriate magazines would reveal the individuals who subscribe to several publications and who therefore may be opinion leaders.

While the best means of locating opinion leaders is not known, creative thought by promotion specialists within a firm would undoubtedly yield other ideas for obtaining direct contact with these consumers.

Once they are located, what sort of communications should be directed to them? The answer to this depends in part upon their demographic and psychosocial characteristics, as revealed by intensive study of a sample of these leaders for a given product. It may be found, for example, that such individuals are high on the psychological trait of dominance and that they diligently seek information as a means to acquiring a power orientation from others in the group. On the other hand, they may tend to be especially cooperative and good-natured and to pass along information in a helpful vein. In any event, once these leaders have been located, communications may be directed to them about forthcoming new products, telling not only that the product will be offered but also giving some background on the development, usage, cost, and availability, which would provide them with the information necessary to secure and perpetuate their positions of leadership in that product category.

Free product usage to opinion leaders may be extremely effective either on a free sample basis (for soft goods) or on a limited trial basis (for hard goods). The offer by Chrysler Corporation of an Imperial automobile for a trial period to professional men such as doctors and lawyers is a good illustration of what may be done. Similarly, Continental automobile dealers in one city offered a highly select group of individuals a $50 bill just to drive their car at a premiere showing of the new model. Of course, free samples of inexpensive household products have been offered many times in the past — but normally to everyone in an area, not *selectively* to opinion leaders. The latter approach might be much less expensive and equally effective.

There is some indication that findings from the Menzel and Katz study on the adoption process for a new drug among doctors has already been put to use, unfortunately to promote sales of the baby-deforming drug, thalidomide. One newspaper article reviewed the materials received by a Senate subcommittee on the instructions given by the drug manufacturer to its salesmen to promote this drug among doctors: "Over and over the [salesmen] were urged to hand-pick 'influential' doctors — get them to use the drug. They, in turn, theoretically, would influence their colleagues." (McCartney, 1963.) While there is no way of knowing for certain, it seems likely that this promotion campaign drew heavily from the study showing how, in the choice of drugs for prescription purposes, key physicians normally exert an influence on colleagues in their own social group.

In summary, there would seem to be a vast, largely untapped opportunity to utilize the two-step flow of communications in introducing and perpetuating consumer products of many types.

Communications and New-Product Adoption

There remains a very interesting body of knowledge about the role of communications in the new-product adoption process. Notice particularly the word *process*, for a consumer normally does not adopt a product or service immediately upon contact.[4] Rather, it is usually the case that a period of time elapses between awareness of a product and purchase of it. Sometimes this inter-

---

[4] Certain types of impulse goods are exceptions, of course.

val is rather long. Several questions, then, arise as to the role of communications in the adoption process:

- Are communications more important in some stages of the adoption process than in others, or are they uniformly important in all stages?
- Are different *types* of communications necessary for different stages, i.e., different sources, different content, and the like?
- If so, what types of communications are most important at each stage of the adoption process?

Lavidge and Steiner suggest that the consumer moves up a series of steps in the adoption of any new product:

1. Near the bottom of the steps stand potential purchasers who are completely unaware of the existence of the product or service in question.
2. Closer to purchasing, but still a long way from the cash register, are those who are merely aware of its existence.
3. Up a step are prospects who know what the product has to offer.
4. Still closer to purchasing are those who have favorable attitudes toward the product — those who like the product.
5. Those whose favorable attitudes have developed to the point of preference over all other possibilities are up still another step.
6. Even closer to purchasing are consumers who couple preference with desire to buy and the conviction that the purchase would be wise.
7. Finally, of course, is the step which translates this attitude into actual purchase. (Lavidge & Steiner, 1961, p. 59.)

These writers believe that certain types of advertising are effective at each of these stages. For example, announcements, descriptive copy, and classified advertisements are most useful at the awareness stage (steps 1 and 2), while slogans, jingles, and teaser campaigns are more useful at the interest stage. (This seems to suggest that for maximum effectiveness of effort it must be that the bulk of the market moves along these steps in unison; it would also be necessary to *measure* repeatedly so that one would know just which stage the market is in at any given time.)

A more definitive article on this subject was presented by Wilkening, who studied the adoption process for new ideas in farming among approximately 600 young farmers in six Wisconsin counties. His views on the differential role of communications are as follows:

> The main assumption of this [work] is that the type of information transmitted about new farm techniques or practices is related to the primary functions and to the structural and operational features of the transmitting agents. Stated another way, different sources are utilized for different types of information. The particular sources utilized will depend upon the way in which they are perceived by the *individual seeking the information* and thus upon the functions performed by those sources for the individual. (Wilkening, 1956, p. 361.)

To investigate this, Wilkening asked each farmer the following questions:

1. Where or from whom do you usually *first hear about* new ideas in farming?

2. After you first hear about some new idea, where or from whom do you get information that *helps you decide* whether to try it out on your farm?

3. If you decide to try out a new idea, where or from whom do you get most help on *how much* material to use, *when* to use it, *how* to go about it, etc.?

Table 9.4 shows the responses to these questions. Notice the large differences in the effects of different sources at different stages in the adoption process. The mass media (farm papers, farm magazines, newspapers, radio, television) play their greatest role in the early stages, when the farmer is first learning about the new idea. In the next stage, the emphasis clearly shifts to others farmers in deciding whether or not to try out the new idea. Finally, the county agent for the United States Department of Agriculture and local universities are the most important communicating agents for getting help on *how* to use the new material or technique, with other farmers and commercial sources (e.g., salesmen) not far behind in terms of influence. (Wilkening, 1956.)

There is, then, an important difference in the part played by communications at different stages of the adoption process. Note, however, that Wilkening's evidence applies to the agricultural

Table 9.4

PERCENTAGE DISTRIBUTION OF RESPONSES TO QUESTIONS
ABOUT THE ROLE OF COMMUNICATING AGENTS

Communicating Agent	*First learn about new ideas*	*Decide whether to try new ideas*	*How to use new material*
Farm papers, farm magazines, newspapers	62.8	3.8	2.2
Radio and television	8.0	0.2	
County agent and universities	7.4	21.1	34.6
Vocational agriculture instructor	6.6	5.2	4.9
Special agencies	0.9	2.0	4.1
Commercial sources	2.2	8.2	21.2
Other farmers	11.0	47.0	23.7
Self, no outside source	0.5	8.6	4.2
No response	0.6	3.9	5.1
Total	100.0	100.0	100.0

situation and to Wisconsin farmers in particular. We know of no similar evidence with respect to new-product adoption by consumers in general.

There is, however, some evidence about the *relative* effectiveness of one medium, television, in the various stages of the product adoption process (as defined by Lavidge and Steiner). This study was conducted by the National Broadcasting Company in Fort Wayne, Indiana, in 1953. In October of that year, Fort Wayne had no television station at all, although 20 per cent of the families owned sets on which they got "fringe" reception from nearby cities. After a television station was approved and installed, approximately 35 per cent of Fort Wayne families bought television sets within six months. By taking before and after interviews in 7,500 homes, NBC was able to measure the impact of television advertising on both "new" owners (who bought sets after the station was installed) and "old" owners (who had sets before the station was installed). Table 9.5 shows before and after percentages for several aspects of product acceptance, from initial awareness to final purchase. While these aspects do not conform exactly with the Lavidge-Steiner steps, they do resemble them; at least they form a sort of progression or continuum from initial impact through final brand purchase.

Table 9.5

Per Cent of Respondents at Various Stages

	Old Owners			New Owners		
	Before TV	After TV	Increase	Before TV	After TV	Increase
Brand Awareness	59	82	23	43	75	32
Brand-Product Association	29	47	18	22	42	20
Trademark Recognition	69	80	11	64	79	15
Slogan Identification	64	86	22	54	83	29
Brand Reputation	29	41	12	24	36	12
Brand Preference Advertised on TV	28	37	9	25	36	11
Not Advertised on TV	29	22	−7	31	21	−10
Brand Purchase*	19	25	6	18	24	6

* Average of brands advertised on TV

By comparing before and after percentages, it appears that television has its greatest impact in the *early stages* of the product adoption process. For example, increases in such early stages as "brand awareness," "brand-product association," and "slogan identification" are far greater than changes in such later stages as "brand preference" and especially "brand purchase." This is true both for old and new owners. We may conclude that television advertising seems to help all along the line but that its influence is greatest at the beginning of the process. As in the case of other studies, it is likely that other information sources come into play at later stages and reduce the *relative* influence of television. (National Broadcasting Company, 1955.)

The evidence strongly suggests that communications have a different role to play at different stages of the new product adoption process and that the types of communications which are most influential vary from one stage to another. It is unfortunate that most of what we know about this important subject comes from studies in areas other than consumer marketing. Research is badly needed to explore the consumer domain, for findings would most certainly be different in at least some respects from those in the agricultural marketing scene, where the greatest amount of research has been done to date.

QUESTIONS
FOR REVIEW

1. What evidence do we have that mass communications ca change attitudes? What, precisely, are the means and pro cesses by which this is accomplished?

2. How does a firm marketing a new line of frozen seafood break the selective perception barrier among both users other brands and nonusers?

3. Are there some consumer marketing situations in which the are more *efficient* ways to change attitudes than by mass com munications?

4. Indicate specifically how the communications principles this chapter are related to each of the following behavior topics discussed earlier:
   Gestalt
   Selective perception
   Learning
   Sensory discrimination
   Cognitive dissonance

5. In general, what industries, products, or brands might bene most from two-sided appeals? Choose one product or bran not already mentioned in the text) and show how a two-side appeal might be used.

6. Under what conditions, if any, is "fear" advertising (i.e., a vertising which is threatening to the consumer) likely to effective? Be specific.

7. Under what conditions might advertising be fully believed a consumer and still not be effective in motivating him action?

8. How might the two-step flow be used by a consumer pro ucts marketer? To illustrate, choose a product and devel a strategy.

References

Abelson, H. I., *Persuasion*. New York: Springer Publishing Company, 1959.

Alderson, W., *Marketing Behavior and Executive Action*. Homewood, Ill.: Richard D. Irwin, 1957.

Alderson, W., "The Analytical Framework for Marketing," in *Proceedings: Conference of Marketing Teachers from Far Western States*, ed. D. J. Duncan. Berkeley: University of California Press, 1958, pp. 15–28.

Alexander, Milton, "The Significance of Ethnic Groups in Marketing New-Type Packaged Foods in Greater New York," in *Advancing Marketing Efficiency*, ed. L. H. Stockman. American Marketing Association, 1959, pp. 557–561.

Allison, R. I., & Uhl, K. P., "Influence of Beer Brand Identification on Taste Perception," *Journal of Marketing Research*, August, 1964, pp. 36–39.

Allport, G. W., & Postman, L. J., "The Basic Psychology of Rumor," in *Readings in Social Psychology*, ed. E. E. Maccoby, T. M. Newcomb, and E. L. Hartley. Holt, Rinehart and Winston, 1958.

Arnheim, R., *Art and Visual Perception*. Berkeley: University of California Press, 1960.

Arrow, K. J., "Mathematical Models in the Social Sciences," in *The Policy Sciences*, ed. D. Lerner & N. D. Lasswell. Stanford: Stanford University Press, 1951, pp. 129–155.

Arrow, K. J., *Social Choice and Individual Values*. New York: John Wiley and Sons, 1951.

Asch, S. E., "Forming Impressions of Personality," *Journal of Abnormal and Social Psychology*, 1946, 41, 258–290.

Asch, S. E., *Social Psychology*. Prentice-Hall, 1957.

Asch, S. E., "Effects of Group Pressure on the Modification and Distortion of Judgments," in *Readings in Social Psychology*, ed. E. E.

315

Maccoby, T. M. Newcomb, and E. L. Hartley, Holt, Rinehart and Winston, 1958.

Baker, S., *Visual Persuasion*. New York: McGraw-Hill, 1961.

Bales, R. F., "In Conference," *Harvard Business Review*, 1954, 32, 44–50.

Banks, S., "The Relationship Between Preference and Purchase of Brands," *Journal of Marketing*, 1950, 145–157.

Barclay, W. D., "The Semantic Differential as an Index of Brand Attitude," *Journal of Advertising Research*, March, 1964, pp. 30–33.

Barron, M. L., *The Aging American*. Thomas Y. Crowell Company, 1961.

Bauer, R. A., & Bauer, A. H., "America, Mass Society, and Mass Media," *Journal of Social Issues*, 1960, 16, 3–66.

Bauer, A., Cunningham, S. M., & Wortzel, L. H., "The Marketing Dilemma of Negroes," *Journal of Marketing*, 1965, 29, 1–6.

Bauer, R. J., "Consumer Behavior as Risk Taking," in *Proceedings of the 43rd National Conference of the American Marketing Association*, ed. R. S. Hancock. Chicago: American Marketing Association, 1960.

Bayton, J. A., "Motivation, Cognition, Learning — Basic Factors in Consumer Behavior," *Journal of Marketing*, 1958, 22, 282–289.

Bealer, C., & Willits, F. K., "Rural Youth: A Case Study in the Rebelliousness of Adolescents," *Annals of the American Academy of Political and Social Science*, 1961, 338, 63–69.

Bell, E., "Consumer Innovators: A Unique Market for Newness," in *Toward Scientific Marketing*, ed. S. A. Greyser. American Marketing Association, pp. 85–107. 1963.

Benedict, R., *Patterns of Culture*. Boston: Houghton Mifflin Company, 1934.

Berelson, B., & Steiner, G. A., *Human Behavior: An Inventory of Scientific Findings*. Harcourt, Brace, and World, 1964.

Berkowitz, L., & Lundy, R. M., "Personality Characteristics Related to Susceptibility to Influence by Peers or Authority Figures," *Journal of Personality*, 1957, 25, 306–316.

Berlyne, D. E., "A Decade of Motivation Theory," *American Scientist*, 1964, 52, 447–451.

Bilkey, W. J., "Psychic Tensions and Purchasing Behavior," *Journal of Social Psychology*, 1955, 41, 247–257.

Bogart, L., & Tolley, B. S., "The Impact of Blank Space: An Experiment in Advertising Readership," *Journal of Advertising Research*, June 1964, pp. 21–27.

Boulding, E., "Orientation Toward Achievement of Security in Relation to Consumer Behavior," *Human Relations*, 1960, 13, pp. 365–382.

Bourne, F. S., *Group Influence in Marketing and Public Relations*. Ann Arbor, Mich.: Foundation for Research on Human Behavior, 1956.

Bowles, J. W., Jr., & Pronko, N. H., "Identification of Cola Beverages: II. A Further Study," *Journal of Applied Psychology*, 1948, 32, pp. 559–564.

Brink, E. L., & Kelley, W. T., *The Management of Promotion*. Prentice Hall, 1963.

Britt, S. H. "How Advertising Can Use Psychology's Rules of Learning," *Printers Ink, September* 23, 1955, pp. 74–80.

Brooks, J., "The Little Ad that Isn't There," *Consumer Reports*, January 1958, pp. 5–11.

Brooks, J., "The Edsel," *New Yorker*, November 26, 1960, pp. 57–102.

Broom, L., "Social Differentiation and Stratification," in *Sociology Today*, ed. R. K. Morton, L. Broom, and L. S. Cottrell, Jr. New York: Basic Books, 1962.

Broom, L., & Selznick, P., *Sociology*, Harper & Row, 1963.

Brown, R. L., "Wrapper Influence on the Perception of Freshness in Bread," *Journal of Applied Psychology*, 1958, 42, pp. 257–260.

Bruner, J. S., "Social Psychology and Perception," in *Readings in Social Psychology*, edited by Maccoby, E. E., Newcomb, T. M., & Hartley, E. L., Holt, Rinehart and Winston, 1958.

Bruner, J. S., & Goodman, C. C., "Value and Need as Organizing Factors in Perception," *Journal of Abnormal & Social Psychology*, 1947, 42, pp. 33–44.

Bruner, J. S., Goodnow, J. J., & Austin, G. A., *A Study of Thinking*, John Wiley and Sons, Inc., 1960.

Bruner, J. S., & Postman, L. J., "On the Perception of Incongruity: A Paradigm," *Journal of Pers.*, 18, 1949, pp. 206–223.

Bullock, H. A., "Consumer Motivations in Black and White," *Harvard Business Review*, May-June 1961, 39, 89–104, and July-August 1961, 39, 110–124.

Burck, G., "How American Taste is Changing," *Fortune*, July 1959, p. 114, ff.

Business News, January, 1965.

Caplovitz, D. "The Problems of Blue-Collar Consumers," in Arthur B. Shostak and William Gombert, eds., *Blue Collar World*, Prentice Hall, 1964, pp. 110–120.

Carter, L. F., & Schooler, K., "Value, Need, and Other Factors in Perception," *Psychological Review*, 1949, 56, pp. 200–207.

Cateora, R., *An Analysis of the Teen-Age Market*, Bureau of Business Research, University of Texas, 1963.

Coleman, J. S., *The Adolescent Society*, The Free Press of Glencoe, A Division of the Macmillan Company, 1961.

Coleman, R. P., "The Significance of Social Stratification in Selling," in Martin L. Bell, ed., *Marketing: A Maturing Discipline*, American Marketing Association, 1961, pp. 171–184.

Colley, R. H., ed., *Defining Advertising Goals for Measured Advertising Results*, New York: Association of National Advertisers, Inc. 1961.

Cooley, C. H., *Human Nature and the Social Order*. New York: Charles Scribner's Sons, 1902.

Combs, A. W., & Snygg, D., *Individual Behavior*, Harper & Row 1959.

Cox, D. F., "Clues for Advertising Strategists," *Harvard Business Review*, Sept.–Oct., 1961, pp. 160–176

Cox, D. F., & Rich, S. V., "Perceived Risk and Consumer Decision Making," *Journal of Marketing Research*, November 1964, 1, pp 32–39.

Crane, E., *Marketing Communications*, John Wiley & Sons, 1965.

Cronbach, L. J., *Essentials of Psychological Testing*, Harper & Row (2nd edition), 1960.

Curtis, J. N., *Social Psychology*, McGraw Hill, 1960.

Davidson, W. R., "Marketing Renaissance," in Stephen A. Greyser ed., *Toward Scientific Marketing*, American Marketing Association 1964, pp. 3–14.

Davis, A., & Havighurst, R. J., "Social Class and Color Differences Child Rearing," *American Sociol. Rev.*, December 1946, 11:698–71

de Grazia, E. (see Grazia)

Dichter, E., "The World Customer," Harvard Business Review, July–August 1962, 40, pp. 113–122.

Dollard, J., Miller, N. E., Dobb, L. W., Mowrer, O. H., & Sears, R. R., *Frustration and Aggression*, Yale University Press, 1940.

Eckstrand, G., & Gilliland, A. R., "The Psychogalvanometric Method for Measuring the Effectiveness of Advertising," *Journal of Applied Psychology*, 1948, 32, pp. 415–425.

Edwards, A. L., *Edwards Personal Preference Schedule Manual*, Psychological Corp., 1957.

Ehrensberger, R., "An Experimental Study of the Relative Effectiveness of Certain Forms of Emphasis in Public Speaking," Speech Monogr., 1945, 12, pp. 94–111.

Engel, J. F., "Are Automobile Purchasers Dissonant Consumers?" *Journal of Marketing*, April 1963, pp. 55–58.

Erlich, D., Guttman, I., & Schonbach, P., "Postdecision Exposure to Relevant Information," *Journal of Abnormal & Social Psychology*, 1957, 54, pp. 98–102.

Evans, F. B., "Psychological and Objective Factors in the Prediction of Brand Choice: Ford versus Chevrolet," *Journal of Business*, 1959, 32, pp. 340–369.

Evans, F. B., "The Brand Image Myth," *Business Horizons*, Fall 1961, p. 19, ff.

Evans, F. B., "You Still Can't Tell a Ford Owner from a Chevrolet Owner," *Journal of Business*, 1961, 34, pp. 67–73.

Evans, F. B., "Correlates of Automobile Shopping Behavior," *Journal of Marketing*, October 1962, 26, pp. 74–77.

Ewing, T. N., "A Study of Certain Factors Involved in Changes of Opinion," *Journal of Social Psychology*, 1942, 16, pp. 63–88.

Ferber, R., Blankertz, D. F., & Hollander, S., *Marketing Research*, Ronald Press, 1964.

Ferber, R., & Wales, N. G., *Motivation and Market Behavior*, Irwin, 1958.

Festinger, L., "Cognitive Dissonance," *Scientific American*, 207:27, October 1962, p. 93 ff.

Flesch, R., *The Art of Readable Writing*, Harper & Bros., 1949.

Foote, N. N., *Consumer Behavior: Household Decision-Making*, Vol. IV, New York University Press, 1961.

320 | References

Forrester, J. W., "Advertising: A Problem in Industrial Dynamics," *Harvard Business Review*, March-April 1959, pp. 100–110.

Freeman, F., Weeks, H. E., Ashley, H., & Wertheiner, W. J., "News Commentator Effects: A Study in Knowledge and Opinion Change," *Public Opinion Quarterly*, 1955, 19, pp. 209–215.

Friedmann, E. A., "The Impact of Aging on the Social Structure," in Tibbitts, *op. cit.*, pp. 120–144.

Gardner, B. B., & Cohen, Y. A., "ROP Color and its Effect on Newspaper Advertising," *Journal of Marketing Research*, May 1964, pp. 68–70.

Gennep van, Arnold, *The Rites of Passage*, translated by Monika B. Vizedom and Gabrielle L. Caffee, University of Chicago Press, 1960, originally published 1908.

Glazer, N., and Moynihan, *Beyond the Melting Pot*, The MIT Press and Harvard University Press, 1963.

Glock, C. Y., & Nicosia, F. M., "Uses of Sociology in Studying 'Consumption' Behavior," *Journal of Marketing*, July 1964, 28, pp. 51–54.

Goffman, E., *The Presentation of Self in Everyday Life*, Doubleday Anchor Books, 1959.

Golin, E., & Lyerly, S. B., "The Galvanic Skin Response as a Test of Advertising Impact," *Journal of Applied Psychology*, December 1950, 34, pp. 440–443.

Gordon, M., *Assimilation in American Life*, Oxford University Press, 1964.

Gottlieb, M. J., "Segmentation by Personality Types," Advancing Marketing Efficiency, ed. L. H. Stockman, Chicago: American Marketing Association, 1959, pp. 148–158.

Graham, S., "Class and Conservatism in the Adoption of Innovations," *Human Relations*, Vol. 9, No. 1, 1956, pp. 91–100.

Grazia, de Sebastian, *Of Time, Work, and Leisure*, The Twentieth Century Fund, 1962.

Guilford, J. P., *Psychometric Methods*, McGraw-Hill, 1954.

Guilford, J. P., "Intelligence: 1965 Model," *American Psychol.*, January 1966, 21, pp. 20–26.

Guilford, J. P., & Zimmerman, W. S., "Fourteen Dimensions of Temperament," *Psychological Monographs*, 1956, 70, #417.

Haire, M., "Projective Techniques in Marketing Research," *Journal of Marketing*, 1950, 14, pp. 649–652.

Havighurst, R. J., & Albrecht, R., *Older People*, Longmans, Green and Company, 1953.

Hayakawa, S. I., "Sexual Fantasy and the 1957 Car," *E.T.C.: A Review of General Semantics.*, 1957.

Helfgott, M. J., "The New Package Research," presented to Marketing Workshop, American Marketing Association (mimeo, Lippincott and Margulies, Inc., 1960).

Heider, F., & Simmel, E., "A Study of Apparent Behavior," *American Journal of Psychology*, 1944, 57, pp. 243–259.

Heller, N., "An Application of Psychological Learning Theory to Advertising," *Journal of Marketing*, January 1956, 20, pp. 248–254.

Hess, E. H., & Polt, J. M., "Pupil Size as Related to Interest Value of Visual Stimuli," *Science*, 1960, 132, pp. 349–350.

Hilgard, E. R., "Methods and Procedures in the Study of Learning," in *Handbook of Experimental Psychology*, edited by S. S. Stevens, Wiley & Sons, 1951, pp. 517–567.

Hill, E. W., "Corporate and Brand Images: A Survey of Current Research with an Example of a Corporate Image Investigation of Soap and Detergent Manufacturers in the Southern California Area," Unpublished Master's Thesis, University of Southern California, Los Angeles, 1961.

Hollingshead, A. B., & Redlich, F. C., *Social Class and Mental Illness*, Wiley & Sons, 1958.

Holloway, R. J., & Hancock, R. S., *The Environment of Marketing Behavior*, Wiley & Sons, 1964.

Homans, G. C., *The Human Group*, Harcourt, Brace and World, 1950.

Homans, G. C., *Social Behavior: Its Elementary Forms*, Harcourt, Brace and World, 1961.

Housing Research Center, Cornell University, *Houses are for People*, Research Publication #3.

Hovland, C. I., "Effects of the Mass Media of Communications," Ch. 28 in *Handbook of Social Psychology*, edited by G. Lindzey, Addison-Wesley Publishing Co., Inc., 1954.

Hovland, C. I., Janis, I. L., & Kelley, H. H., *Communication and Persuasion*, Yale University Press, 1953.

Hovland, C. I., Lumsdaine, A. A., & Sheffield, F. D., *Experimentation on Mass Communications*, Princeton University Press, 1949.

Hovland, C. I., & Weiss, W., "The Influence of Source Credibility on Communication Effectiveness," *Public Opinion Quarterly*, 1951, 15, pp. 635–650.

Howard, J. A., *Marketing: Executive and Buyer Behavior*, Columbia University Press, 1963.

Hull, C. L., "The Influence of Tobacco Smoking on Mental and Motor Efficiency," *Psychological Monographs*, 1924, 23, 161.

Hull, C. L., *Principles of Behavior*, Appleton Century, 1943.

Hunt, J. McV., "Traditional Personality Theory in the Light of Recent Evidence," *American Scientist*, 1965, 53, pp. 80–96.

Husband, R. W., & Godfrey, J., "An Experimental Study of Cigarette Identification," *Journal of Applied Psychology*, 1934, 18, pp. 220–251.

Inkeles, A., and Levinson, D. J. In *Handbook of Social Psychology*, ed. G. Lindzey, Camb. Addison-Wesley, 1954.

Inkeles, A., & Levinson, D. J., *Social Psychology*, Vol. II, Harvard University Press.

Inkeles, A., & Rossi, P. H., "National Comparisons of Occupational Prestige," *American Journal of Sociol.*, 1956, 61, pp. 329–39.

Janis, I. L., & Feshbach, S., "Effects of Fear-Arousing Communications," *Journal of Abnormal & Social Psychology*, 1953, 48, pp. 78–92.

Jersild, A., "Primary, Recency, Frequency, and Vividness," *Journal of Experimental Psychology*, 1929, 12, pp. 58–70.

Kaplan, M., "The Uses of Leisure," in Tibbitts, *op. cit.*, pp. 407–443.

Kassarjian, H. H., "Social Character and Differential Preference for Mass Communication," *Journal of Marketing Research*, May 1965, 2, pp. 146–153.

Katona, G., "Rational Behavior and Economic Behavior," *Psychological Review*, 1953, 60, pp. 307–318.

Katona, G., *The Powerful Consumer*, McGraw Hill, 1960.

Katz, E., "The Two-Step Flow of Communication: An Up-to-Date Report on an Hypothesis," *Public Opinion Quarterly*, Spring 1957, pp. 61–78.

Kelley, H. H., "Salience of Membership and Resistance to Change of Group-Anchored Attitudes," *Human Relations*, 1955, 8, pp. 275–289.

Kelley, H. H., & Volkart, E. H., "The Resistance to Change of Group-Anchored Attitudes," *American Sociological Review*, 1952, 17, pp. 453–465.

Kelly, G. A., "Man's Construction of His Alternatives," in *Assessment of Human Motives*, ed. Lindzey, G., Holt, Rinehart & Winston, 1964.

Kelman, N. C., & Hovland, C. I., " 'Reinstatement' of the Communicator in Delayed Measurement of Opinion Change," *Journal of Abnormal & Social Psychology*, July 1953, 48, pp. 327–335.

Klein, G. S., Spence, D. P., & Holt, R. R., "Cognition Without Awareness; Subliminal Influences upon Conscious Thought," *Journal of Abnormal & Social Psychology*, 1958, 57, pp. 255–266.

Koffka, K., *Principles of Gestalt Psychology*. New York: Harcourt, Brace & Co., 1935.

Köhler, W., "Relational Determination in Perception," in *Cerebral Mechanisms in Behavior*, ed. by Jeffress, L. A., John Wiley & Sons, 1951, pp. 200–243.

Krech, D., Crutchfield, R. S., & Ballachey, E. L., *Individual in Society*, McGraw Hill, 1962.

Krugman, H. E., "Affective Response to Music as a Function of Familiarity," *Journal of Abnormal & Social Psychology*, 1943, 38, pp. 338–392.

Krugman, H. E., "Some Applications of Pupil Measurement," *Journal of Marketing Research*, November 1964, pp. 15–18.

Krugman, H. E., & Hartley, E. L., "The Learning of Tastes," *Public Opinion Quarterly*, Winter 1960, pp. 621–631.

Lansing, J. G., & Kish, L., "Family Life Cycle as an Independent Variable," *American Sociological Review*, October 1957, pp. 512–519.

Lasswell, H. D., *World Politics and Personal Insecurity*, McGraw Hill Book Company, 1935.

Lasswell, H. D., *The Analysis of Political Behavior*, Routledge & Kegan Paul Limited, 1948.

Lavidge, R. J., & Steiner, G. A., "A Model for Predicting Measurements of Advertising Effectiveness," *Journal of Marketing*, October 1961, pp. 59–62.

Lazarsfeld, P. F., Berelson, B., & Gaudet, H., *The People's Choice*, University Press, 1948.

Lazarus, R. S., & McCleary, R. A., "Autonomic Discrimination Without Awareness: A Study of Subception," *Psychological Review*, 58, 1951, pp. 113–122.

Leavitt, H. J., "A Note on Some Experimental Findings about the Meanings of Price," *Journal of Business*, July 1954, 27, pp. 205–210.

Levy, A., *Life*, July 16, 1965.

Levy, S. J., "Symbols by Which We Buy," Advancing Marketing Efficiency, L. H. Stockman, ed., Chicago: American Marketing Association, 1959, pp. 409–416.

Lewin, K., *A Dynamic Theory of Personality*, McGraw Hill, 1935.

Lewin, K., *Principles of Topological Psychology*, McGraw Hill, 1936.

Lewin, K., "Group Decision and Social Change," in *Readings in Social Psychology*, ed. Maccoby, E. E., Newcomb, T. M., and Hartley, E. L., Holt, Rinehart & Winston, Inc., 1958, pp. 197–211.

Lindzey, G., ed. *Assessment of Human Motives*, Holt, Reinhart, & Winston, 1964.

Linton, H. B., "Dependence on External Influence: Correlates in Perception, Attitudes and Judgment," *Journal of Abnormal & Social Psychology*, 1955, 51, pp. 502–507.

Lipset, S. M., & Bendix, R., *Social Mobility in Industrial Society*, University of California Press, 1959.

Los Angeles *Times*, February 16, 1964.

Lucas, D. B., & Britt, S. H., *Measuring Advertising Effectiveness*, McGraw Hill, 1963.

Luh, C. W., "The Conditions of Retention," *Psychol. Monographs*, #142, 1922.

Lumsdaine, A. A., & Janis, I. L., "Resistance to 'Counter-Propaganda' Produced by a One-Sided versus a Two-Sided 'Propaganda' Presentation," *Public Opinion Quarterly*, 1953, 17, pp. 311–318.

Maloney, J. A., "Is Advertising Believability Really Important?" *Journal of Marketing*, October 1963, pp. 1–8.

Martineau, P., *Motivation in Advertising*, McGraw Hill, 1957.

Martineau, P., "Social Classes and Spending Behavior," *Journal of Marketing*, October 1958, 23, pp. 121–130.

Maslow, A. H., "The Influence of Familiarization on Preference," *Journal of Experimental Psychology*, 1937, 21, pp. 162–180.

Maslow, A. H., "A Theory of Human Motivation," *Psychological Review*, July 1943, pp. 370–396.

McCartney, J., "Drug Promotion Appeal Directed at Doctors' Ego," by-lined column in Chicago Daily News, Post-Dispatch, February 25, 1963.

McCrary, J. W., Jr., & Hunter, W. S., "Serial Position Curves in Verbal Learning," *Science*, February 6, 1953, pp. 131–134.

McVey, J., "Are Channels of Distribution What the Textbooks Say?" *Journal of Marketing*, January 1960, pp. 61–65.

Media/Scope, "How Important is Position in Consumer Magazine Advertising?" June, 1964, pp. 52–57.

Menzel, H., & Katz, E., "Social Relations and Innovation in the Medical Profession: The Epidemiology of a New Drug," *Public Opinion Quarterly*, Winter 1955–56, pp. 337–352.

Merton, R. K., "The Environment of the Innovating Organization: Some Conjectures and Proposals," in Gary A. Steiner, ed., *The Creative Organization*, The University of Chicago Press, 1965.

Miller, R. L., "Dr. Weber and the Consumer," *Journal of Marketing*, January 1962, pp. 57–61.

Mills, C. W., *The Power Elite*, Oxford University Press, 1956.

Morgan, J., "A Review of Recent Research on Consumer Behavior," in *Consumer Behavior*, ed. by Clark, L. H., Harper & Bros., 1958, pp. 93–219.

Murray, H. A., ed., *Explorations in Personality: A Clinical Experimental Study of Fifty Men of College Age*, Oxford University Press, 1938.

Myers, J. H., "A Competitive Edge in Marketing Communications," in *Competition in Marketing*, ed. by Meloan, T. W., & Whitlo, C. M., produced under grant from Sperry & Hutchinson Foundation, New York, 1964. (Copies available from University of Southern California)

National Broadcasting Company, *How Television Changes Strangers into Customers*, New York, 1955.

Newcomb, T. M., "Attitude Development as a Function of Reference Groups," in *Readings in Social Psychology*, Maccoby, E. E., Newcomb, T. M., and Hartley, E. L., Holt, Rinehart & Winston, 1958.

Newman, J. W., *Motivation Research and Marketing Management*, Plimpton Press, 1954.

Ogilvy, D., *Confessions of an Advertising Man*, Atheneum Publishers, 1963.

Opinion Research Corporation, *America's Tastemakers*. Report No. 1, Princeton, N.J., April 1959.

Osgood, C. E., Suci, G. J., & Tannenbaum, P. N., *The Measurement of Meaning*, University of Illinois Press, 1957.

Oxenfeldt, A., Miller, D., Shuchman, A., & Winick, C., *Insights Into Pricing*, Wadsworth Publishing Co., 1961.

Paranka, S., "Marketing Predictions from Consumer Attitudinal Data," *Journal of Marketing*, July 1960, pp. 46–51.

Parsons, T., *Essays in Sociological Theory*, Glencoe, Ill.: The Free Press, 1949.

Parsons, T., Bales, R. F., Olds, J. Zelditch, M., & Salter, P. E., *Family, Socialization, and Interaction Process*, The Free Press of Glencoe, 1955.

Pelz, E. B., "Some Factors in 'Group Decision'," in *Readings in Social Psychology*, (see Lewin reference)

Pflaum, J., "Smoking Behavior: A Critical Review of Research," *Journal of Applied Behavioral Research*, April-May-June 1965, 1, pp. 195–209.

Postman, L. J., & Rau, L., "Retention as a Function of the Method of Measurement," University of California Publications in Psychology, 8, No. 3, 1957.

Pronko, N. H., & Bowles, J. W., Jr., "Identification of Cola Beverages: I. First Study," *Journal of Applied Psychology*, 1948, 32, pp. 304–312.

Pronko, N. H., & Bowles, J. W., Jr., "Identification of Cola Beverages: III. A final Study," *Journal of Applied Psychology*, 1949, 33, pp. 605–608.

Pronko, N. H., & Herman, D. T., "Identification of Cola Beverages: IV. Postcript," *Journal of Applied Psychology*, 1950, 34, pp. 68–69.

Rainwater, L., Coleman, R. P., & Handel, G., *Workingman's Wife*, Oceana, 1959.

Ramond, C. K., Rachal, L. N., & Marks, M. R., "Brand Discrimination Among Cigarette Smokers," *Journal of Applied Psychology*, 1950, 34, pp. 282–284.

Reichara, S., Livson, F., & Petersen, P. G., *Aging and Personality*, John Wiley and Sons, Inc., 1962.

Reinecke, J. A., "The Older Market — Fact or Fiction?" *The Journal of Marketing*, January 1964, 28, pp. 60–64.

Riesman, D., with Glazer, N., & Denney, R., *The Lonely Crowd*, Yale University Press, 1950.

Rohrer, J., & Sherif, M., eds., *Social Psychology at the Crossroads*, Harper, 1951.

Rosberg, J. W., "How Does Color, Size Affect Ad Readership," *Industrial Marketing*, May 1956, 41, pp. 54–57.

Ruch, F. L., *Psychology and Life*, Scott, Foresman and Company, (Fifth edition) 1958.

Rudolph, H. J., *Attention and Interest Factors in Advertising*, Funk & Wagnalls, New York, 1947.

Sharp, H. & Mott, P., "Consumer Decisions in the Metropolitan Family," *The Journal of Marketing*, October 1956, 21, pp. 149–162.

Sherif, M., "A Study of Some Social Factors in Perception," Archives of Psychology, 1935, No. 187.

Shibutane, T., "Reference Groups as Perspectives," *American Journal of Sociology*, 1955, 60, pp. 562–569.

Simmons, L. W., "Aging in Preindustrial Societies," in Tibbitts, *op. cit.*, pp. 62–91.

Simon, H. A., & March, S. G., *Organizations*, John Wiley & Sons, 1958.

Smith, E. A., *American Youth Culture*, The Free Press of Glencoe, 1962.

Sommers, M. S., "Product Symbolism and the Perception of Social Strata," in Stephen A. Greyser, ed., *Toward Scientific Marketing*, American Marketing Association, 1964, pp. 200–216.

Star, S. A., & Hughes, H. M., "Report on an Educational Campaign: The Cincinnati Plan for the United Nations," *American Journal of Sociology*, 1950, 55, pp. 389–400.

Starch, D., "What is the Best Frequency of Advertisements," *Media/scope*, December 1961, 5, pp. 44–45.

Staudt, T. A., & Taylor, D. A., *A Managerial Introduction to Marketing*, Prentice Hall, 1965.

Stone, G. P., "City Shoppers and Urban Identification: Observations on the Social Psychology of City Life," American Journal of Sociology, July 1954, 60, pp. 36–45.

Streib, G. F., & Thompson, W. E., "The Older Person in a Family Context," in Tibbitts, *op. cit.*, pp. 447–488.

Survey Research Center, University of Michigan, Ann Arbor, Michigan.

Tannenbaum, P. H., "Initial Attitude Toward Source and Concept as Factors in Attitude Change Through Communications," *Public Opinion Quarterly*, 1956, 20, pp. 413–426.

Thistlethwaite, D. L., de Haan, N., & Kamenetsky, J., "The Effects of 'Directive' and 'Non-directive' Communication Procedures on Attitudes," *Journal of Abnormal & Social Psychology*, 1955, 51, pp. 107–113.

Thomas, William I., *The Unadjusted Girl*, Little, Brown, 1923.

Thompson, V. A., *Modern Organization*, Alfred A. Knopf, 1961.

Thorndike, E. L., *Animal Intelligence: Experimental Studies.* New York: Macmillan, 1911.

Thumin, F. J., "Identification of Cola Beverages," *Journal of Applied Psychology*, 1962, 46, pp. 358–360.

Thurstone Temperament Schedule, Science Research Associates, Chicago, 2nd edition, 1953.

Tibbitts, C., ed., *Handbook of Social Gerontology*, University of Chicago Press, 1960.

Time, July 24, 1964, p. 77.

Tucker, W. T., *The Social Context of Economic Behavior*, Holt, Rinehart & Winston, Inc., 1964.

Tucker, W. T., & Painter, J. J., "Personality and Product Use," *Journal of Applied Psychology*, 1961, 45, pp. 325–329.

Tull, D. A., Boring, R. A., & Gonsior, M. N., "A Note on the Relationship of Price and Imputed Quality," *Journal of Business*, April 1964, pp. 186–191.

Ulin, L. G., "Page Size Influence on Advertising," *Media/scope*, July 1962, pp. 47–50.

Veblen, T. *The Theory of the Leisure Class.* New York: Macmillan, 1899.

van Gennep (see Gennep, van)

Venesian, A. R., "New Products' Strongest Ally," *Printers Ink*, May 29, 1964.

Warner, W. L., & Abegglen, J. C., *Occupational Mobility in American Business and Industry 1928–1952*, University of Minnesota, 1955.

Warner, W. L., & Lunt, P. S., *The Social Life of a Modern Community*, Yale University Press, 1941.

Webster, F. E., "The 'Deal Prone' Consumer," *Journal of Marketing Research*, May 1965, 2, pp. 186–189.

Weinberger, M., "Does the 'Sleeper Effect' Apply to Advertising?" *Journal of Marketing*, October 1961, pp. 65–67.

Weiss, W., "Opinion Congruence with a Negative Source on One Issue as a Factor Influencing Agreement on Another Issue," *Journal of Abnormal & Social Psychology*, 1957, 54, pp. 180–186.

Wells, W. D., "Measuring Readiness to Buy," *Harvard Business Review*, July 1961, 39, pp. 81–87.

Wertheimer, M., "Gestalt Theory," in *A Source Book of Gestalt Psychology*, edited by Ellis, W. O., Rontledge & Kegan Paul, Ltd., 1955.

Westfall, R., "Psychological Factors in Predicting Product Choice," *Journal of Marketing*, April 1962, pp. 34–40.

Westfall, R. L., Boyd, H. L., Jr., & Campbell, D. T., "The Use of Structured Techniques in Motivation Research," *Journal of Marketing*, October 1957, 22, pp. 134–139.

White, C. M., "Multiple Goals in the Theory of the Firm," in *Linear Programming and the Theory of the Firm*, edited by Boulding, K. E., and Spivey, W. A., Macmillan, 1960.

Whyte, W. H., Jr., "The Language of Advertising," *Fortune*, September 1952, pp. 98–101 ff.

Whyte, W. H., Jr., "The Web of Word of Mouth," *Fortune*, November 1954, pp. 140 ff.

Wiebe, G. D., "Sampling-Motivation Research Merger: How Will it Aid Ad Men?" *Printers Ink*, November 28, 1958, p. 23 ff.

Wilkening, E. A., "Roles of Communicating Agents in Technological Change in Agriculture," *Social Forces*, May 1956, pp. 361–367.

Winick, C., "How to Find Out What Kind of Image You Have," in *Developing the Corporate Image*, edited by Bristol, L. H., Jr., Scribners, 1960.

Winick, C., "Anthropology's Contribution to Marketing," *Journal of Marketing*, July 1961, pp. 53–60.

Winick, C., "Three Measures of the Advertising Value of Media Context," *Journal of Advertising Research*, June 1962, 2, pp. 28–33.

Wolgast, E. H., "Do Husbands or Wives Make the Purchasing Decisions?" *Journal of Marketing*, October 1958, 23, pp. 151–158.

Woods, Sister Frances Jerome, *Cultural Values of American Ethnic Groups*, Harper and Brothers, 1956.

Woods, W. A., "Psychological Dimensions of Consumer Behavior," *Journal of Marketing*, January 1960, 24, pp. 15–19.

Woodworth, R. S., & Schlosberg, H., *Experimental Psychology*, Holt & Company, 1960.

Yamanaka, J., "The Prediction of Ad Readership Scores," *Journal of Advertising Research*, March 1962, 2, pp. 18–23.

Young, K., *Social Psychology*, Appleton-Century-Crofts, Inc., 1956.

Ziller, R. C., "Toward a Theory of Open and Closed Groups," *Psychological Bulletin*, 1965, 64, pp. 164–182.

Index

3